The Human

Also available from Bloomsbury

Traces of Racial Exception, edited by Ronit Lentin
The Aesthetico-Political, edited by *Martín Plot*
Democracy and Its Others, edited by Jeffrey H. Epstein
Posthumanism, edited by Stefan Herbrechter
Conflicting Humanities, edited by Rosi Braidotti and Paul Gilroy

The Human

Bare Life and Ways of Life

John Lechte

Macquarie University, Australia

BLOOMSBURY ACADEMIC
LONDON • NEW YORK • OXFORD • NEW DELHI • SYDNEY

BLOOMSBURY ACADEMIC
Bloomsbury Publishing Plc
50 Bedford Square, London, WC1B 3DP, UK

BLOOMSBURY, BLOOMSBURY ACADEMIC and the Diana logo are trademarks of
Bloomsbury Publishing Plc

First published 2018
Paperback edition published 2020

© John Lechte, 2018

John Lechte has asserted his right under the Copyright, Designs and Patents Act,
1988, to be identified as Author of this work.

For legal purposes the Acknowledgements on p. viii constitute an extension of this
copyright page.

Cover design: Irene Martinez-Costa
Cover image © LoudRedCreative/Getty Images

Bloomsbury Publishing Plc does not have any control over, or responsibility for,
any third-party websites referred to or in this book. All internet addresses given
in this book were correct at the time of going to press. The author and publisher
regret any inconvenience caused if addresses have changed or sites
have ceased to exist, but can accept no responsibility for any such changes.

A catalogue record for this book is available from the British Library.

A catalog record for this book is available from the Library of Congress.

ISBN: HB: 978-1-3500-2813-5
PB: 978-1-3501-4388-3
ePDF: 978-1-3500-2812-8
ePub: 978-1-3500-2815-9

Typeset by Integra Software Services Pvt. Ltd.

To find out more about our authors and books visit www.bloomsbury.com and
sign up for our newsletters

For Peetra and Simon
In memory of Kathryn Lechte (1923-2018)

Contents

Acknowledgements

Sections of Chapter 3 appeared in the journal Theory Culture and Society (35(1): 3–22, 2018) under the title 'Rethinking Arendt's Theory of Necessity: Humanness as Way of Life or the Ordinary as Extraordinary'. Also, parts of Chapter 5 appeared online on 28 July 2017, again in *Theory Culture and Society* under the title 'Heterology, Transcendence and the Sacred: On Bataille and Levinas'.

A shorter version of Chapter 6 was published under the same title in the journal *Philosophy Today* (66(3): 655–678, 2017).

The writing of this book has been made possible by an Australian Research Council Discovery grant awarded for the period 2013–2015. I offer here my grateful acknowledgement of this grant.

An earlier version of Chapter 3 was given as a paper at Goldsmiths, University of London, in the Department of Sociology Global Justice programme on 2 March 2015. I thank Dr Kirsten Campbell for inviting me to give this paper.

Also, a very early version of Chapter 6, entitled 'The Human and the Animal', was given in the Department of Politics at Goldsmiths on 17 November 2014. I thank Professor Saul Newman for inviting me to give this paper.

Note on the Text

Except where otherwise indicated, all translations from French texts are my own.

1

Introduction

In the following study, two syntagmas will be permanently in play: 'way of life' (to become 'ways' of life) and 'bare life', taken from the work of Giorgio Agamben (1998). The implications of the ideas that lie behind these syntagmas will be investigated in the texts of a select number of thinkers as a range of themes are addressed in relation to the human,[1] or humanness: freedom and necessity, the animal, animality as nature, politics as *polis* life in relation to inclusion and exclusion, the sacred, death and the moment of death, technics and nature, the Same and the Other, the everyday as extraordinary. These themes reverberate, as will be shown, in the texts of Agamben, Arendt, Bataille, Derrida, Hegel, Heidegger, Husserl, Leroi-Gourhan, Levinas, Mauss, Schelling, Simondon, Stiegler and others. How is it that the play of bare life against the idea of way of life is so crucial in coming to a deeper understanding of the human? This is the question to which I endeavour to give a response.

To consider bare life today is important, for, as will become apparent in light of Agamben's thinking, bare life has enduring political implications. These stem, Agamben suggests, from a theory of sovereignty as much as from a theory of the putative biological and economic origins of bare life. It is necessary to reveal the significance of bare life because this syntagma evokes the way that the human status of certain societies and individuals has been, and perhaps still is, brought into question, thereby limiting access to the accoutrements of civil identity, which include human rights. Stateless people in particular are vulnerable to such discrimination.

The demonstration of the embeddedness of bare life in key texts in philosophy and theory constitutes the main project of this book. If the pervasiveness of bare life in the texts of astute thinkers can be proven, a prima facie case exists for saying

---

[1] The argument is that 'the' human does not exist. Nevertheless, the phrase will still be employed to avoid awkwardness, and because it is actually addressing the theme of 'the' human, it becomes clear 'the' human as a general type does not exist.

that an exclusivist strand (quite explicit, it will be argued, in the work of Hannah Arendt) runs through European-inspired thought. On this basis, it would be quite mistaken to deny that bare life has political implications. However, the implications are not quite what Agamben has proposed in the asymmetry of sovereignty and *homo sacer* as bare life, or at least the political implications are not limited to the issues surrounding sovereignty. They are much more potently present in the opposition from Aristotle that Agamben also invokes, namely the difference between – as this has been interpreted in modernity – *zōē* as biological life and *bios* as way(s) of life, or qualified life.[2]

Let us now turn then to a more detailed examination of 'bare life'.

Bare life

At least two factors that Agamben presents in relation to *homo sacer* and bare life seem to throw into doubt the idea that bare life, from the beginning, is minimal biological life. The first of these is that bare life 'makes its appearance in the Western world' (Agamben 1998: 100) as 'sacred life', which does not have any essential link to biological life. Secondly, Agamben says, 'from the beginning this sacred life has an eminently political character' (100) and as such is linked to sovereign power. This might explain Agamben's dissatisfaction with the anthropological explanation of the sacred as ambivalent[3] in terms of content, but as clearly separated from profane life. To this separation, Agamben gives a *political* instead of a religious inflection. In Ewa Ziarek's words: 'bare life – wounded, expendable, and endangered – is not the same as biological *zoē*,

---

[2]   There is scholarly argument against Agamben's interpretation of the *zōē/bios* opposition in Aristotle. Thus, it has been argued by Derrida (2008a: 431–443), Debreuil (2006) and Finlayson (2010) that *zōē* is not reducible to biological or instinctual life and that certain animals can be included in the category of *bios*, even in Aristotle. Agamben, of course, largely follows Arendt on this point, so that an analogous criticism could be made even more strongly of her conceptual choices. The issue, however, is not just about language and an interpretation of Aristotle, but also about the reality of exclusions from civil and political life based on a distinction between bare life and qualified life, where certain human beings are relegated to the domain of bare life (also called 'subsistence life'). That, for his part, Finlayson seems, like Arendt, to accept the separation of (bare) life from politics, is suggested by the following passage: 'Thus, *man's political nature has a biological, instinctual, and material basis*, but also a deeper and more specifically human essence. If there is a definition here, it is that man is an animal with speech and reason, a capacity for ordering his political existence on the rational basis of mutual advantage and justice' (Finlayson 2010: 113; emphasis added). The point is that whether or not Agamben's reading of Aristotle is correct, the distinction between biological and qualified life has been a potent one in the modern era and it is this with which we will be concerned in what follows.
[3]   Agamben thus designates as a 'mythologeme' (1998: 75) the theory of the sacred as ambivalence.

but rather it is the remainder of the destroyed political bios' (2008: 90). Other commentators have drawn the same conclusion (cf. Husain and Ptacek 2000: 496–497 and Lemke 2005: 5). Bare life on this basis does not necessarily begin as some kind of minimal biological existence (which might be assumed to be implied with Agamben beginning his study with a reading of Aristotle on *zōē* and *bios* – the 'Greek' connection – and following up with *homo sacer*, bereft of civil identity, being the 'Italian' connection), but may effectively be reduced to this by the force of sovereign power. As Thomas Lemke says of *homo sacer*: 'While even a criminal could claim certain legal rights and formal procedures, this "sacred man" was completely unprotected and reduced to mere physical existence' (Lemke 2005: 5). Here, 'mere physical existence' means bare life. It is as a physical body that *homo sacer* is included in the political sphere as that which is fundamentally excluded and in a zone of indistinction that marks the absoluteness of sovereign power. Of course, being reduced to a physical body does not necessarily mean that *homo sacer* was *originally* a physical body. My argument, however, is that this is the case in modernity. Initial reference to something like *zōē* thus makes sense because the tradition of Western theory takes the purely physical being that must first attend to its biological needs as the *origin* of human and animal life.

Bare life as natural life has the features of a 'narrative effect' or of a retrospective illusion. Or it could be said that it is the product of veridiction, where the truth is strategically proclaimed (i.e., has a political effect) within a certain discourse, but is far from being proven.[4] As I shall argue, there is no bare life *as such*. This would be even more so for beings who would be 'the remainder of the destroyed political bios', for they would be irrevocably marked by *bios* – by forms of language and thought, social practices, a biography – even if treated as entirely expendable. Stateless people today exhibit similar traits even if they evoke *homo sacer* and thus bare life when confronting sovereign power. This, indeed, is what I take to be the deeper sense of bare life in Agamben's theory, whether or not he would specifically acknowledge the version of it that I shall present. In principle, I argue that, against bare life, there is no life that is not – or does not evoke – a *way* of life.

---

[4] Here, I am not using 'veridiction' in exactly Michel Foucault's sense, for he emphasizes above all the way that an uttering of the truth is existentially produced, as with the Greek *parrhēsia* as an essential saying of the truth without holding back (see, for example, Foucault 2011), whereas I am more concerned with the *function* of truth in relation to the false. However, the notion of bare life appears in a specific discourse (biology) at given historical moment (nineteenth century) and has definite political effects (exclusion of non-citizens from the *polis*). The claim to truth serves to bolster political effects.

Even though it is not essential to be guided specifically by Agamben in what follows, it is instructive to consider the terms of his assertion that bare life as sacred life is the 'originary' consequence of sovereign power and that 'from the beginning this sacred life has an eminently political character' (1998: 100). Here, there are all the hallmarks of a founding myth where the political relation (sovereign power and *homo sacer*) would have been there from time immemorial. What has been there, we can assume, is the asymmetrical incarnation of the power relation, where sovereignty would be equivalent to absolute power and the sacred as *homo sacer* would be equivalent to absolute powerlessness. As we shall see in more detail, this is, on the surface, very different even from Hannah Arendt's approach, where politics and freedom are the essential outcome of transcending necessity as the satisfaction of biological needs (Arendt 1958). And yet we may ask what it is exactly that constitutes *homo sacer* qua *homo sacer* if not a purely biological essence. To kill *homo sacer* is in fact to kill bare life as the last vestige of physical aliveness.

Consequently, it happens that in relation to sovereignty, *homo sacer* is what such an entity is *destined* to become – that is, bare life – in order that sovereignty as such can be confirmed. But, clearly, bare life – if not *homo sacer* – is what also can function (and I say, does function) as an origin. This is the status it assumes in biology and economics, two domains where the notion of utility in relation to necessity is privileged. Probably more than bare life as destiny, then, it will be bare life as origin that is the main concern of our subsequent deliberations.

With regard to utility, it is instructive to recall how important this notion is in the work that is of such founding significance in modern biology, Darwin's *On the Origin of Species* (Darwin 1981).[5] Thus, in the 'struggle for existence' – the essential principle driving 'natural selection' – Darwin argued that 'geometrical increase' in populations leads to a shortage of space in which to live and therefore to a competition for survival. Only the best adapted members of a species will survive. As Darwin readily admits, this 'is the doctrine of Malthus applied with manifold force to the whole animal and vegetable kingdoms' (1981: 63). And he makes the importance of utility absolutely transparent, and were it to be shown to be false, he says that it 'would be absolutely fatal to my theory' (199).

Clearly, the struggle for existence is premised on the assumption of economic theory that the relative scarcity (of land and all other resources) drives natural

---

[5] The impact of Darwin's work is emphasized by Ernst Mayr in his introduction to the facsimile edition of *On the Origin of Species*, first published in 1859: 'The intellectual revolution it caused and the impact it had on man's concept of himself and the world were greater than those caused by the works of Copernicus, Newton, and the great physicists of recent times' (Mayr 1981: vii).

selection. In this regard, it is ironic that Elizabeth Grosz, in a rereading of Darwin's theory of evolution, first of all notes Darwin's affinity with Malthus, and then, approvingly, points to the coalescence of the disciplines of biology and economics: 'The interchange between biology and economics – the study of living systems and the study of the production, circulation, and exchange of objects or commodities – is not fortuitous insofar as the two disciplines have long borrowed models, images, metaphors, and techniques from each other' (Grosz 2004: 38). Significantly, Grosz does not consider the fact that both disciplines are founded, in relation to the pursuit of life, in the concepts of scarcity and utility and that these have profound implications for understanding why bare life is ultimately such a dominant motif in theories of humanness and animality. As will become clear in Chapter 2, the scarcity-utility conceptual couple allows the basis of consumer society to be theorized in terms of the dialectic of freedom and necessity which, in the final analysis, means that bare life (= necessity in relation to scarcity) is at the origin of this society.

Rather than conceptualizing bare life in relation to sovereignty, it will instead be treated primarily as it appears in relation to utility and subsistence, where life is deemed to be sustained at its most minimal level. The approach of Marshal Sahlins, in criticizing the validity of the notion of subsistence, is in keeping with the spirit of the approach to be adopted here. Thus, in his famous chapter, 'The Original Affluent Society' (Sahlins 1974: 1–40), Sahlins shows that the term 'subsistence' is derived entirely from Western economic theory, the main presupposition of which is that there is scarcity in relation to a potential infinity of wants: 'Modern capitalist societies, however richly endowed dedicate themselves to the presupposition of scarcity. Inadequate economic means is the first principle of the world's wealthiest peoples' (1974: 3). Especially societies such as hunter-gatherer Australian Aboriginal society are deemed to be of a subsistence nature because, to all (European) appearances, the members could only 'manage to eke out a bare existence' (6). More fully, as one observer, cited by Sahlins, put it: 'A man who spends his whole life following animals just to kill them to eat, or moving from one berry patch to another, is really living just like an "animal"' (Braidwood 1957: 122, cited in Sahlins 1974: 5). Indeed, the pervasiveness of the conflation of supposedly subsistence living with animality, together with the idea that the truly human is the being that transcends animality, will be noted frequently in the course of this study.

Sahlins's approach is to argue that subsistence is the product of the concept of scarcity that underpins Western economic theory, a theory that has inappropriately become the lens through which certain non-Western societies have been evaluated: 'Yet scarcity is not an intrinsic property of technical means' (5). And Sahlins adds, 'The hunter, one is tempted to say, is "uneconomic man"' (13). This is because the life of the hunter is based on the principle that 'wants are scarce' and 'means (in relation) plentiful' (13).

Subsistence implies that people are, as Braidwood put it, exclusively concerned with finding enough food and resources to live on, the battle being about staying physically alive, that is, in being (at minimum) bare life. Whatever it takes to achieve this, regardless of *how* it is done, must be done. For only *after* the problem of staying alive has been solved (the problem of necessity) and only after bare life (the level of animality) has been transcended can culture and political and civil society emerge.

The 'banal' to be understood here as a constitutive part of a way of life is different from both 'everyday life' studies and anthropological observation, to the extent that the latter often presupposes (as in the work of Leroi-Gourhan) a distinct biological substrate that would correspond to the zoological (or animal) essence of humans.

Such, then, is the thesis most frequently underlying explanations of culture and politics in relation to many non-Western contexts, for example, as has just been seen, in relation to Australian Aboriginal culture. Sahlins's point of course is that such peoples are not 'stone age', but the economic theory that makes them so is.

The philosophical and political purport of bare life

Today, the current view is that only after economic justice has been rendered in relation to the fulfilment of needs can there be full political participation, especially as this applies to the economically disadvantaged of society, as the seminal analysis of social, material rights for the development of citizenship rights by T. H. Marshall ultimately implies.[6]

Here, one could suggest that precisely because of its unique emphasis on freedom and equality in the *polis*, Arendt's thought is aberrant and *sui generis* and not at all in keeping with the current emphasis on equality in relation to socio-economic issues. I will endeavour to show, however, that if in reality latter-day economics is essentially concerned with utility with the consequence that economic activity is never an end in itself but is always about escaping bare life –

---

[6]   Cf.: Marshall (1977).

always a means to an end, where this end is the overcoming of scarcity and making the economic sphere ultimately redundant – then a case can surely be made for the autonomy of politics in the sense that Arendt intended.

To succeed in showing that current economics is about bare life and utility and not about the political, it will behove us to attempt to plumb depths of consumer society – the society of the commodity and of the spectacle in Guy Debord's sense. Although often theorized in terms of the dialectic of 'use' and 'exchange' value, it is necessary to show that, indeed, consumerism constitutes, for better or for worse, a culture – or, more precisely, a *way* of life[7] – and is not ultimately reducible to an elaborate strategy for solving the problem of necessity (bare life). In other words, it is necessary to wrench consumer society from the vice-like grip of the measure of a 'standard of living', which can be high (Western countries) or low ('developing' or Third and Fourth World countries). With his theological approach to *oikonomia*, Agamben offers a serious argument as to the non-utilitarian basis of the *oikos*, and a later part of this study will be devoted to giving some consideration to this, as well as to Agamben's studies of liturgy as 'way if life'.[8]

To be clear, what is at stake at all times in this study is the human, or rather humans and humanness. For, as Bernard Stiegler says, 'the' human does not exist. Only humans exist.[9] And the argument concerning economics is entirely geared to this. But in order to provide a more solid background to our concerns, I will also consider the way that the human–animal relation has been understood historically, and archaeologically, especially in the work of Leroi-Gourhan.[10] The background of modern humanism will come into view along with the idea that that what is human (and perhaps what is animal) is without essence, such as is evoked by Foucault's famous statement in *The Order of Things* (1982), and that 'man is an invention of recent date. And one perhaps nearing its end' (387). This study will thus endeavour to explain why it is essential that a consideration of the human in no sense should lead to any form of humanism.[11]

---

[7] Walter Benjamin went as far as one could here by calling capitalism a religion, that is, at minimum, a particular way of life (see Benjamin 2004).

[8] See Chapter 10.

[9] 'If *the* human existed it would be terrifying. It does not exist anymore than *the* natural language [*la langue*]. Humans exist' (Stiegler 1996: 187).

[10] See Chapter 8.

[11] To clarify this a still further, I refer to Heidegger's term 'Dasein' (being there). Let us say that Heidegger chose this term because it is bereft of any fixed content. One can never assume to know who (or what) Dasein is. In principle, Dasein is not the human. However, a slippage has been noted in Heidegger on this point, so that, by default, Dasein becomes the human and has certain qualities. Humanism, then, would be equivalent to reducing the human to a fixed set of qualities that are assumed a priori. By contrast, even though transcendent, the human that I shall be concerned with is essentially unfounded.

This theme will be elaborated upon in detail throughout the following chapters. Suffice it to say now that humanness qua humanness is a transcendence and that current thought indebted to the European tradition cannot acknowledge this. To paraphrase Hegel: for European philosophy, only some are truly human (only some can be citizens, for example, even if this is not part of the orthodoxy). The point is to ensure that all are treated as truly human. Or rather, that modern political community does not by any means exhaust the being of the human being, that being human is itself enough to warrant the deepest respect – that being human is, qua human, what opens the way to transcendence. It is a matter, then, of developing a case for showing that the human (and maybe certain forms of animality) is a transcendence. Important for introducing what is at stake in this regard is the philosophy of Emmanuel Levinas. Let me indicate briefly as to how Levinas is relevant here in relation to the questions that he raises, the question concerning humanness.

Levinas and the question of human being

If 'human' here means to think the human qua human as distinct from any form of humanism that would attribute a priori a fixed content to humanness, it is clear that a philosophical approach needs to be taken, even if philosophy, too, has not been exempt from objectifying and of reducing things to the order of the Same, as Levinas has argued. In a sense, we are engaging in philosophy in order to go beyond (a certain) kind of philosophising.

To some extent, Agamben has laid out the political terrain relating to exclusion through his distillation of bare life in the European tradition. With regard to Levinas and humanness, the approach is not one of philosophy as contemplation but rather of thinking humanness as part of an immediate engagement: 'To think is no longer to contemplate, but to be engaged, merged with what is launched – the dramatic event of being-in-the-world' (Levinas 1998b: 3). Thus, to think the human is to be already involved with it, much as being and thinking coalesce in Heidegger. This is to say that thinking is not *about* the human or humans (which would produce an objectification), but that *in* thinking the human, something else appears, something that is without essence, without foundation.

Even at a more naïve level, we can easily understand that we are always already 'in the world' and never at a remove from it, except imaginarily. From this, Levinas goes on to say that 'we are responsible beyond our intentions. It is impossible for the attention directing the act to avoid inadvertent action' (1998b:

3). And our inadvertent actions leave traces. To erase the trace is leave another trace. Or, the psyche, composed of the unconscious as well as consciousness, is the domain of the ego and the order of the Same, the order that includes the ego. Because he sees the self-regard of Western philosophy as dominating notions of otherness, Levinas has dubbed this philosophy an 'egology' – a term, as we shall see in Chapter 9, Levinas in fact owes to Husserl. Whether inadvertently or not, the Same rubs out all traces of difference, of the Other, of multiplicity. In this effort, though, it betrays itself. For, to reiterate, to erase a trace is also to leave a trace. Before Agamben came to study gesture (see Agamben 2000: 49–60), Levinas pointed to gesture as the scene of inadvertent traces: 'The comedy begins with our simplest gestures', he says. In acting, one leaves traces whether in the putative everyday life or in other contexts. In wiping away the traces, one leaves others (Cf. Levinas 1998b: 3). Levinas's approach here will be commented upon in Chapter 9, devoted to the philosopher's notion of the human and transcendence. But we note here that the trace is also the basis of 'a transcendence that cannot be reduced to an experience of transcendence' (Levinas 1998b: 89).

That is, it occurs in the human whether or not consciousness is involved. Against this, commentaries on everyday life talk about banality, the inconsequential, utility, the mundane, the minor and the ordinary. On this basis, the everyday would seem to be anything but a harbinger of transcendence, just as the domain that Agamben has designated as bare life is similarly deemed to be anything but transcendent. Of course, bare life is transcendence understood as gesture and trace. But as gesture and trace it becomes part of a way of life and ceases to be bare life. We have then, with regard to transcendence, sketched out the rudiments of the extended discussion that will take place in Chapter 9.

Heidegger and transcendence

Again, as concerns transcendence, Heidegger's observation in *Being and Time* can be noted to the effect that 'the idea of "transcendence" – that man is something that reaches beyond himself – is rooted in Christian dogmatics' (Heidegger 1978: 74). For Heidegger, the Christian heritage has limited the possibility for establishing an ontological understanding of 'man's Being'. In order for this understanding to occur, the later part of *Being and Time* proposes that if '*Dasein is its disclosedness*' (1978: 171; Heidegger's emphasis), in 'care is grounded the full disclosedness of the "there"' (402). If, in addition, the most general feature of Dasein is its 'Being-in-the-*world*', the question arises as to the ontological possibility of 'world'. Thus, '(i)n what way must the world *be*, if Dasein is to be able to exist as Being-in-the-World?' (415; Heidegger's emphasis). Part of the answer is that Dasein's Being is 'care' and the 'ontological meaning of care is temporality' (416). Temporality 'constitutes the disclosedness of the "there" [...]. In the disclosedness of the "there" the world is disclosed along with it' (416). Crucially: 'Having its ground [gründend] in the horizontal unity of ecstatical temporality, the world is transcendent' (417). But it must be understood that '(i)f no *Dasein* exists, no world is "there" either' (417; Heidegger's emphasis). So, the 'there', 'world', 'disclosedness', evoke transcendence, which is also the transcendence of Being vis-à-vis beings. The totality – if there is a totality – is Being as such. Even though this account remains incomplete, clearly, transcendence ushers in a domain irreducible to materiality, objectification, or to being as a specific entity.[12]

According to Heidegger's seminar on Parmenides, disclosedness and the revealing of truth (aletheia) take place for the Greeks in the *polis*. It will thus be necessary to consider this in some detail, as it has implications for understanding the nature of politics today, especially if, at the same time, Arendt's approach to the *polis* is taken into account.[13]

Transcendence and politics in Levinas

For Levinas, however, the approach of ontology, where Being would be revealed in the openness of the *polis*, inhibits a deeper appreciation of transcendence. This is so in the sense that, for the philosopher of responsibility, *'being's other'* gets concealed (Levinas 1998b: 16; Levinas's emphasis). There is, it is claimed, an implicit totalising effect in Heidegger's notion of Being.

Nevertheless, the notion of transcendence ensures that the human is not reduced to any given empirical or material manifestation, and especially not to bare life. It will be necessary to examine the extent to which this notion is applicable to all beings, not just to human being. Transcendence gives rise to versions of the sacred and becomes an important point of reference.

---

[12] As many have noted (e.g., Agamben), Heidegger's approach in no way embraces any version of biologism and, indeed, it is this that Heidegger opposes in showing that Being is never what is 'Being-present-at-hand' as the self-evident; nor is life (for the human) 'mere-aliveness' (Heidegger 1978: 75).

[13] See Chapter 7.

Thus, Levinas says that he must return to responsibility for the other in the 'heteronomy of ethical obedience' where obedience occurs prior to any order, 'to the "imperativity", so to speak, of that original imperative, that original *transcendence*' (Levinas 1999: 33; emphasis added). Indeed, the 'true essence of man is presented in his face' (1969: 290). The face gives rise to the necessarily open-ended 'face to face' encounter, where the enactment of language as 'saying' leads to a transcendence that cannot be totalized. Nor can beings separated in an exteriority which is a plurality be totalized (1969: 295).[14] This is a plurality, Levinas says, which is distinct from a homogenising multiplicity – thus distinct from a multiplicity which totalizes and englobes its content.

Most of all, transcendence features in Levinas's philosophy as the infinite that is opposed to the lot of finitude incorporated within a totality. Within finitude (and thus within the sphere of history as a permanent state of war) the other is effaced within the order of the Same – the order lacking transcendence. The order of the Same is one of immanence. To do justice to the other and to the human as such, therefore, we are obliged to go beyond finitude, totality or objective knowledge – beyond the order of the Same, which gives them life. The project of history as the overcoming of necessity cannot do justice to the other as Autrui (the Absolute Other as the other person) because the order of the Same constitutes a totality that includes both the Same and the Other – albeit an Other constructed by the other of the Same. This is the situation which, as already mentioned, gives rise to the effacement of the Other (*Autrui*). Transcendence becomes the way out of this situation, even though it can never be an object of knowledge. Thus, Levinas writes: 'Infinity is characteristic of a transcendent being as transcendent; the infinite is the absolutely other' (1969: 49). The infinite is a transcendence on the same plane as the Other. The aim should be to see transcendence as including the way to justice – justice as nothing more nor less than an encounter with the Other.

To engage with Levinas on the human is thus to engage with the human as the absolute other. The advantage of this (if we can speak in these terms) is that the historical phenomenon of war (the key element of finite material history) ceases to be the focal point for defining the human. The Other cannot be thematized since thematization is part of the objectivizing approach of epistemology (knowledge). To be a theme is to be an object and, therefore, part of the order of the Same. The Same, the realm of finitude and of death, while defining finitude, also transcends

---

[14] 'The unity of plurality', Levinas continues, 'is peace, and not the coherence of the elements that constitute plurality' (1969: 306).

it.[15] There are grounds for saying that Levinas's approach to the human is one that refuses to limit the human to finitude and to violence. How, though, might it be possible – if at all – for transcendence and the infinite to communicate with those other domains? Specifically, how might political experience (as the management of conflict and a striving for equality and happiness) be linked to transcendence? This is a crucial question if transcendence and infinity are to be important forces *in the world*. The difficulty here is that the world emerges as a spectacle – as a domain ripe for objectification and thus for the dominance of the Same. What place, we need to ask, can the Same have in the encounter with the Other in the 'face to face', in language and discourse, with regard to the face as the incarnation of transcendence? Part of Levinas's response is to say that the Other can and does have an encounter with the Same, with the ego, and that this constitutes a kind of relationship, but it is not one that is totalizing. Be this as it may, does it not need to be said that the human is that which does engage in totalizing, in englobing and in homogenizing the Other – that Western philosophy, as an index of this, has to be included in the essentially human, even if this 'essentially human' must be understood to include the inhuman?

To establish his ethical approach as responsibility for the face of the Other as the Infinite and as transcendence, Levinas, as others have pointed out, leaves the question open as to what place the political (in the colloquial sense) might play in human experience (cf. Critchley 2004). Is it a matter of bypassing the political completely as the seat of finitude or of seeing it as a part of a negative passage enabling the lineaments of transcendence and infinity to become in some sense manifest? Even more pointedly, we need to know what becomes of the order of the Same vis-à-vis the ethical order? Suffice it to say that a remark by Derrida on what is effectively the political realm, cited by Critchley in his essay on Levinas, puts what is at stake in sharp relief: 'Without the possibility of radical evil, of perjury, and of absolute crime, there is no responsibility, no freedom, no decision' (Derrida 1997: 219).

To be persuaded by Levinas's evocation of the transcendent in relation to the human still requires us to establish whether or not it is possible to see transcendence as associated with the human as a *way of life*. Could a way of life be governed by infinity and transcendence rather than by history and finitude? Even while placing finitude in a new perspective by relativizing it, Levinas, too,

---

[15] In his lectures just after the war, Levinas addresses the status of death in relation to finitude, which, he says, is not part of the order of the Same because it is the future. The future is 'altérité', 'l'autre': 'Il est absolument autre et nouveau' (Levinas 1979: 71)

in *Totality and Inifinity*, summarizes the fact that the accoutrements of life are not simple *means* of subsistence, but are part of the fact that '[l]ife is the *love of life*' (1969: 112; Levinas's emphasis).[16] As the sacred and religion are key defining characteristics of a way of life – of the content of life – these are clearly important, but do not give the whole story. Language, art and all poetic practices (including music) must also be considered. It is, incidentally, necessary to *believe* (i.e., not just rely on knowing) in words, or symbolic forms, in order for language to work.[17]

The human and death

In a milieu where the word is 'life' and where transcendence is hardly in vogue,[18] it is appropriate to spare a thought for death. Is human life, qua life, essentially a resistance to death? Or is an affirmative response here indicative, once again, of the dominance of bare life in the play of power, where power would ultimately be the capacity to ensure, within sovereign borders, that life, however minimal, prevails? Power, in this sense, is about the repression of death as that which has to do with being as such. For this study, the question is to know to what extent death *transcends* life (but not in a religious sense), whether religious or non-religious. Much depends, to be sure, on how death is to be understood. If it is understood in strictly biological terms, the idea of 'transcendence' would seem to be irrelevant. However, once life ceases to be reducible to bare life, death is also irreducible to biology. Could there, then, be such a thing as a *quasi*-secular form of the sacred and of transcendence? On the face of it, Deleuze's notion of immanence seems to be is in opposition to this. But is this really so? I give a response to Deleuze later in this chapter – Deleuze who, in his final published work, homes in on the notion of '*a* death'. Before coming to this, let us first consider briefly aspects of Heidegger's 'being-towards-death'.

Dasein and death

In the much discussed notion of 'being-towards-death', an attempt is made to embrace death as a possibility more than as an actuality. Thus, against the scenario

---

[16] This is a key point in relation to Levinas's philosophy and will be elaborated upon in Chapter 9.
[17] On this, see Deleuze's notion of belief, evoked in *Cinema 2: The Time Image* (1989) and in 'Immanence: A Life' (2001), where it is a matter of *believing* in the real (à la Godard) and *believing* in *a* life [not in life tout court], in its immanence, which then confers on this life an aura of transcendence.
[18] However, Deleuze says that 'transcendence is always a product of immanence' (2001: 31).

painted above where the actuality of death is confused with its possibility, and so is repressed, Heidegger argues, that, for Dasein, death is essentially futural and its own-most possibility. The question that arises, however, is whether, in attempting to provide a purely philosophical approach to death, Heidegger is reliant (and perhaps phenomenology as a whole), after all, on anthropological and psychological data that deals with actuality. At least this is what needs to be investigated in some detail, which is not possible here. In a preliminary way, though, we can say, in the first place, that there is the isolation of the individual subject who experiences a death which no one else can experience. Death is always essentially 'my' death.[19] No one can die in my place. This comes across, in an everyday sense, as a modern psychological fact. It is always 'me' who dies, never the other: 'The dying of Others is not something which we experience in a genuine sense' (Heidegger 1978: 282). For, it is contained in the very being and in the very idea of death that it is mine. Philosophically, the death of the other is unthinkable. Yet, 'dying is not an event' (1978: 284) and must be understood existentially, that is, as part of the being of existence. This is its philosophical status. Secondly, the view that death arrives to all beings is seemingly empirically derived by Heidegger – or, at least it is an already-given piece of knowledge – before being encapsulated in the notion of finitude – 'the authentic Being-come-to-an-end [Zuendegekommensein]' (Heidegger 1978: 282). Here, we need to know precisely what 'come-to-an-end' means. Is it a purely biological end, or something more? In principle, it is indeed the latter. Heidegger acknowledges that dying is part of Being; but this is not simply a 'physiological' or 'biological' event. For life 'is not a mere Being-present-at hand, nor is it Dasein. In turn, Dasein is never to be defined ontologically by regarding it as life (in an ontologically indefinite manner) plus something else' (Heidegger 1978: 75). Furthermore, in a statement confirming that Dasein's death is more than the extinguishing of biological life, Heidegger famously says:

> *Dasein's* going-out-of-the-world in the sense of dying must be distinguished from the going-out-of-the-world of that which merely has life [des Nur-lebenden]. In our terminology the ending of anything that is alive, is denoted as 'perishing' [Verenden]. We can see the difference only if the kind of ending which Dasein can have is distinguished from the end of life. (Heidegger 1978: 284)

Here, Heidegger clearly distinguishes between death as merely perishing, which can be attributed to animals, compared to dying, which constitutes human

---

[19] Indeed, 'any Dasein whatsoever is characterized by mineness' (Heidegger 1978: 68)

death. Ultimately the distinction between 'perishing' and 'dying' contributes to the confirmation of Heidegger's humanism (= the human as a given type of entity), the other being, as we shall see (c.f. Chapter 6), the fact that the animal, in opposition to the human, is excluded from the *polis* because it is defined as being bereft of the word.

Being-towards-death, then, is signalled by anxiety as existentially and not empirically founded and to be distinguished from the fear before empirical death typical of the inauthentic everyday sense attributed to death (the sense of the 'They'). In this way, Being-towards-death becomes one's own-most possibility – the possibility (futural) of impossibility. Dasein lives essentially in light of the future where death awaits. Death thus takes Dasein out of itself, beyond itself – ecstatically[20] – in time. In effect, time is futural (Being-towards-death), not of the present (now). In this sense, and only in this sense, does death become linked to a form of transcendence, the authentic being of the human. Being-towards-death, then, is, for Heidegger, a mark of the human – a quality of the human! – that no animal can come to incarnate. As such, it is also the mark of a humanism.

The death penalty as the mark of the human

In the history of Western thought, the human has often been marked by a particular quality or characteristic. Language is the most obvious. But capital punishment has been also. In his seminar on capital punishment, Jacques Derrida (2012) shows how, from Plato to Rousseau and Kant, capital punishment has been intimately implicated in understanding the human. Thus, in Plato's *Laws*, only the truly human can be condemned to death, whereas an animal, by contrast, cannot be. As Plato and the tradition he inaugurated presents it, there is even something ennobling in condemning to death the one who has transgressed social laws or norms. In a long passage from Plato's *Laws*, cited by the philosopher, those who commit a crime due to folly rather than viciousness will be condemned by the judge to a five-year period of incarceration:

> Throughout this period, they shall have no communication with any citizen except the members of the nocturnal council, who shall visit them with a view

---

[20] Cf., 'Ecstatico-horizontal temporality temporalizes itself *primarily* in terms of the *future*' (Heidegger 1978: 479).

to admonition and their souls' salvation. When the term of confinement has expired, if the prisoner is deemed to have returned to his right mind, he shall dwell with the right-minded, but if not, and he be condemned a second time on the same charge, he shall suffer the penalty of death. As for those who add the character of a beast of prey to their atheism or belief in divine indifference or venality, those who in their contempt of mankind bewitch so many of the living by the pretense of evoking the dead and the promise of winning over the gods by the supposed sorceries of prayer, sacrifice and incantations, and thus do their best for lucre to ruin individuals, whole families, and communities, the law shall direct the court to sentence a culprit convicted of belonging to this class to incarceration in the central prison, where no free citizen whatsoever shall have access to him, and where he shall receive from the turnkeys the strict rations prescribed by the curators of the laws. At death he shall be cast out beyond the borders without burial, and if any citizen has a hand in his burial, he shall be liable to a prosecution for impiety at the suit of any who cares to take proceedings. (Plato 1980 Book X a-e)

As Derrida notes, the price paid for a fate worse than being formally condemned to death is to have (like Antigone's brother) no customary or official burial – to be nothing more than refuse, to be non-human. Not death, then, but *how* one dies is the mark of the human in Ancient Greece: 'For here, it is the right (*doit*) to a sepulchre which marks the difference between man and beast, between a man condemned to death who still has the right to a sepulchre, to be honoured by men, and those who do not even merit the name of man, and who therefore do not even merit the death penalty' (Derrida 2012: 33). This point is crucial because it implies that capital punishment 'is a sign of access to the dignity of man, something that distinguishes man' and raises the human to a level above life itself. Capital punishment as the 'condition of the human law and of human dignity, one could almost say of the nobility of man', arises again in Kant's argument, where there can be no justice or law 'in a system which would exclude capital punishment' (Derrida 2012: 33).

Theoretically, at least, one is truly human who qualifies within the law to be condemned to death. Those outside the law become inhuman. In its most striking form, the question (already evoked) is whether the inhuman is part of the human. For Aristotle, the question is whether a slave could qualify as being human. The answer is that in order to assume the inferior position of the property of a master and to be possessed of a slave nature, the slave has to be defined as human, albeit of the lowest order (see Aristotle 1995: 1259b and 1260a). But overall, the question of the human is the question of those *outside* common legal, social and political structures.

Human and inhuman: Inside and outside the law

Inside and outside political community and the law

When, in a key argument to be addressed in this study, Hannah Arendt broaches the issue of human rights in *The Origins of Totalitarianism* (1968), it is to argue that the notion of human rights is inadequate because stateless people – people external to any political community – cannot find protection – cannot find it by definition, so to speak. For protection implies membership of a political community (*polity*). And so, in the period between the two world wars, it seemed futile for stateless people to call upon the 'abstract nakedness of being human. Not the loss of specific rights, then, but the loss of a community willing and able to guarantee any right whatever, has been the calamity which has befallen ever-increasing numbers of people. Man, it turns out, can lose all so-called Rights of Man without losing his essential quality as man, his human dignity. Only the loss of a polity itself expels him from humanity' (Arendt 1968: 177). In these terms, if there are inevitably some for whom there is no place within a polity, and if, furthermore, those peoples deemed to be mired in necessity also, by this very fact, must suffer from not being part of a viable *polity*, which is the only place, according to Arendt, where freedom can flourish, there will thus always be humans who are not fully human – who are 'expelled from humanity'.

Fully stateless people, it is hardly necessary to say, cannot be condemned to death since they do not figure within any given legal system. Indeed, when wholly outside the law, and having no legal status, as was the case for many between the two wars, committing a crime and thus becoming the focus of legal procedures was often the only way to gain 'some kind of human equality' (Arendt 1968: 166). Again, the issue to be addressed is the inhuman in the human, rather than the human as defined within a Eurocentric conception, where human always means human within a political community, or at least within a sphere where Western-style law is applicable. Just as, for Agamben, *homo sacer* was that being who could be killed without the perpetrator committing homicide, so those outside the European political community become vulnerable to all kinds of harm – and not to all kinds of injustice because justice, if one follows Kant as representative of European thought on this matter, can only be obtained within a given legal system.

In an example as telling as Arendt's claims about political community, Kant refers, quite remarkably, to infanticide and to duelling as instances where the legislature faces extreme difficulty in imposing the death penalty. We shall, for the moment, leave duelling to one side and focus on Kant's response to infanticide. The type of infanticide at issue is the one committed by an unwed mother. As Kant notes, the child victim is thus 'illegitimate'. The explanation as to why it is difficult, if not impossible, to impose the death penalty in such circumstances is as follows:

> The child that comes into the world apart from marriage is born outside the law (for the law is marriage) and therefore outside the protection of the law. It has, as it were, stolen into the commonwealth (like contraband merchandise), so that the commonwealth can ignore its existence (since it was not 'right' that it should have come to exist in this way), and can therefore also ignore its annihilation; and no decree can remove the mother's shame when it becomes known that she gave birth without being married. (Kant 1998: 109)

Here is another instance where the one outside the law – and thus outside civil life – is also deemed to be outside humanity, in a state of nature and exposed to death, and, as a result, should, in the said circumstances, be destroyed without this being murder (the latter, for Kant, would entail the mandatory implementation of the death penalty, according to the law of retribution (*ius talionis*)).

In commenting on this example (along with that of duelling), Derrida, in his seminar on capital punishment, emphasizes the 'double bind' dilemma resulting from Kant's all too rigorous logic, a logic that tries to marry a recognition of the importance of a sense of honour with the law of talion. The issue of the humanness (or otherwise) of the victim is not Derrida's concern (as it is not generally the concern of European thought). Or rather, Derrida recognizes that this is a *human* victim (otherwise there would be no dilemma), but not a citizen; it is thus a question of a kind of non-human human (Derrida 2012: 182). The most important point of Derrida's commentary on Kant's dilemma is captured in the following passage:

> there are moments where people obey subjective motives [...] which are in disagreement with objective rules; [...] this state of fact or again this state of nature, this residue of a state of nature translates a lack of education or a barbarism which is reflected in the disagreement between the subjective and the objective, between the primitive [*sauvage*] desire or the state of nature of citizens and the law, with the result that the civil constitution which registers or reflects this inadequation itself remains, to this extent at least, barbarous or uncivilised [*inculte*], still rooted in a state of nature that it should have surpassed. (Derrida 2012: 184)

Clearly, for Kant, infanticide is not murder (i.e., is not a criminal homicide). Is it even homicide (the criminal killing of one human being by another)? If the victim is human, homicide has been committed. However, if not being present or visible within the terms of any given legal system means that one is not fully human, the victim in the example referred to by Kant is, for all intents and purposes, not human. As such, not only has murder not been committed, but there has not even been a homicide! The situation is, however, still more complicated. For, as we know, Kant says that a human being should always be treated as an end, never as a means, even (and this is the crucial point) when that being is 'condemned to lose his civil personality' (Kant 1998: 105), since he has an 'innate', or 'inherited', personality which transcends any civil identity. How, then, are we to reconcile this with the example of infanticide, where it seems that (1) an infant is killed as a *means* of salvaging the mother's honour after having a child out of wedlock (the infant is not treated as an end), and (2) the infant's death can be ignored by the commonwealth, as it has no civil status and is therefore not fully human (its 'innate' personality can seemingly be disregarded). Even though Kant proposes that those without a 'civil personality' should be treated in accordance with something like their original humanity, in practice, as Arendt indicated, to be treated as fully human requires that a being have a *civil* status. In sum, Kant does not resolve the dilemmas raised by the human but only reinforces a certain Eurocentrism.

Homo sacer Outside the Law and Statelessness

Kant's discussion of infanticide evokes the situation of Agamben's *homo sacer*. Let us return to this for a moment.

In Sextus Pompeius Festus's interpretation of Verrius Flaccus's Latin dictionary, *De uerborum significatu* (translated as *On the Meaning of Words*),[21] Agamben reads an entry on *homo sacer* as saying that anyone who kills the 'sacred man' cannot be held liable for homicide. The Latin text which Agamben cites is ambiguous, as it refers, in its nominative form, to '*parricidium*' rather than '*homicidium*'. Agamben then complicates things by saying that *parricidium* originally meant the 'killing of a free man'[22] (1998: 72). His commentary attests

---

[21] The reference is Agamben (1998: 71), where *De verborum significatu* is given as *On the Meaning of Words*. Agamben does not mention the connection to Verrius, on whose work Festus relies. See Glinister (2007: 11).

[22] To Numa Pompilius has been attributed, Agamben goes on to say, the inauguration of the law against murder (Agamben 1998: 81). The historian Judy Gaughan comments in regard to *parridas* (the key term here): 'the difficulty for modern scholars, unlike the Romans living under Numa's rule, results from not knowing what the word *parridas* means. But even though we know neither the specific derivation of the word nor its precise meaning, it is probably safe to say that in Numa's law, *parridas* indicated a person subject to a capital penalty' (Gaughan 2010: 10).

to the fact that, with regard to *homo sacer*, the one who is killed has become an inhuman human. In a slight variation on Agamben's take on this, which follows up the anthropological literature on the sacred, we could say that *homo sacer's* ambiguous human status derives from him being outside any legal or social system, like the child victim Kant describes. Both can be killed with impunity because they lack any civil, or community identity and are thus not fully human (although they are human enough to be the subject of an exclusion).

Way of life and necessity

If the human always exists within a way of life, as has been argued thus far, how is it that bare life and biopolitics dominate the current era? The answer is in the assumption that the human qua human exists *prior* to a way of life, that the human is based in 'necessity' and a struggle for existence, which it needs to transcend, as the tradition would have it, where the brute body is found, bereft of all insignia, or indices of a way of life. In this regard, Gilbert Simondon shows how, in modern thought, the individual is assumed to be prior to individuation, whereas, Simondon argues, individuality is the outcome of forms of individuation (Simondon 2013: 1 and *passim*). Life, prior to a way of life, and the individual prior to individuation are surely the most enduring myths of modern Western culture. Although aspects of this argument are not new, it reaches the height of poignancy when human rights are at stake, or when we are forced to confront the 'nothing but the human' in everyday life. Of particular importance in this regard is the human caught up in situations of utter degradation, or of extreme oppression – as witnessed by those who are enslaved by whatever power, be it political, economic or social. As mentioned earlier, Aristotle struggled with the question of whether slaves are human and had to conclude that they are. For slavery only makes sense – only has significance and a capacity to elicit indignation and compassion – if the slave is also human.

Approaches to indigenous Australian Aborigines raise further questions about the nature of the human and bare life. To a European vision shaped by colonialism, the situation of Australian Aboriginal people, particularly those least Westernized, is to see them as being so materially impoverished as to be on the verge of extinction. Spiritual needs apart, a huge effort has been directed towards assisting indigenous Australians achieve a material equilibrium (a 'standard of living') thought to allow the flowering of a certain degree of freedom. To the typically concerned person, the aim, then, is to ensure that the debilitating fact of a merely 'subsistence' life is overcome. For the assumption of modernity is that culture and knowledge are only possible after basic needs have been satisfied.[23]

But the essential human is not arrived at through economic, material, political or social liberation. For one must always already be human in order that the forces of liberation can be directed and called upon to do their liberating work. To repeat: one liberates someone from slavery because they are essentially *not* a slave (they, are instead, 'prisoners'). But again, what of necessity? Would it not be that efforts to bring about the liberation from necessity as the satisfaction of basic needs only makes sense because those marked out to be helped are *already* free. Freedom here is what one already is. Thus, it would only make sense to talk about animal liberation (within the usual meaning of the term 'animal') if animals were essentially free beings. The scandal occurs when an essentially free being is in shackles. In this sense, what the animal is becomes a question of equal importance with that of the nature of the human. Indeed, given that, at least within the frame of historical legend, the destinies of the human and the animal have been inextricably bound together, the question of the animal becomes even more urgent.[24]

Human being and violence: Politics and ethics

Investigating the human leads inexorably to the question of how war, conflict, violence, power, death, finitude, the Same and history are not its key defining elements. And if they are – if politics is the management of conflict and violence and human beings are essentially political – how could transcendence, infinity, the Other, responsibility and Desire (Levinas's key terms) be part of the human? Can we hold onto the political as it is evoked here, the political in its often awful current manifestations? Or is it a matter of going beyond it – of approaching the political as we might approach the institution of slavery or Mediaeval warfare

---

[23] In the 'Appendix' to his *Lectures on the Philosophy of World History* (1993), Hegel evokes Aristotle's point that 'man turns to universal and exulted things only after his basic needs have been satisfied' (1993: 155). The passage from Aristotle cited in the Appendix runs as follows: 'therefore since they [the earliest philosophers] philosophized in order to escape from ignorance, evidently they were pursuing science in order to know, and not for any utilitarian end. And it is confirmed by the facts; for it was when almost all the necessaries of life and the things that make for comfort and recreation were present, that such knowledge began to be sought' (Aristotle 1995 Bk I (A) 982b 20–25). What is cited here is so because it indicates the 'taken-for-grantedness' in philosophy of the satisfaction of basic needs prior to culture.

[24] See Chapter 6.

considered as things to be excluded from the human understood in its deepest sense as transcendence? Or, again, maybe we need to acknowledge, as others have done, the possibility of humanity as having a fundamentally self-destructive disposition. Thus understood, the human's fundamentally inhuman impulse would be an essential part of the human, an impulse that would give meaning to freedom. Is this the terrible dilemma we must face? To fight the human in the name of humanity! This fight could also be called a fight for (a certain version of) human rights.

For many, the violence of political struggles in all their forms calls for political action as the realization of a project to change the world – to make it more just. The violence of (what is called) politics is very real and perhaps explains the current interest in the Messianic as, in Benjamin's terms, the relation of a philosophy of history to politics as quest for happiness in the profane world.[25] To sharpen what is at stake here, calls, I argue, for further reflection on the notion of the human qua human. Certainly, in this endeavour I want to go beyond the very question-begging definition of human rights as the rights one has by virtue of being human. To get at the dynamics of the human qua human, the issues raised in the wake of this phrase call to be examined and developed in as full and elaborate a way as possible so that the clichés that abound with respect to this theme can at least be put under pressure, if not brought to the point of collapse. Clichés hide; they do not reveal. The points that, in my view, we need to keep in mind again come from Levinas. These are: 'When man truly approaches the Other [*Autrui*] he is uprooted from history' (Levinas 1969: 52), and that politics 'ensures happiness' as the search for equality as the struggle for recognition; while religion 'is Desire and not struggle for recognition. It is the surplus possible in a society of equals, that of glorious humility, responsibility, and sacrifice' (1969: 64).

Politics as happiness is the quest for the good life of the self. It is also the quest for freedom as freedom of the self. It does not, for Levinas, fundamentally concern justice because the latter is about responsibility in an encounter with the Other where, consequently, freedom is secondary. Politics and ethics thus seem to be irreconcilable. One is political to the extent that one is concerned with freedom and equality – which, in the end, is always *my* freedom and *my* being equal through recognition. Can there be a crossover of justice and freedom? Of

---

[25] As readers of Benjamin are aware, the situation of the relation of the profane, political world to the Messianic is complex, even if actors often pass over this complexity. Benjamin says, for example, that if the profane is represented by an arrow of history pointing 'to the goal toward which the profane dynamic acts and another marks the direction of Messianic intensity, then certainly the quest of free humanity for happiness runs counter to the Messianic direction' (Benjamin 1986: 312).

ethics and politics? Certainly, if justice as responsibility for the Other (Autrui) as the other person defines itself against freedom, ethics might thus be seen to define itself against politics – that is, in a certain sense, politics becomes necessary to ethics. But if ethics is 'first philosophy', as Levinas says, does this give rise to an origin of the human? The question of the origin of the human will be of particular import in the following chapters, but particularly in Chapter 8 on technics.

The question of origin has for many thinkers raised the issues of the biological status of humans in relation to animals and to a perception of nature. Darwin's struggle for existence, as we have seen, places the emphasis on utility in relation to survival. And even for Levinas, as commentators have noted (e.g., Gehrke (2006: 429) and Simmons (1999: 92)), animals are essentially biological beings engaged in a struggle for life and bereft of any ethical capacity (see Levinas 1988: 172). On this basis, human and animal would be essentially separate. While the animal clearly originates in bare life, the human is distinct from biology. Nevertheless, we will want to know whether being distinct from biology really means having overcome biological determinations in order to assume full humanness, in which case, bare life might still serve as a concealed origin, or whether, on the other hand, there is no biological entity that is not a participant in a way of life.

The issues posed in relation to the human raise the need to consider exactly how politics and the human are constituted with regard to specific events such as the proliferation of statelessness, events of torture and other forms of violence generated notably by the conflicts in Afghanistan, Iraq, Gaza, Syria, Africa and elsewhere.

In approaching actual political events that seem to be utterly intractable, we can revisit the well-known tradition in political thinking going back to Machiavelli, one that argues that the end justifies the means; in other words, to achieve a politically important result (e.g., the equality of all members of society), certain acts (e.g., killing), doubtful from a (Christian) moral point of view, might be required. This is often called a 'realist' approach to politics. Max Weber explains what is at issue here:

> No ethics in the world can dodge the fact that in numerous instances the attainment of 'good' ends is bound to the fact that one must be willing to pay the price of using morally dubious means or at least dangerous ones – and facing the possibility or even the probability of evil ramifications. From no ethics in the world can it be concluded when and to what extent the ethically good purpose 'justifies' the ethically dangerous means and ramifications. (Weber 1970: 121)

The point is, Weber adds, '[t]he decisive means for politics is violence' (121). It is known that Levinas proposes that, inscribed in the face of the Other, is the commandment, 'Thou shalt not kill'.

It has for a long time been said – and Weber underlines this – that ethical purity and political action do not mix. For one is concerned with the salvation of the soul, while the other is concerned with bringing about changes in this mundane world. Levinasian ethics also tends in this direction, so that in conceding the profound insights one is led to ask about how these insights could bring about changes in the 'real' world. Even more pointedly, it is said in the 'poem' of 'The Grand Inquisitor' in Dostoyevsky's great novel that for people to be virtuous they need first to have bread (Dostoyevsky 1982: 296). Does this principle also govern Levinas's philosophy, namely, that material needs must be met before spiritual needs can be satisfied? We shall see later (cf. Chapter 9) that the answer is in the negative. For now, it is simply appropriate to note that it is with the themes of hospitality and responsibility that Levinasian ethics of the other person may well introduce a crossover between ethics and politics.

But even Weber shows that a politics as extreme realism only concerned with ends and not with means brings about an impossible 'inner burden' to the individual political actor, so that only a machine-like demeanour of superhuman proportions would be capable of continuing to act in such a climate. Ultimately, then, politics and ethics cannot be separated, even if they remain distinct.

Perhaps the most important point is that for Weber, like Levinas, the human is only constituted existentially; it is not given essentially in an a priori, totalizing fashion. Only in acting (Weber) and only in saying (Levinas) do we see the human emerge as human.

Human as inoperativity

From a different angle, I have, in collaboration with Saul Newman, examined Agamben's notion of 'inoperativity', a term evoking Georges Bataille's '*désoeuvrement*' (see Lechte and Newman 2013: 90–93). Within the scope of inoperativity, the human is fundamentally self-constituting and is not defined by a 'struggle for existence' (Darwin), but always manifests a way of life – even in the face of death. Inoperativity evokes, then, Bataille's 'general economy', an economy that is not based on utility or the most efficient achievement of ends useful to the ultimate survival of the species, as is the case with the 'restricted economy' of balanced books and the accumulation and conservation of resources. This is, then, the domain of necessity. It has to be said against Bataille that the so-called restricted economy is not at all isolated from the dynamics of a *way* of life. For, if the very notion of bare life as 'struggle for existence' is to be found wanting in light of the fact that there is only a way of life, the idea that there can be – due to its utilitarian logic – a restricted economy totally distinct from the general economy becomes problematic. And so, just as there is no bare life, so, too, there is no truly restricted economy based exclusively on a means–ends rationality and the overcoming of the so-called necessity. Indeed, the restricted economy of everyday life – the conventional economy endlessly cited in the media and vaunted by economists – is a way of governing, not a credible model of human life as such.

There is, then, no human without a certain transcendence. Only when transcendence is brought into the picture can work begin on an adequate defence of such things as human rights. While, for some, introducing transcendence also evokes the distinction between transcendence and immanence, this is not the case here. On the other hand, there is a risk that emphasizing transcendence obscures the fact that, at a fundamental level, the difference between transcendence and immanence begins to become blurred.

'Immanence: "A" life': The plane of immanence and transcendence

The notion of transcendence may be further clarified by reference to a certain understanding of immanence. Thus, in Deleuze's philosophy, 'the transcendental field is defined by a plane of immanence and the plane of immanence by a life' (Deleuze 2001: 28). Against Heidegger, Deleuze says that the being of 'a' life (an individual life) cannot be ruled out of the sphere of the authentic human, as Heidegger's dying as 'present-at-hand' would imply. But a number of key questions remain unasked in Deleuze's scenario of 'a' life. What, for example, is a 'life' in the field of immanence? In a sense, Deleuze, strategically, does not give a full answer to this question, except to say that 'a' life is in the world and is a play with death. Life is always 'a' life, as has been noted, a singularity, or collection of singularities, prior to individuality, prior to a self or an ego. In Hume's terms, this is 'a' life of sensations before they are contingently organized into a form of subjectivity. Simondon's domain of preindividuality is in play out of which forms of individuation would subsequently emerge (see Simondon 2013). Thus, when discussing the 'plane of immanence' in relation to philosophy, Deleuze and Guattari also invoke, like Simondon, the pre-Socratic Greek philosopher, Anaximander and his notion of the indefinite and indeterminate 'Apeiron' (Deleuze and Guatteri 1991: 46), the pre-Socratic Greek term for 'nature' (Simondon 1989: 196). It is this that gives rise to individuations. As we shall see in our subsequent discussion of Simondon,[26] there is an issue with regard to how nature seems to be implicit in it and that it is *out of* preindividuality that individuations emerge, this being the hallmark of a kind of origin.

With life as collections of singularities derived from preindividuality, children can be seen to exemplify this notion of singularity to a high degree: 'small children all resemble one another and have hardly any individuality, but they have singularities: a smile, a gesture, a funny face – not subjective qualities' (Deleuze 2001: 30). Singularities are immanent – *in* the world – and Deleuze wants *this* to be a kind of marker of the human per se. As a marker, however, singularity seems to take on a transcendental quality, one that fuels the notion that 'transcendence is always a product of immanence'. Immanence, or 'in the world-ness', is what Deleuze advocates – that in which he urges us to believe. A passage from the second volume of Deleuze's cinema books, referred to by Deleuze's translator, John Rajchman, reinforces the idea of a belief in the world, or in singularity, or, simply, in immanence: 'The modern fact is that we no longer believe in this world. We do not even believe in the events which happen to us, love, death, as if they only half concerned us' (Deleuze 1989: 171). And so the 'link between man and the world is broken. Henceforth, this link must become an object of belief: it is the impossible which can only be restored within a faith' (172). In short: 'Only belief in the world can reconnect man to what he sees and hears' (172). Belief in the world is belief in (the plane of) immanence; and such a quasi-paradoxical belief means that immanence evokes its other: transcendence. A belief in immanence (belief in the world) is a vehicle, I would argue, of transcendence.

On the one hand, Deleuze goes 'beyond' Bataille (if one can speak in these terms)[27] in his approach because he does not get bogged down in a proof of, and justification for, the materialism of the world. In short, belief is in no sense foreign to Deleuze's idea of pure immanence as the world. On the other hand, life as a play of experimentation, contingency and with it, finitude, seems

---

[26] On Simondon and preindividuality, see Chapter 8.

[27] Because it does not go 'beyond' the world, immanence is seen by many interpreters of Deleuze as distinct from transcendence, where the subject, object, being, God – in effect the a priori concepts of Kant's noumenal sphere – are over and beyond the empirical world (on this, see, for example, Smith (2003) and Spindler (2010)).

to be incidentally promoted. To be rooted in finitude in this sense was what Heidegger's 'Being-toward-death' was geared to overcome. Deleuze, of course, could be said to have developed the notion of 'pure immanence' precisely to avoid the kind transcendence seemingly present in 'Being-toward-death'.

It is clear that for Deleuze and Guattari there has to be a plane of immanence as some sort of raw material out of which concepts in philosophy are created, and, apparently, this material cannot just be the refashioning of existing concepts.[28] And this is what raises difficulties. On the other hand, immanence is a way of avoiding false universalizations, or overbearing totalizations (such is entailed in the idea of life given as essentially biological or as essentially spiritual), so that the focus is on *a* life, a life as singular and unique. This is precisely the approach to be taken in the following investigation. On the other hand, because an understanding of immanence as pure immediacy and continuity with an environment is so prevalent – Bataille's animal 'in the world like water in water' (Bataille 1994: 24) – it seems to me that to employ a notion of immanence that becomes a kind of foundation – the 'prephilosophical' or philosophy's unthought – is to submerge it in, or make it beholden to, the plane of immanence. This is despite the fact that Deleuze and Guattari implicitly recognize this problem in as much as they work to render their thought concerning the plane of immanence more subtle by saying that pre-philosophy signifies 'nothing which pre-exists, but something *which does not exist outside of philosophy*' (Deleuze and Guattari 1991: 43; Authors' emphasis), that 'the non-philosophical is perhaps at the heart of philosophy' (43), that it is what cannot be thought yet must be thought, that it is the 'non-thought in thought' (59). This effort towards subtlety and complexity is, however, undermined by references to the plane of immanence as the duality of 'Thought' and 'Nature', of 'Physis' and '*Nous*' (41). Certainly, this is a Nature as 'fractalised' and, as such, a force for complexity rather than simplicity, a simplicity evoked by conventional geometry.[29] Nevertheless, thought itself is not fractal, thus reinforcing the impression that we are in fact dealing with an opposition.

But, in any event, in the context of immanence, is it really feasible that infinity, responsibility, Autrui (the Other as others, and in particular the other person) and the like could be thought? It seems doubtful as such concepts would be conceived not as creations of immanence, but the outcome of transcendence.

---

[28] Deleuze makes it quite clear that old concepts become 'useless' and 'inadequate' and that it is better to create new ones (1988: 111).

[29] On 'Fractal', see Lechte (2003: 85–87).

On this basis, immanence comes to be pursued for its own sake, regardless of the cost.

The real question that must be asked, however, as concerns Deleuze's 'plane of pure immanence' is: What would bare life be in relation to immanence and transcendence? The answer is that bare life would be equivalent to absolute immanence in that it is indistinguishable from pure nature as the environment, absolutely without transcendence in the sense that it would be the object of no language, of no signs, of no externalization, thus, of no technics. It would be – as will be shown in Chapter 8 – simply an absolute interiority.

Conclusion

In his commentary on Deleuze's, 'Immanence: A Life …', Agamben goes to the nub of the problem regarding an understanding of the term 'life'. Thus, he writes that '"life" is not a medical and scientific notion but a philosophical, political, and theological concept, and […] many of the categories of our philosophical tradition must therefore be rethought accordingly' (Agamben 1999: 239). Analogously, we could say that human is not a biological or scientific notion but now should be understood as being precisely, philosophical, political and theological. The human, in short, cannot be reduced to bare life as a purely material nutritive substance. This is particularly the case once power becomes interested – as has been the case since the nineteenth century – in the biological basis of human societies. Such an interest alone brings the human into the orbit of power and the political.

More pointedly, the human is that entity in relation to which transcendence is essential. Does this mean that animals are excluded from what is essentially human? It would seem that animality *is* essentially distinct from humanity if one accepts Heidegger's claim that only Dasein dies (is transcendent), while the animal perishes (is a mere immanence). However, the animality–humanity double is of a much more complex hue than Heidegger's formulation would suggest. And we will explore this in some detail in relation to Heidegger, Descartes, Derrida and Simondon.

Most of all, however, it remains to be seen the extent to which human transcendence (and thus the human as such) is tied to a 'way of life' (*bios*) that cuts across the *bios-zōē* distinction. Thus, it is a matter of interpreting the notion proposed by Nietzsche in *The Will to Power* (1968) when he says that: '*Consciousness is present to the extent that consciousness is useful*' (1968:

Sect 505; Nietzsche's emphasis). Is the notion of 'use' (related to 'necessity') at all sustainable when it comes to the human? We must continue to pursue this question throughout the entirety of what follows; for the response we give will have the profoundest consequences for the human and the way it is understood.

2

Consumer Society and Necessity

The guiding point of reference for this chapter is captured in a statement by Maurice Merleau-Ponty in his course on Nature at the Collège de France, to the effect that: 'It can be perfectly argued that life is not uniquely submitted to the principle of utility' (2003: 183). Utility, we shall see, is tied irrevocably to necessity.

Before undertaking a study of the human in relation to political exigencies, it makes sense to clarify exactly what is at stake in focusing the notion of the human in relation to utility and necessity in general and, in particular, on Arendt's notion of necessity as the satisfaction of basic needs, exemplified for Arendt by the activities in the Greek *oikos*. Here, we can summarily note that in *The Human Condition* (1958) Arendt argues that, in ensuring the sustainability of biological life, the *oikos* functions as the material support for the *polis* because it is thought that the care of the body and the assurance of reproductive life are the conditions of possibility of political life (*bios*). In this light, the question posed in relation to contemporary consumer society is that of whether or not the underlying rationale of consumer society (which may well be different from its truth or reality) is identical or similar to that given by Arendt for the Greek *polis*. That is to say, is the rationale of consumer society that of solving the problem of necessity, even to an excessive degree, as we saw intimated by Marshall Sahlins? My argument will be that, at an unconscious level, the logic of this society implies the effort of distancing consumers from the necessity to the greatest extent possible. The opposition between wealth and poverty is nothing else but this. Wealth and affluence are thus based on the degree to which a consumer is distanced, as it is thought, from the 'basic needs for survival', or from subsistence.

In the BBC programme *The Super-rich and Us*, presented by Jacques Peretti (2015),[1] the issue addressed is the ever-widening gap in capitalist societies between the wealth of the 1 per cent 'super-rich' and the rest of the population.

---

[1] TV programme broadcast on ABC2, Australia, on 30 April and 7 May 2015.

Nick Hanauser, American entrepreneur and venture capitalist, whose company, aQuantive, was acquired by Microsoft for US$6.4 billion, fears that if the wealth of people like himself continues to increase while the incomes of the remainder do not, there may well be social disruption on a grand scale. What Hanauer's view implies is that the wealth of the super-rich is so vastly removed from a mere survival or subsistence level that it engenders the possibility of revolt by those whose income and resources are much closer to subsistence level. In other words, the great debate about inequality turns on the extent to which people are or are not close to what is called the poverty line, where life becomes close to mere physical survival. Traditional economic theory, as we saw earlier, of course refers to a fundamental scarcity of resources relative, if not to human needs, then certainly in relation to wants or desire. Scarcity drives the whole economic edifice of human society. If it were not for scarcity, the theory goes, there would be no subsistence existence, for *everyone* would have as much as they wanted.

In the first part of his 1970 study, *The Consumer Society*, Jean Baudrillard (1998) addresses the issues that I want to develop further here. In the first place, Baudrillard recognizes that it is appropriate to compare the social logic of Western behaviours regarding consumerism to those of non-Western cultures. In this way, the excess and waste (exemplified in the West by paying £100,000 for a single dress (cf. Peritti (2015)) or by the 'destruction' of objects – by the fact that they are used for only a fraction of their potential before being discarded and replaced) are characteristic of all societies, and that the North American potlatch finds its correlate in, among other things, expenditures in Western societies on art (cf., US$300 million for Gauguin's *When Will You Marry?*), on sport, on dining at luxurious restaurants, on military weapons, on luxury cars (US$4.5 million for a Lamborghini Veneno Roaster), on the stock market and so on. Waste thus characterizes all societies. The counterpart of affluence is waste. We can see, then, that Baudrillard assimilates Western societies ('societies of growth') to the model of the 'general economy' (expenditure without return) proposed by Georges Bataille. The element of (self) destruction and 'useless prodigality' implicit in the general economy is thus also detected in societies thought to harbour economies based on pure utility and the conservation of resources for future investment – what Bataille called the 'restricted economy'. While Bataille tended to locate the general economy in non-Western societies, Baudrillard *also* locates it, as we have seen, in developed economies.

In his study, Baudrillard is led to pose the question that precisely concerns us here, namely: 'Do human beings [les êtres] organize themselves for purposes of survival, or in terms of the individual or collective meaning they give to their lives?' (1998: 44). Valéry, as cited by Baudrillard, says that only after having satisfied the needs of animal necessity is it possible to evolve to another level: 'Foresight and the laying of provisions gradually freed us from the rigours of our animal necessities and the "word-for-word" character of our wants' (1998: 44). For his part, Baudrillard declares in opposition to Valéry that 'this value of "being", this structural value may involve the sacrifice of economic values' (1998: 44). Survival – bare life – is thus not the driving force of human being.

It is noteworthy, perhaps, that Valéry's way of presenting the human condition largely mirrors Arendt's argument in *The Human Condition*, where, in light of the Greeks, it is said that the problem of necessity must be solved before it is possible to enjoy the freedom of word and deed in the *polis*. We will have occasion to return to Arendt's argument, but it is worth recalling here that labour for Arendt (as opposed to work) is only ever implicated in necessity, or pure survival.[2] Baudrillard's point, by contrast is, as we saw, that survival is not the driving force of the human condition, that the economic as utility can be sacrificed, that the idea that there is a measurable and influential level of subsistence in human affairs is a myth and that, ultimately, Western and non-Western cultures alike are affected by the general economy of expenditure without return. To consume as if there were no tomorrow is a mark of consumption, not production, the latter being the domain political economy had privileged in its understanding of capitalism. Political economy's claim to credibility and plausibility only works on the basis of the division of societies into developed (Western) capitalist and underdeveloped (non-Western) societies. Bataille's approach, which influences Baudrillard, does not work with this division. All societies, to a greater or lesser degree, are constituted, not just by production, but also by the excessive consumption of the general economy.

Despite this, Baudrillard seems to undermine his position regarding the non-determinate status of necessity and survival when he writes: 'All production and expenditure *beyond the means of strict survival* can be termed waste' (1998: 45; emphasis added). This seems to imply that there *is* a basic level of survival – the level of necessity – which is ultimately determinate – that *homo economicus* does exist – and that Arendt and Baudrillard on consumer society might be closer on this point than was initially thought. Baudrillard also argues that waste can be defined only in relation to utility – utility being ultimately evocative of necessity. He does this because he is under the sway of Bataille's distinction between the

---

[2] Thus, while work is not antipolitical, labour is because its sole concern is the labourer, 'alone with his body, *facing naked necessity* to keep himself alive' (Arendt 1958: 212; emphasis added).

general and the restricted economy as the economy of utility. This opposition proposed by Bataille will be examined in detail in Chapter 5; for now, let us simply say that when Baudrillard separates waste, as the element most characteristic of consumer societies, from utility (which, in his view one has to do because, as we saw, waste has meaning only in relation to utility), the opposition between 'developed' and 'under-developed' societies is reinforced. For while it may, from a certain angle, be possible to show excess and waste are a driving force in Western societies, it leaves wide open the question of utility in non-Western societies, such as those of the 'indigenous Melanesians' evoked by Baudrillard. The clear implication is that while societies of a modern industrial type can mime the excess and potlatch logic of certain traditional economies, the fact remains that non-industrial economies are seen to be incapable of imitating the drive for utility so characteristic of post-Enlightenment industrialized societies.

Baudrillard brings a degree of whimsy to his study when he invokes the fantasmatic aspect of the consumer object: it performs 'magic' – it brings happiness, or rather, it becomes the incontrovertible *sign* of happiness. It is thus all that anyone could ever want in this life. As such, it is pursued with religious fervour. Here, let us not leap to the conclusion, plausible as it might be, that the object as the sign of happiness and the magic that it weaves in bringing happiness (this is the message of all advertising) – that this world of fantasy is governed by an underlying sense that poverty and penury – starvation and homelessness – are as far as can be from being reality for the consumer-individual. Quantitatively, *all* needs are more than met: they are fulfilled to overflowing. But the fear is that one day they might not be met. Phantasmatically, one might lose everything, become bereft of resources and returned to nature's embrace. Nature for the consumer is a mark of an objectless world.

Ultimately, then, there is an underlying quantitative assumption in the term 'consumer' itself. It is really unnecessary to venture far from the established script to press home the point. For it is well known that to live a subsistence existence is the very opposite of that of the life of a consumer, the basis of what has come to be called the 'consumer society'. In subsistence existence, all needs are not met, only those deemed to be necessary for survival or the preservation of life. To live a subsistence existence is to be in a condition of bare life. We can say that to keep bare life at bay nevertheless presupposes that bare life is what drives the system called 'consumer society'.

This thesis is effectively hegemonic. It governs the economic and social history of the West – the question being: When did Western society begin to become consumerist? For the Marx of *Capital*, the answer is fairly straightforward:

consumer society emerges when forces of production emerge so that 'exchange-value' comes to take precedence over 'use-value'. The dominance of exchange-value obviously is at its height when art sells for apparently astronomical prices, when housing is the value from the profit one can make from it, when the price of a means of transport can be in millions of dollars, when cuisine becomes the same as gastronomy, etc. All this despite appearances pivots on the quantity of resources deemed to support bare life.

If we have here an indication of how bare life determines the history of consumer society, what might it do to the future of the said society? The answer is contained in the term 'development', as in the phrase 'societies on the way to development'. To become a developed economy is to become one in which the greater majority of members are no longer living a subsistence existence (are in poverty) but have become consumers. Even though, clearly, uneven development (inequalities) complicates the picture, all economies are – or are not – on the way to development, are – or are not – developed.

A key point noted by Baudrillard (along with many others) is that inequalities in consumption dominate developed economies. Indeed, a system in equilibrium where all consumed equal amounts is, says our analyst, an illusion. Rather, the system is structurally, not conjuncturally, founded in the difference between wealth and poverty, so that it produces as many dissatisfactions as satisfactions (1998: 70). Equilibrium is thus always 'to come' and never arrives, so that in this sense, all societies are on the 'way to development'. Western and non-Western societies begin to resemble each other. And we will see subsequently that it is a matter of reformulating Baudrillard's thesis a little in order to make the link between the so-called developed and not-developed societies even closer.

Baudrillard, clearly under the influence of the structuralist ascendency of the 1970s, invokes 'code', 'system', 'differences' in his analyses. In other words, the idea of substantive differences or real qualities that may be isolated in themselves is not, on the face of it, part of his approach.

'Necessity' and Pierre Bourdieu's theory of taste

The pervasiveness of 'necessity' as an explanatory tool is seen in the call for the satisfaction of basic physical needs – as defined by the existing state of society – as a human right as well as in Pierre Bourdieu's very influential notion of *habitus*, where a 'taste for necessity' (Bourdieu 1986: 374–396) is characteristic of those who have grown to accept 'self-imposed constraint' – luxury not being 'for the likes of them' – so that they are grateful to have a roof over their head and enough food to survive on. Luxury, as Bourdieu conceives it, then, is the 'distance from necessity', so that we have 'two contrasting ways of defying nature, need, appetite, desire' (1986: 254). Certainly, Bourdieu's whole theory of taste depends on those whom he observes taking it absolutely for granted that there is a level of subsistence in which basic needs alone are satisfied – the level at which scarcity operates – as opposed to luxury and abundance, the other (necessary) terms in the opposition: 'necessity/luxury'. Only in this way does it make sense to refer to 'the unbridled squandering which only highlights the privations of ordinary existence and the ostentatious freedom of gratuitous expense' (1986: 254–255).

It is of course perfectly possible that it is the socio-economic strata analysed who accept the 'necessity/luxury' opposition, where, effectively, necessity is equivalent to bare life, not the researcher himself. How plausible is this statement? At first reading, it would seem that, as structuralist as he is, Bourdieu would be unlikely to accept that there is an actually objective level of bare life in relation to which all else is in play. Difference is the factor to bear in mind, not the qualitative truth of a reality 'in itself', so that what would be determinate would be the differential relation between those who have a 'taste for the necessary' and those who live a life of luxury; not absolute but relative poverty would rule, just as we would be dealing not with absolute but with relative wealth.[3] Consumption patterns would only have validity on this reading from a strictly comparative perspective. Or, to put it in Bourdieu's own words, when he refers to the fields of 'pursuit of distinction', 'none is more obviously predisposed to express social differences than the world of luxury goods' (226). But then, when it comes to the issue of privation, Bourdieu repeats a common refrain: that there is a level of pure, natural biological need that must be satisfied before any participation in high culture is possible. Thus: 'the aesthetic disposition tends to bracket off the nature and function of the object represented' (1986: 54). Further, the conditions of existence of an aesthetic disposition in relation to cultural goods (which entail a certain mode of consumption) 'are characterised by the suspension and removal of economic *necessity* and by objective and subjective distance from *practical urgencies*, which is the basis of objective and subjective distance from groups subjected to those determinisms' (1986: 54; emphasis added). What would 'practical' or 'ordinary' (as Bourdieu later puts it) 'urgencies' be here? The

---

[3] It is perhaps worth noting that 'relative wealth' implies a competition for wealth and resources where there would always be 'winners' and 'losers', while, theoretically, a level of absolute wealth could be the basis of general equality, as it would be a level that remains the same for all.

answer may be derived from the meaning Bourdieu deduces for the aesthetic disposition. For, if there is a single characteristic that defines it even more than the content of a certain cultural capital (knowledge and appreciation of classical music and literature, etc.), it is that aesthetic activity is done exclusively for its own sake. Indeed, a 'high culture' lifestyle is what is done for the sake of doing it. In fact we could almost be speaking of a watered-down version of Bataille's 'general economy'. The following passage from *Distinction* (1986) well captures the purport of what is at stake:

> The aesthetic disposition, a generalised capacity to neutralise ordinary urgencies and to bracket off practical ends, a durable inclination and aptitude for practice without a practical function, can only be constituted within an experience of the world freed from urgency [Bourdieu emphasizes yet again!] and through the practice of activities which are ends in themselves, such as scholastic exercises or the contemplation of works of art. In other words, it presupposes the distance from the world […] which is the basis of the bourgeois experience of the world. (1986: 54)

Bourdieu adds, by way of elaboration:

> The scholastic world of regulated games and exercises for exercise' sake is at least in this respect, less remote than it might appear from the 'bourgeois' world and the countless 'disinterested' and 'gratuitous' acts which go to make up its distinctive rarity, such as home maintenance and decoration, occasioning a daily *squandering* of care, time and labour (often through the intermediary of servants), walking and tourism, movements without any other aim than physical exercise and the symbolic appropriation of a world reduced to the status of a landscape, or ceremonies and receptions, pretexts for a display of ritual luxuries, décors, conversations and finery, not mention of course, artistic practices and enjoyments. (55; emphasis added)

In sum, the manifestation of the 'general economy' is a sign that:

> Economic power is first and foremost a power to keep economic necessity at arm's length. This is why it universally asserts itself by the destruction of riches, conspicuous consumption, squandering and every form of *gratuitous* luxury. (1986: 55; Bourdieu's emphasis)

Domination occurs, in effect, when those who live a life of (relative?) luxury can afford to ignore necessity – who can affirm their 'power over a dominated necessity' (56) – compared to those who are dominated *by* necessity, that is, 'ordinary interests and urgencies' (56). That is, 'The tastes of freedom can only assert themselves as such in relation to the tastes of necessity' (56).

Despite there being no absolute standard for the judgement of taste as one finds in Kant and against whom Bourdieu takes up the cudgels, there is little doubt that there is, in Bourdieu's framework, the equivalent of a subsistence level of existence, evoked by the notion of 'economic necessity'. To be sure, it might be objected that such necessity is only ever relative to freedom – the distance from economic necessity and that, in a different context, what here counts as economic necessity might there count as luxury. How plausible is this objection? Is it true that there is, for Bourdieu, no absolute level of subsistence, which would also be a basic level of utility?

As a starting point, compare the point made by Bourdieu that the foods of those living in the realm of necessity will be the 'heaviest, grossest and most fattening', 'bread, potatoes, fats' (179). In other words, we are moving to the point of the *objective* nature of food of poor people. The foods cited are the poor person's staple. By implication, they are the cheapest available, even if they are not essentially unattractive to the gourmand – although it is hard to believe that this is not also what is implied. At any rate, there can be little doubt about the assumed purely utilitarian nature of such foods. They simply function to keep 'mind and body alive'. In fact, Bourdieu does indeed follow Marx – not just in privileging the terms 'freedom' and 'necessity' as his key analytical terms in *Distinction*, but in believing with Marx that there is a level of basic subsistence, represented for Marx by labour, as is shown by the following passage from *Capital, Volume III*:

> the realm of freedom actually begins only where labour which is determined by necessity and mundane considerations ceases; thus in the very nature of things it lies beyond the sphere of actual material production. Just as the savage must wrestle with Nature to satisfy his wants, to maintain and reproduce life, so must civilized man, and he must do so in all social formations and under all possible modes of production. With his development this realm of physical necessity expands as a result of his wants; but, at the same time, the forces of production which satisfy these wants also increase. Freedom in this field can only consist in socialised man, the associated producers, rationally regulating their interchange with Nature, bringing it under their common control, instead of being ruled by it as by the blind forces of Nature; and achieving this with the least expenditure of energy and under conditions most favourable to, and worthy of, their human nature. But it nonetheless still remains a realm of necessity. Beyond it begins that development of human energy which is an end in itself, the true realm of freedom, which, however, can blossom forth only with this realm of necessity as its basis. (Marx 1977: 820; cited in Klagge 1986: 770)

Labour is always a 'means' never an end in itself. Thus, Klagge says that, [t]he realm of necessity can never be eliminated, but it should be minimized as much as possible' (1986: 774). Again: 'Material production is required to meet our physical needs, to provide for our physical necessities. Indeed, Marx also calls it the "realm of physical necessity"' (775).

And so, with Marx in mind, even if Bourdieu moves on from focusing on particular foods to talk about different food régimes – régimes related to different ideas of the body (fat, or solid, for the working class and slim for the more privileged classes), there remains an underlying assumption of what might constitute a bedrock level of sustenance, even if, for the most part, this bedrock is not explicitly described. In other words, relative privation (the privation of the working class, a privation that has meaning only in relation to the relative sumptuousness and distance from privation or necessity of bourgeois consumption) evokes absolute privation, the level at which starvation would ensue due to the total deprivation of nourishment.

Here it is worth noting the somewhat intricate manner in which Bourdieu treats the *way* that food is eaten by different social groupings. He refers, for instance, to 'working-class and bourgeois ways of treating food, of serving, presenting and offering it, which', he says, 'are infinitely more revelatory than even the nature of the products involved' (Bourdieu 1986: 193). It is almost as though gestures were the key element in the depiction of a *way* of life where necessity would cease to be the defining factor. Consequently, two régimes of gestures would confront each other, two régimes which would contribute to defining social identities, but not on the basis of one or other being closer to nature or necessity. Popular culture might often be criticized by the proponents of 'high' culture for being banal but not for being closer to necessity.

Be this as it may, Bourdieu seemingly recoils from pursuing the implications of this mode of analysing régimes of gestures that constitute a way of life and instead reiterates, in later sections of *Distinction*, his initial invocation of necessity and all that that implies regarding natural, 'primary needs'. It could even be said that 'primary needs' to which the working class have close proximity are also to be closer to reality, or even to truth. For the working class can be characterized by 'being' (the way things are) as opposed to bourgeois 'seeming' (the way things appear to be); they opt for material substance as against the opposing classes 'pure form, done only for form's sake' (1986: 199); they incarnate 'reality' as against 'sham' (199); they embody 'simple, common ways of speaking' as opposed to rhetorical elegance and stylistic accomplishment, which have distinctive value. The bourgeois class, unlike Rousseau, explicitly treat raw nature as 'brutish necessity' (254), as barbaric and unrefined – the domain from whence 'taste' is lacking. This, of course, would also imply that the working-class comportment is also closer to animal behaviour. Eventually, Bourdieu will summarize this by saying: 'Ease [as opposed to anxiety and uncertainty] is so universally approved only because it represents the most visible assertion of freedom from the constraints which dominate ordinary people, the most indisputable affirmation of capital as the capacity to satisfy the demand of *biological nature* or of the authority which entitles one to ignore them' (255; emphasis added).

If we were to follow Bourdieu's own precept, we would say that in classifying social reality (e.g., that bourgeois taste entails a distancing from necessity – from animality, in effect), Bourdieu classifies himself. In the polarization of working class and bourgeoisie, it would not be difficult to show that Bourdieu takes the part of the working class, to the extent in particular, I suggest, that he – like Marx – considers that there is truly is a level of necessity equivalent to subsistence[4] which is evoked by working-class experience, if the members of this class are not in all essentials the incarnation of necessity. In short, privation is not absolute even if the possibility of the latter always exists. Thus, in classifying the world in the way he does, Bourdieu reveals his adherence to the principle enunciated by Marx, namely that freedom begins only where labour done for physical survival ceases, it being understood here that all classes and all peoples must first satisfy, whether directly or by proxy (slavery), the needs of biological life. It might be objected, however, that Bourdieu, far from subscribing himself to what we have stated rather provides a map of the way that, in social reality, the world is represented; it has nothing to do with Bourdieu's own philosophical or political position, or, for that matter, with his own *relation* to social reality.

But just as the fact that 'no appeal' being made in *Distinction* to 'the tradition of philosophical or literary aesthetics' is a 'deliberate refusal', so we must assume that the key coordinates of his study, the terms 'necessity' and 'freedom', were the outcome of a deliberate decision, and that it would be disingenuous in the extreme to assume that this decision was made in ignorance of the history of these terms, especially in Marx, but also in Arendt. In this light, the key assumption and question of Bourdieu's study becomes: Given that all humans must first solve the problem of necessity as pure survival, how do different occupational groupings,

---

[4] In an effort to criticize 'Maslow's hierarchy of needs' (which has basic needs of food and shelter at the bottom of the hierarchy), Trigg (2004) is forced to acknowledge that there is a similarity on this point between Maslow and Bourdieu: 'at low levels of income, there is a close relationship between the choices of individuals and their primary needs' (2004: 401). Trigg fails to follow through the possible implications of this because he turns to analyse '*habitus*' rather than the dialectic of 'necessity and freedom'. But *habitus* is what gives one a taste for necessity, not what eliminates 'primary needs'.

ultimately classifiable in terms of working class and bourgeois class, live their respective relation to necessity and to its counter point, freedom? *Distinction*, focusing on patterns of consumption of all kinds, is Bourdieu's answer to this question, where the working class live in intimate proximity to necessity and the bourgeoisie define themselves through their distance from necessity – this distance being equivalent to the degree of freedom one experiences.

But if freedom is also domination because 'distance from necessity' also means manifesting one's disdain for necessity – 'stigmatising' it – and, by implication, disdain for those unwilling or unable to rise above necessity, is this not a significant limit to freedom? Indeed, all the indices point towards the re-emergence of the master–slave dialectic, where, ultimately, it is the slave as labourer who, historically, holds all the shots. That Bourdieu himself does not recognize this is seen in the fact that, effectively, he valorizes the freedom that the bourgeoisie have acquired. Because necessity is a truth, the freedom that is inseparable from it is also a truth. Were this not so, the whole schema of the dominant and the dominated class would become meaningless. Recall that a key element of the experience of members of the dominant class is that they have the luxury (which in this case is the luxury of symbolic capital) of doing things entirely for their own sake and not for any utilitarian motive. For to be free is essentially to be free of utility grounded in necessity.

The main reason for examining Bourdieu's argument is in order to show that, despite its level of sophistication and subtlety, it is ultimately governed by the assumptions governing explanations of modernity, namely that what drives the human is the urge to survive, that until basic or primary needs have been satisfied – until Man has settled his accounts with Nature, as Marx would say – no other form of life is possible. In short: freedom presupposes the overcoming of necessity.

It is clear, then, that reference to 'primary needs' not only implies the whole gamut of secondary needs upon which, for many commentators, consumer society is based, but it also implies that there is a level of natural need – the needs of living beings as part of nature. The notion of technics, as we shall see (cf. Chapter 8), is tied to the idea of the human's separation from, or integration in, nature. It is only in the seventeenth century that nature emerges with the natural sciences in its modern guise as the object of study. Nature has its own laws; 'Man', to the extent that he has natural needs, is part of nature. 'Man', to the extent that he is part of nature, also manifests his animal nature: or his being in immanence.

Nearly half a century ago (1970) Baudrillard signalled that the notion of basic or primary needs was part of the ideology of *homo economicus* dominating economic science, including political economy. Ultimately, argued Baudrillard, the whole idea of utility stems from the positing of primary needs, such as the satiating of hunger, etc. While it might be true that hunger, and even more, starvation, do not signify and have no symbolic status, they pertain to individuals in a traumatic state rather than to communities as historically and culturally constituted. In a certain sense, then, starvation and even famine are traumatic and tend not to signify. But they do signify and become very different when, within communities, individuals sacrifice for each other, or where there exists inherited strategies for dealing with difficult times. Thus, the economic theory which attempts to situate the genesis of consumption in the initial satisfaction of primary needs forgets that human life is essentially social, cultural, political – in a word, 'communal', even where disruption, or even revolution, characterizes communities. We can thus say, in light of Baudrillard's prescient essay, that '[e]ven before survival has been assured, every group or individual experiences a vital pressure to produce themselves meaningfully in a system of exchange and relationships' (1981: 74). Three key terms should thus be marked here: 'meaning', 'exchange' and 'relation' – each of them connoting the humanness of the human, each of them putting primary, biological needs out of the picture. We can thus conclude that, were they to exist, primary needs would not have meaning, would not exist in a system of exchange, like language, and would not be part of any relation, whether this be social, cultural or political. Baudrillard puts it well: 'It would appear that a "theory of needs" has no meaning' (1981: 79). Even more importantly, Baudrillard says (and Sahlins (1974) only echoes this in more detail): 'There have never been "societies of scarcity" [i.e., subsistence societies] or "societies of abundance"' (1981: 81). This is because scarcity and abundance are structurally constituted; they do not exist in themselves. They are, in other words, relational. To say this is to say that the economist's 'scarcity' is relative to abundance as constituted in a given system of meaning and exchange. Thus, '[i]t is impossible to isolate an abstract, "natural" stage of poverty or to determine absolutely "what man needs to survive"' (1981: 81).

It is, however, the ideology of primary need and fundamental utility, and the abstracting of individuals out of their socio-cultural and group milieu, that has characterized modernity. Modernity, in short, has been explained as the system that overcomes primary deprivation, and that satisfies primary needs, thereby enabling individuals to engage in a full social and cultural life. In this sense, we could almost say that modernity coincides with the invention of poverty and certainly of the notion of subsistence. As will be shown below, such an approach has not been without certain advantages from a political point view, for it has paved the way for the idea of project as progress and change. The point being that if one does accept that there is no absolute privation, what justification can there be to pursue a course that aims to bring about a more just state of affairs for living beings? This is the question that will concern a later chapter of this study. For now, it is necessary to show how the concept of nature has contributed to the ideology of primary needs.

The issue of nature

We have already seen that, for Marx, labour, in its essential form, is the means through which human beings subdue and come to dominate nature. This, of course, is the nineteenth-century culmination of a process that began in the seventeenth century and that produces the concept of Nature. No doubt, with Newton, Francis Bacon and Descartes in the seventeenth century, Nature is yet to appear as a general field for study in its own right, being rather the study of individualities. But with the arrival of natural history and the emergence of what will become, especially in light of Newton and Bacon, the 'scientific method', Nature as an object is on the way to being distinguished as the general field it will become with the refinement of the natural sciences in the second half of the nineteenth century.

With regard to the eighteenth century, one can talk about the aetheticization of nature with Kant (cf. the sublime), or a more profoundly bucolic nature with Rousseau and the romantics. Even if Rousseau says at the beginning of his *Essay On the Origin of Language* (1986: 11) that passion and not need elicited the first words uttered by humans, it is still the case that Nature, as a broad field of interest and object of inquiry, is being further delineated. Indeed, in Rousseauian terms – as we shall see in more detail later[5] – natural man is the true man; social man is but a corrupt form of humanity. The 'golden age', says Rousseau, is the age when humanity lived in a state of nature. Natural man alone is free, the *Social Contract* will claim, while social man is 'everywhere in chains'.

Hegel, in his *Philosophy of Right* (1975), also addresses the relation between man and Nature. Man only realizes his destiny in freedom, says Hegel, after making the drives and impulses of nature his own, that is, only after transcending his natural animal being and assuming his truly human being.

---

[5]   See Chapter 8.

On this basis, freedom is not to be equated with arbitrary and indeterminate freedom to act on impulse, which is derivative of man's natural condition and highlighted as true freedom in theories of the 'state of nature', but is only realized through the unity of 'right' (as the law in its broadest sense) and will, and freedom as such becomes the determinate goal of action. Arbitrary, natural freedom can only be freedom 'in itself', while determinate action opens the way to freedom 'for itself'. Whatever might be the merits or otherwise of Hegel's notion of freedom, it is important here to note the fact of the overcoming of nature (nature taken in charge by the conscious ego[6]) *before* authentic freedom can be a possibility Indeed, to this end, Hegel – still in the *Philosophy of Right* – refers to the science of political economy and to the 'the system of needs':

> An animal's needs and its ways and means of satisfying them are both alike restricted in scope. Though man is subject to this restriction too, yet at the same time he evinces his transcendence of it and his universality, first by the multiplication of needs and means of satisfying them, and secondly by the differentiation and division of concrete need into single parts and aspects which in turn become different needs, particularized and so more abstract. (Hegel 1975: 127 §190)

Hegel thus views nature as that which must be overcome, or taken possession of, if the human is to become both truly human and the incarnation of will as will to freedom. Although it might appear that Hegel reserves the term 'necessity' exclusively as a synonym for contingency in his *Science of Logic* (1966: 183), when the meaning of contingency is set out, it is clear that necessity is in fact another term for 'nature'. Like nature, contingency is 'determinate', 'immediately actual', what 'contains Necessity as its Being-in-Self' (1966: 183).[7]

Foucault's *The Order of Things* (1970) gives priority to changes in the *episteme* in the evolution of science over changes in the object of science, so that it would not be the discovery of plant life in the eighteenth century that gives rise to Botany as new modes of classification, but that the appearance of new modes of classification made plant life the appropriate object for Botany. In short, for

---

[6]   As will become clear in Chapter 4 on freedom, Hegel judges that the idea of 'natural' freedom is false, 'because to be confined to mere physical needs as such and their direct satisfaction would simply be the condition in which the mental is plunged in the natural and so would be one of savagery and unfreedom, while freedom itself is to be found only in the reflection of the mind into itself, in mind's distinction from nature, and in the reflex of mind in nature' (Hegel 1975:128 §194).

[7]   A great deal has of course been written, from the perspective of the Logic, on both Nature and contingency in Hegel, especially in terms of clarifying whether Hegel's 'Nature' is but a part of the whole system of ideas that is Hegel's philosophy.

Foucault, changes in the subjective side transform knowledge, not the discovery of new objects. Nevertheless, even within an 'archaeological' approach it is possible to see that in the nineteenth century, life as natural life emerges at the same time as political economy posits labour as the means of ensuring human biological survival.

All through the eighteenth century – most notably with the physiocrats – the notion of labour as satisfying, in the first instance, basic needs began to come to the fore. The labour theory of value, in short, emerged. Thus, if, for the physiocrats agricultural wage-labour is the key to the satisfaction of all needs and basis of the labourer's subsistence, this is no doubt because, in addition, such labour is closest to a direct encounter with nature. 'Before exchange', says Foucault in analysing the thought of the physiocrat, Quesnay, 'there is nothing but that rare or abundant reality provided by nature' (Foucault 1982: 192). The wage received by the agricultural labourer enables the satisfaction of basic needs and the surplus product, should there be any, would satisfy the basic needs of others. For the physiocrats, the 'fruit I am hungry for, which I pick and eat, is a *commodity* presented to me by nature' (192: Foucault's emphasis). Subsistence, as a result, is the norm rather than the exception, while in the nineteenth century subsistence will come to be seen, from Adam Smith onward, as the exception rather than the norm. But, in any case, everyone must satisfy the primary needs of subsistence before other needs and desires can be addressed, even if, in the new theory, the subsistence level is no longer the end of the system and rather becomes the means of gravitating to other things, as occurs with abundance and the play of desire in consumer society. For the seventeenth- and eighteenth-century economic theories, the 'value of things is [...] founded on their utility' (1970: 196). It is utility which will come to incorporate primary and secondary needs, the latter always retaining an echo of the former; for secondary needs, to use Bourdieu's terms, are nothing but the sign of the distance from necessity.

On the working of nature, it can be said that, with the development of science in the seventeenth and eighteenth centuries, 'wealth, nature, or languages' are not thought of as having been bequeathed by preceding ages' (1970: 208). Instead, there is a break, or caesura, between the Renaissance and the Classical Age (seventeenth and eighteenth centuries) and, again, between the Classical Age and the nineteenth century. But this latter break only exists, as I have said, because subsistence no longer comprehends the entire logic of the system. Profit, or surplus value, corresponding to production that satisfies secondary needs comes to occupy centre stage with the development of political economy in the nineteenth century.

However, Foucault emphasizes that the issue of primary need remains integral also to political economy: 'in the last resort, need – for food, clothing, housing – defined the absolute measure of the market price' (1970: 222). And he continues by pointing out: 'All through the Classical Age, it was *necessity* that was the measure of equivalences, and value in use that served as absolute reference for exchange value' (1970: 222; emphasis added). With Adam Smith, exchange is no longer expressed in terms of need (even if need is still at the basis of the system); instead, labour becomes, through the ever-increasing number of divisions in it, an absolute measure of value and not just a measure of the cost of maintaining a worker in a condition of subsistence (although it is also this). In short, the productivity of labour, compared to what it was in the Classical Age, increases to an almost unimaginable degree: to cite Foucault's example: one worker producing 20 pins in a day compared with ten workers, each with a given task, producing 48,000 pins in a day (1970: 224). Despite this, '[n]eeds, and the exchange of products that can answer to them, are still the principle of the economy; they are its prime motive and circumscribe it; labour and the division that organises it are merely its effects' (1970: 224).

In his commentary on Smith and Ricardo, Foucault points to the way that scarcity becomes the key notion in economic discourse. Because scarcity is the fundamental lot of man, economics is necessary. In all cases, the human is that being who lives in light of scarcity (unknown to the animal). Scarcity forces 'living beings' to 'run the risk of not finding in their natural environment enough to ensure their existence' (Foucault 1970: 257). Regardless of whether or not basic needs are *represented*, satisfying a subsistence needs level is still the key concern. Foucault goes further in reading Ricardo by saying that, what scarcity and subsistence production imply is that 'he is the human being who spends, wears out, and wastes his life in evading the imminence of death' (Foucault 1970: 257). The pragmatic concern about death thus joins subsistence, scarcity and utility as the key terms in economics.

The key point for Ricardo is that while, originally, nature provided humanity with all that was necessary to satisfy primary needs without the need for labour, increased population changes all this and people, to survive, are forced to engage in productive labour.

The emergence of economics thus arises with the simultaneous emergence of a concern to solve, for humanity, the problem of subsistence, that is, the problem of how all human beings can initially survive physically before proceeding to live culturally that is, potentially, in freedom. Possibly, for the first time in history, to be poor – where poverty is equivalent to living a subsistence life – is, albeit by default, to be excluded from culture and from the possibility of freedom.

All of this serves to reconfirm that labour and its correlate in Marx of 'labour power' is, is essentially and exclusively utilitarian, rooted in the idea of subsistence as the satisfaction of the primary needs of physical life – food, clothing and shelter – and is bereft of any symbolic or cultural significance. The injustice of labouring that Marx points to is that labourers expend labour-power at a rate often far in excess of what is needed for subsistence and yet only receive enough in return to allow subsistence life.

Overall, then, labour is universal and applicable to all human situations to the extent that the essential human is mere life, finite life, or bare life, as we have said after Agamben. The irony is that, far from primary needs being an ancient idea rooted, for example, in the Greek *oikos* or in the so-called primitive societies, it uniquely emerges in the essentially modern context of the European eighteenth and nineteenth centuries. Only a notion of primary need can give rise to a truly consumer society, a society, as economic theory says, founded on utility. Arendt's view of economy as originally *oikos* is entirely in keeping with this principle. It is a view that ultimately will prove to be the foundation of the exclusion of those deemed to be mired in subsistence. Of course, such people are the very ones in need of being brought into the fold of the European *polis*, or its equivalent. Such an exclusion is in no way entirely explicit or conscious. In fact, every effort is made to ameliorate the conditions of those in economic distress (overseas aid funds do nothing else). Human rights organizations, similarly, are devoted to defending the rights of those in poverty. NGOs attempt to improve basic health and welfare (including education) of those often on the brink of death. The extreme situations implied are thought to be exactly those of all peoples when the basic resources of food, clothing and shelter are reduced to a minimum. Only when such conditions have been satisfied can the world standard of living improve. To this end, new food technologies are being developed with the aim of bringing about a future increase in protein levels.[8]

But just as Merleau-Ponty's insight, gained from a careful reading of ethnological research, that there is often a very narrow 'relation between instinct

---

[8] In the French weekly, *L'Obs*, a French agronomist is quoted as saying that, given the future world deficit of protein, the prospect of deriving the latter from insects (e.g., scarab beetles, crickets and cicadas) becomes ever more plausible (Nora and Couter 2015: 50–52).

and symbolism' (Merleau-Ponty 2003: 195) and that even animals can have a certain culture and manifest a style, so that, even here, life as mere subsistence is false. This is why the remainder of this study will, as a key theme to be addressed, dispute the supposedly utilitarian basis of the human.[9]

In a study of the relation between politics and nature that entails that the sciences be brought into democracy, Bruno Latour begins clearing the ground for the new role of science by pointing out that political ecology must let go of representations of nature in Western society. Such representations, says Latour, do not relate to an objective reality (even though the quintessential object of science has been nature), but are about the way politics is, and has been organized in industrial societies. 'Non-Western cultures', says Latour, '*have never been interested* in nature; they have never adopted it as a category; they have never found a use for it. On the contrary, Westerners were the ones who turned nature into a big deal, an immense political diorama' (Latour 2004: 43; Latour's emphasis). The diorama includes what nature represents for the political forces at play. Latour does not say this, but it is entirely plausible to propose bare life as essentially nature and it is this which undoubtedly has political implications.

Nature, then, has to do with the way that the political field is organized.[10] The dialectic of freedom (politics) and necessity (nature) participates in this field. It does not refer to a rigorously objective reality that determines the range of possibilities for human life. Through a series of mediations, both transparent and oblique, the notion of consumer society participates in the dialectic in relation to which, in Latour's terms, we need to abandon 'the notion of nature' (2004: 41) and, I would add, its synonyms: necessity, subsistence, primary needs, bare life. Such, then, is the task that lies before us.

---

[9] In a passage already partly cited from his Collège de France course on Nature dealing with the idea that 'an organism has no other function than preserving itself', Merleau-Ponty's says: 'Yet there is only a very small part of the forms of the organism that fills these conditions. We must criticize the assimilation of the notion of life to the notion of the pursuit of utility' (Merleau-Ponty 2003: 188).

[10] Latour elaborates on 'Nature' by saying: '"Nature", as we know, does not refer to a domain of reality but to a particular function of politics reduced to a rump parliament, to a certain way of constructing the relation between necessity and freedom, multiplicity and unity, to a hidden procedure for apportioning speech and authority, for dividing up facts and values' (2004: 133).

3

Rethinking Arendt's Theory of Necessity and Freedom: The Ordinary as Extraordinary

We will now reconsider Hannah Arendt's notion of the Greek *oikos* (household) as the sphere of necessity with the aim of challenging the idea that there is a condition of necessity or mere subsistence, where life is reduced to a struggle to satisfy basic biological needs. For Arendt, the Greek *oikos* is an illuminating model because it shows that necessity activities were to be kept quite separate from action in the *polis*. The ordinary and the undistinguished happens in the *oikos* and its equivalent, with the *polis* being reserved for extraordinary acts done without any regard for life.[1] The exclusionary nature of this theory of the *polis* as action has, at best, been treated with kid gloves by Arendt's commentators who are often fascinated by the idea of extraordinary and glorious political acts in the *polis* and who often prefer to see Arendt as genealogist – pointing to determinant moments in the history of political practice without necessarily endorsing these practices. However, as the notion of Nature has governed theories of political association, so, in Arendt, the notion of *oikos* is a key determinant in her political theory. It is not the *oikos* as such that Arendt is concerned to champion, but what it signifies: the eternal division of human life into spheres of necessity and freedom. Whether or not the necessity and freedom dichotomy in modern society takes the form it did in Greece is beside the point. Rather, the point, for Arendt, is that a form of necessity and freedom is clearly manifest in the modern era, just as there is a contemporary incarnation of what counts as the ordinary and the extraordinary.

While the thought of Hannah Arendt on the human and politics has often been contested for its view of the social – most notably by certain strands of feminist discourse – it remains an important pillar of Western

---

[1] For Heidegger, by contrast: 'At bottom, the ordinary is not ordinary; it is extraordinary' (Heidegger 1993a: 179). We will be following up on this point, not just in relation to Heidegger.

political and social theory. Indeed, I would go further and say that it has been extraordinarily influential since the Second World War in relation to the Western polity's self-understanding of citizenship as the essential basis of politics. For although Arendt poignantly noted the tragic plight of stateless people between the two world wars and spelled out the futility of human rights advocacy beyond the borders of the nation state, her conception of politics ultimately privileges citizenship *in* the nation state; for it is only there that the 'right to have rights' can be satisfied (Arendt 1968: 147–182). Indications are that, privately, Arendt wished that this were not so and that her hope was that this tragic situation could be assuaged by the stateless person being respected simply on the basis of his or her humanity. Publicly, however, in her writings, Arendt proceeds as though the only meaningful and effective approach to statelessness is to enable the stateless person to become a citizen. But, as it has turned out, this has meant (because most now follow Arendt on this point) that to be outside citizenship is to be in a kind of nether region where one is treated as neither fully human nor entirely non-human. The issue at stake concerns the way that non-citizens are often cast by Arendt and the Western tradition of political theory as those unable to activate their 'right to have rights' because, having only their humanity to fall back on, they are deemed to be reduced to a struggle for biological survival (the realm of necessity) giving them the status of bare life. The question is: How can the situation of non-citizens be rethought so as to counter their being reduced to bare life?

A response to this question will entail a detour through Heidegger's notions of *oikos* and *polis*, where the boundary between the two domains becomes fluid due to the fact that both are in language. Heidegger thus differs from Arendt because of this. So, too, will we see that Agamben's elaboration of the term *oikonomia* (Agamben 2011b) brings 'glory' into focus, the same term that Arendt said was characteristic action in the *polis*.

As Arendt's thought evolved from *The Origins of Totalitarianism* first published in 1951 to her later works of the 1960s and early 1970s, the very idea of the human outside the nation state – that is, outside citizenship or the pathway to it – very much recedes into the distance. From her writings on politics and the notion of the *polis* that is central to it, Arendt associates the idea of humanness simpliciter with mere biological survival and all that this entails. In other words, humanness – or the human as an 'animal species' – evokes the inspiration Arendt gains from the Greek *oikos* as the place of the satisfaction of basic needs and the assurance of the reproduction of the species. The *oikos* is the domain of subsistence or the domain of 'necessity'.[2] With Saul Newman, I have already shown (Lechte and Newman 2012: 526–529) that only beyond this domain can politics as freedom and the play of artifice take place.[3] Politics as the enactment of freedom within a community of equals is put under threat, Arendt argues, as soon as the concerns of the *oikos* assume a public face. This, as is known, is her complaint in *The Human Condition* regarding 'the victory of the *animal laborans*', or of pure labour, and she elaborates by saying that this is equivalent to the rise of society where, 'it was ultimately the life of the species which asserted itself' (1958: 321). After the secularization that came with the 'Modern Age', '[w]hat was left was a "natural force", the force of the life process itself, to which all men and all human activities were equally submitted [...] and whose only aim, if it had an aim at all, was the survival of the animal species man' (321). And, our author, continues: 'What was not needed, not necessitated by life's metabolism with nature, was either superfluous or could be justified only in terms of the peculiarity of human as distinguished from other animal life' (321). Earlier in *The Human Condition*, Arendt had set the scene for the putative victory of the *animal laborans* by claiming that the human 'is subject to need and necessity' (121). And '[m]an cannot be free if he does not know that he is subject to necessity, because his freedom is always won in his never wholly successful attempts to liberate himself from necessity' (121). 'Necessity' is the summary term that brings together all that is related in human and animal life to survival as a biological entity, or as a being possessed of life. In itself – and this is what I will contest – necessity, for both Arendt and the Western contemporary era's self-understanding, has (almost by definition) no transcendent aspect; it cannot of itself constitute a *way* of life, but is seen as the essential element or the condition of possibility of a way of life (life as action, for example). Women or slaves, or those whose horizon has been circumscribed by labour in the *oikos* or its equivalent, cannot realistically harbour designs of an active political life (a '*bios*' in Aristotle's terms), but must remain immured in a sphere that nonetheless paves the way for the experience

---

[2] Here, it is incorrect to think that Arendt's references to the Greek *oikos* are simply a nostalgic return to the origins of Western thought. Rather, the *oikos* provides, as Arendt sees it, an illuminating model of necessity that every social and cultural formation has to deal with. That is, humanity as such – whether ancient or modern – has to solve the problem of necessity before anything like politics as action is possible – or, indeed, before a life of contemplation is possible. My argument is that the so-called sphere of necessity is far more complex than Arendt shows it to be.

[3] Here it is not being suggested that Arendt necessarily had a narrowly circumscribed vision of public space. Rather it is perfectly feasible that a private space where a salon was held could indeed function as a creative public space. To say this, however, does not at all minimize the effect of the necessity-freedom opposition. Moreover, it is the *kind* of activity undertaken more than where it is enacted that is pertinent. Or better: it is the *kind* of activity that creates the space.

of freedom by others in the *polis*. It is this dichotomy (*oikos-polis*) derived from Arendt's interpretation of the Greek model, which governs the Arendtian theory of politics. But of course not only Arendt; for reference to the Greeks is just her way of arriving at the predominance of utility in secular modernity. Others, such as Weber, have reached a similar conclusion without bemoaning the ascendancy of labour. Or again, if we turn to the example of the field of pre-history, we can see that the human is *first* destined to overcome purely subsistence existence as a struggle to survive *before* evolution enables higher forms of life based in culture to emerge.[4]

Arendt's negative view of the social as the 'victory of the *animal laborans*' has been challenged by feminist thinking. Mary Dietz (1995) provides an incisive overview of key feminist positions on Arendt, and is critical of the thinking that reduces the issue of Arendt's championing of the *polis* to the detriment of the *oikos* or the social to one of gender; that is, according to Dietz, gender critics have often characterized Arendt as a woman thinking like a man, thus explaining her hostility to feminist aspirations, or as Arendt, a woman, thinking like a woman and thus open to feminist recuperation.[5] For Dietz, what has been missed is that Arendt's thought on politics as action cannot be reduced to an *animal laborans*/action dichotomy, but must be seen in terms of the more complex, tripartite frame of 'labor-work-action' – activities which merge into one another (1995: 29). Nevertheless, Dietz, seemingly, cannot fail to recognize the temporal priority of necessity, whether this be satisfied by labour or work, or a combination of the two: 'Action requires *animal laborans* and *homo faber*; for in order to act, human beings must *first* [my emphasis – J.L.] satisfy the demands of life and achieve stability' (Dietz 1995: 31)

For her part, Hanna Pitkin has shown (see Pitkin 1995: 51–81 and Pitkin 1998: 52–68) that the concept of the social in *The Human Condition*, while embracing the idea of necessity, is not reducible to it. The meaning of this term also includes the social as 'high society', in the eighteenth-century sense, as well as the social as '*das Man*', or the 'They' in Heidegger's sense, where *das Man* implies the external conventions of the collectivity to which one attempts to

---

[4] For example, the prehistorian, André Leroi-Gourhan (whose work will in part be the subject of Chapter 8), takes it for granted that the starting point for the study of tools of consumption would be those which 'satisfy *the most elementary needs of man*: his food, clothing and shelter' (1973: 140; emphasis added). The point here is that it is possible (even *necessary*) to satisfy these needs independently of other activities, those linked, for example, to sociality, religion or art. As such, Leroi-Gourhan's position is not vastly different in its basic assumptions to that of Arendt and her view of necessity; it is just that Arendt draws from this very different conclusions.

[5] See Dietz (1995: 17–50)

comply. The broadest meaning of the social, as Pitkin explains, is as the 'absence of politics' (Pitkin 1998: 197) and the sentiment that one cannot do anything that would change things. Politics as action disappears in the social, hence Arendt's disquiet. Granted all this, however, it is still clear that, for Arendt, the physical condition of possibility of *das Man* is the satisfaction of the so-called basic needs necessary for survival. Everything is premised on this, the broader connotations of the term 'social', notwithstanding.

In a recent work, Philip Walsh also emphasizes the tripartite nature of human life in *The Human Condition* (see Walsh 2015). Both Walsh and Dietz want to show, then, that Arendt's argument is more subtle than has hitherto been acknowledged. It is not simply a matter of a negative sign over the social as dominated by labour and a positive one over action. Instead, the *way* that labour, work and action interrelate to each other needs to be analysed and understood. Thus, Walsh argues that 'activities cannot be simply ordered into one or other of these categories; the triade of activities is not a *territorial* division [...]. Rather, *homofaber* and *animal laborans* are *lifeworlds*, which operate as models or archetypes, which activities may approximate to more or less. In any given society these activities are given their meaning, the "proper place", via *institutions*' (Walsh 2015: 5–6. Walsh's emphasis). Once having introduced this call to a more subtle reading of Arendt, Walsh, in his turn, also seems unable to avoid emphasizing the temporal priority of necessity. For he says that: 'labour is bound to biological conditions of human life' (Walsh 2015: 6). That is, Walsh, too, cannot avoid recognizing the temporal priority of necessity in Arendt because the evidence in Arendt's texts in favour of such recognition is overwhelming.

Broadly speaking, in the Arendtian scenario, one leaves the comfort of the private household, where the preservation of life is the key concern, for the risks of action in the public sphere. Action is always risky because the results and consequences of it can never be assured. Arendt:

> as such the public realm stands in the sharpest possible contrast to our private domain where, in the protection of family and home, everything serves and must serve *the security of the life process*. It requires courage even to leave the protective security of our four walls and enter the public realm, not because of particular dangers which may or may not lie in wait for us, but because we have arrived in a realm where the concern for life has lost its validity. (1960: 35; emphasis added)

Without the 'security of the life process', no politics is possible. Yet, within the *oikos* and its equivalent, anything approaching action is impossible. Let us acknowledge that *oikos*-type activities in the service of life do not have to be rigorously spatially demarcated. What is exclusive is not necessarily the household as a welcoming hearth where children are raised. Rather, what is exclusive is that there are *types* of activity that are of entirely separate essences and cannot be fused. On this basis, the slogan 'the personal is the political' would have made absolutely no sense to Arendt. Life activities and political action are *essentially* different from one another.

Space does, however, become relevant in relation to authentic political activity because the latter can only take place for Arendt within the confines of the nation state. Thus, in her lectures on Kant's political philosophy, she argues that while thinking and scholarship for Kant are essentially *public* activities (cf. Arendt 1982: 39–40.), they are the activities of a world citizen – of a spectator of events – not those of a true political actor. To be a political actor is only possible in the circumscribed public sphere of the nation state: 'To be a citizen means among other things to have responsibilities, obligations, and rights, all of which make sense only if they are territorially limited. Kant's world citizen was actually a *Weldtbetrachter*, a world-spectator. Kant knew quite well that a world government would be the worst tyranny imaginable' (1982: 44).

If genuine political activity can only be undertaken by citizens in the public sphere in a nation state, what of stateless people today – asylum seekers and refugees cut adrift on the high seas? What of those from non-Western cultures for whom the distinction of private and public, life and action, necessity and freedom make no sense? What of those deemed to live an irreversible subsistence existence? Here, Arendt's view of a genre of activities being entirely concerned with life and survival is entirely misplaced and leads her to make statements of the following sort in Part Two of *The Origins of Totalitarianism*, where she says that certain peoples, 'since they are no longer allowed to participate in the human artifice, they begin to belong to the human race in much the same way as animals belong to a specific animal species' (1968: 182). This passage implies that to live in such a way as to be uniquely in the service of life (life as 'mere existence' (1968: 181)), to live a life that does not rise above 'mere givenness' (181), to live a life that 'is a permanent threat to the public sphere' (181), a life unworthy of civilization – this life can never be a 'way of life'. For this is a life without even a modicum of extraordinariness or transcendence.

In a statement published almost a decade after *The Origins of Totalitarianism*, Arendt reiterates:

> Where men live together but do not form a body politic – as, for example, in tribal societies or in the privacy of the household – the factor ruling their actions and behavior is not freedom but the necessities of life and concern for its preservation. (Arendt 1960: 30)

Arendt's tone in this and similar passages often emits sympathy for those bereft of a political community or *polis*. All the more so because she suspects that they exist in the 'abstract nakedness of being nothing but human' (1968: 179), which was the condition of those in the extermination camps. Here, no doubt, is the greatest of challenges: to be able to determine what remains of a transcendent form of the human even after the formal accoutrements of civil identity have been – as far as this is possible – expunged. Insight is possible here only if we challenge the idea that there can be a totally non-transcendent human existence – a human existence reduced to 'mere existence' or to 'bare life' (cf. Agamben).

To this it might be objected that there is no need to give up the approach initiated by Arendt, an approach that would call on us to enable all peoples to experience political community, which would also be the basis of an experience of freedom. From human life as pure subsistence to human existence as more than this: namely, human existence as the freedom of the citizen in a nation state.

In response, we need to recognize that the world of today is, at least in part, the result of an approach such as we find in Arendt. It is a world where indigenous cultures are still recovering from the traumas of European colonialism and religious proselytizing, as well as from the agonies of 'ethnocentrism, racism, genocide' (see Lechte 1988). The issues in this domain are of course enormous and complex. And it would be wrong to claim that one can do justice to them here. Suffice it to say that I have initiated an approach quite different to Arendt's and will continue to do so in what follows. Such an approach attempts to show that, for essential reasons, there is no uniquely subsistence society, that the research now available regarding the origins of the terms *oikos* and 'economy' are at odds with Arendt's perspective and that, in lieu of 'bare life', or life as necessity, there is *always* a way of life. And this in the sense that the latter is always inscribed within what is called the economy.

To address the issue of necessity in Arendt and to argue against the theorist's characterizations is not to say that biological survival and the *oikos* should be understood as political in the colloquial meaning of this term, as Beltrán and others have argued (Beltrán 2009). Rather, it is to say that there is no biological survival *in itself* for the human, or for the *oikos*, or for labour in a pure state.

In Beltrán's terminology, there is no 'undocumented subjectivity' (seen as equivalent to statelessness) other than within the European perspective, even if there might be the undocumented residency of people living inside and outside certain forms of legality. For, at minimum, subjectivity is formed in and through language, of which the 'undocumented' are never bereft. Human visibility is not uniquely equivalent, as Kant claimed, to being within the sphere of European law; it is not uniquely equivalent to being a citizen; it is not uniquely equivalent to having 'rights'; it is not uniquely equivalent to being a member of a *polis* and the freedom of the performance, of 'new beginnings' (Arendt) – even if it might also be all of these things.

On another level, Beltrán recognizes the problematic nature of Arendt's adherence to the 'freedom-necessity' opposition. Thus, she states: 'The ongoing failure to rethink the relationship between freedom and necessity provides a deeper understanding of why it remains so difficult for the undocumented to appear as individuals engaged in acts of political freedom' (Beltrán 2009: 600). While I argue that this failure is endemic in modern political theory, of which Arendt is a clear representative, Beltrán's view is that Arendt's theory of action in the *polis* as 'new beginnings' can be adapted to address the plight of stateless people, even if their being immured in necessity stretches things to their limit. Labour has somehow to become constitutive of citizenship, whether in a de facto sense, where rights are accorded on the basis of residency in a specific location, or where, by contrast, certain rights are formalized. The point is that the condition of labouring *as such* has to become the basis for the acquisition of certain rights, which means that it has to become the basis of access to (a forms of) citizenship (cf., 2009: 615). But this means that those initially excluded will, at a certain price, be included in the *polity*. The problem with such a position is similar to that of bringing the 'right to have rights' to those apparently bereft of political community (i.e., certain non-European, if not non-Western, societies). The paternalism implicit in such an approach hardly needs repeating.

Thus, just as we saw in the previous chapter, which is that concern about 'Nature' (in which the opposition of necessity and freedom is implied) reflects a form of political organization, so the idea that the rightless, the non-citizens, and those who have nothing to sell but their labour power are without any political status is a reflection of the existing state of politics in industrial and post-industrial societies. Just as Latour, as we saw, urges us 'to let go of nature', so we must let go of the idea that non-citizens are bereft of any political status.

The ordinary, the extraordinary and the 'darkness' of difference

I am arguing, in effect, that Arendt's interpretation of the Greek *polis* can be approached from three different angles. The first has to do with the political theorist's view of the *polis* as the sphere of extraordinary acts and her concomitant denial that any political significance attaches to the sphere of necessity. In relation to this, it has been pointed out that labour is a noble activity for humanity. Indeed, labour as an activity can be a legitimate *political* concern. But, let it be emphasized again, labour always occurs in a given context as part of a *way* of life – or, as Agamben calls it, a 'form of life'. There is no life that is not essentially a *way* of life. A way of life would be 'beyond' necessity, if the latter ever existed in a pure form.

Another approach is to point out that Arendt had a nuanced idea of the Greek *polis*, which included the recognition that slave labour, upon which the freedom of the *polis* was predicated, was indeed a high price to pay. Roy Tsao, in an essay that engages with Arendt's *The Human Condition*, cites the following passage that acknowledges the injustice of slaves labouring to enable privileged citizens to perform their freedom in the *polis*:

> The price for the elimination of life's burden from the shoulders of all citizens was enormous and by no means consisted only in the violent injustice of forcing one part of humanity into the darkness of pain and necessity. Since this darkness is natural, inherent in the human condition – only the act of violence, when one group of men tries to rid itself of the shackles binding all of us to pain and necessity, is man-made [Tsao excludes this parenthesis] – the price for absolute freedom from necessity, is, in a sense, life itself, or rather the substitution of vicarious life for real life. (Arendt 1958: 119–120)

The phrase in this passage, 'Since this darkness is natural' calls for analysis. Nature, which drives necessity, is dark. Evoked here is the phrase from *The Origins of Totalitarianism* of the '*dark* background of mere givenness' (1968: 181; emphasis added). And Arendt also refers to 'public life' as 'eliminating or reducing to a minimum the *dark* background of difference' (1968: 182; emphasis added). 'Difference', then, is dark – what is deemed natural is dark – while equality, we might assume, comes into the light (into the 'clearing'?) in the *polis*, the latter being, as we know, the only domain where one can reveal *who* one is, and where the extraordinary can appear.

The last approach I shall mention is to recognize the sphere of necessity in Arendt in passing, but to focus primarily on the notions of politics, freedom and, to a lesser extent, democracy. Such is characteristic of much of Dana Villa's and David Marshall's writing on Arendt.[6] While, before them, Sheldon Wolin argued against the anti-democratic nature of Arendt's theory of the *polis*, he still interprets 'common life' much as Arendt interprets 'necessity': 'Common life resides in the cooperation and reciprocity that human beings develop in order to survive, meet their needs, and begin to explore their capacities and the remarkable world into which they have been cast' (Wolin 1983: 17).

That the full implications of Arendt's position regarding the *polis* and natural difference have not been fully appreciated almost goes without saying. It thus remains to spell out exactly what these implications are.

'Necessity', the ordinary and statelessness

The argument to be considered is that Arendt's particular appropriation of the 'necessity-freedom' dialectic has profound implications for the way that Western politics relates to the plight of certain non-Western peoples. We have already given some indication of this. Indeed, Arendt's thinking itself confronts us with the plight of those without a *polis* or a 'political community':

> Not the loss of specific rights, then, but the loss of a community willing and able to guarantee any rights whatsoever, has been the calamity which has befallen ever-increasing numbers of people. Man, it turns out, can lose all so-called Rights of Man without losing his essential quality as man, his human dignity. Only the loss of a polity itself expels him from humanity. (Arendt 1968: 177)

The plight of the 'stateless' is the plight of all those who have suffered 'the loss of a polity', or it might be the plight of those yet to experience a political community.[7] But statelessness is about more than this. It also evokes those who live in the darkness of 'mere givenness'. Statelessness is for many (and I include myself) a decidedly political issue and yet it is difficult to see how it can be so within the frame of Arendt's thinking – at least not if we are to accept that, for

---

6   See, for example, Dana Villa (1996) and David Marshall (2010). Perhaps the subtitle of Villa's undoubtedly scholarly and, in many respects, nuanced book, *Arendt and Heidegger* says it all: *The Fate of the Political*. The 'Fate of the Political' can only be the fate of an essentially Western humanity, which builds its heritage on a certain interpretation of Athens in Ancient Greece. The fate of the political, indeed, is also about the fate of those excluded from the Western political sphere (from Arendt's 'political community'), an exclusion constitutive of the Western political sphere. Not to talk about this, as political theory does not, is to neglect the main part of the reality in question.

7   As Andrew Schaap succinctly says: 'For Arendt, politics is possible only within a public sphere in which individuals already recognize each other as equal and distinct and this is precisely what stateless people are deprived of' (Schaap 2011: 34).

her, politics can only take place in the circumscribed space of the *polis*. While it is feasible to suppose that, following Kant, Arendt would agree that as a scholar – that is, as a spectator – one can point publicly to the plight of the stateless (which is precisely what Arendt did), the amelioration of the lot of those without a political community can never be the achievement of political action – the outcome of an extraordinary act or acts.

Even more to the point, however, the Arendtian frame, it has been argued, does not allow that statelessness people themselves can act politically.

Commentators have assumed that the main issue in relation to Arendt's theory of freedom and politics is her failure to recognize the political importance of the socio-economic domain in her valorization of action – or the *vita activa*. If Arendt had acknowledged that politics is also about 'who gets what when and how', her theory for advocates of labour might have been at least vaguely tolerable. As it is, it appears that the key element of politics gets left out of account.

However, pushing for due recognition of the socio-economic sphere is itself part of the problem and not part of the solution. This is because, like Arendt, those who promote the socio-economic sphere also see it as essentially a sphere of utility. In itself it can never be a sphere of freedom or transcendence. Like Arendt, therefore, promoters of the importance of labour and the economy also believe that (the equivalent of) necessity must be overcome in the first instance, the main difference being that they think such overcoming should be part of the political project, whereas Arendt does not. Necessity – which includes the ordinariness of life in its repetitiveness, in its banality – must be overcome, Arendt argues; only then is a truly authentic form of political action possible. But difference, for its part, has nothing to do with the idea of politics that Arendt promotes because, almost by definition, necessity cannot be part of a play of freedom, and therefore of the *polis*. Or, to use the Greek terms, which Arendt and, after her, Agamben, have popularized: *zōē* as biological survival or as pure life (necessity) cannot ever be the basis of *bios*, or a way – or form – of life (freedom).

Another thing common to both those who agree and those who disagree with Arendt is the view that, above all, her approach is, to use Villa's words, 'extraordinarily radical and profoundly original' (Villa 1996: 11).[8] From what

---

[8]   Here, mention should be made of Jacques Taminiaux's essay '*Bios politikos* and *bios theoretikos* in the Phenomenology of Hannah Arendt' (1996), which sees Arendt as the only contemporary thinker to argue for the value of *praxis* (*bios politikos*) as against the *poiesis* (to make) and *theoria* (to see) of the tradition of political and philosophical thinking of the West.

has been argued thus far, it should be clear that precisely the opposite is the case: that Arendt's view of politics essentially goes to the heart of the current Western theory and practice of politics, and that the Heideggerian inspiration that informs this is more ambiguous than Arendt had thought was the case. In the current political climate, for example, it is still a matter of excluding those who are not citizens or legitimate residents from the practice of politics – hence the seemingly irresolvable issue of statelessness today.

The notion of '*polis*' provides an indication as to how this notion contains an exclusivist aspect. Moreover, how this term is understood has implications for how '*oikos*' is understood, so further attention also needs to be given to this.

The *polis*

Heidegger contends, especially in his *Parmenides* seminar (Heidegger 1992), that the Greek πόλις (*pōlis*) is not reducible to the current meaning of 'politics' as envisaged in the West. The *polis* provides the place for the taking place, as it were, of the unconcealedness of beings in their being, or of αλήθεια (*alētheia*). The *polis* would be the domain where the human as such shows itself and can be comprehended by those beings gathered together.

For her part, Arendt agrees with Heidegger that disclosure is freedom: 'For, to disclose, i.e., to let appear in the open, can only be accomplished by what gives in advance this open and thus is in itself self-opening and thereby essentially open, or as we may also say, is of itself already "free". The still concealed essence of the open as the primordial self-opening is "freedom"' (Heidegger 1992: 143).

What, then, does Heidegger say of the *oikos*? Stuart Elden (2005) has indicated, in this regard, a key passage in Heidegger's reading of Aristotle that shows speech (language) to be the basis of both the *polis* and the *oikos*:

> 'It is the sharing of a common view [*koinonia*: association, i.e., being-with-another] in *these* matters that makes an *oikos* and a *polis*' (*Politics*, 1253a9.17). Heidegger's paraphrasing translation of this sentence is important: 'This being-together in that way (i.e., the way they are in the world, that they speak with you) forms the household and the *polis*'. (GA18: 47)[9]

---

[9] GA = Heidegger, Martin (1975) GA18 = Heidegger, Martin (2002a). The Metcalf and Tanzer translation of the Aristotle passage translated here by Elden is as follows: ' "The being-with-one-another of such beings (i.e., beings that are in the world in such a way that they speak with it) makes for household and πόλις"' (Heidegger 2009: 33).

In a further passage from the English translation of Heidegger's 1924 course on Aristotle, we read:

> It is shown that the κοινωνία [*koinonia*] which forms the household (*οἰκία*) is only possible on the ground of λέγειν [*legein*], on the basis of the fact that the being of the human being is speaking with the world – expressing itself, speaking with others. (Heidegger 2009: 35)

Thus, *legein* as speaking/discoursing and, in an older form, as 'gathering together', is a key quality of the human whether the latter is understood within the *oikos* or the *polis*. On this basis, it would not be possible to withhold the status of human from women or slaves, as Arendt's interpretation of Greek thought tends to do, even though neither group can enter the *polis*.

Heidegger is also interested in the way that Aristotle invokes *legein* as what marks the human as human, and how this distinguishes the human from the animal. Because the animal lacks language, it cannot address the 'world as world'. And it is this deficit that entails its exclusion from the *polis*.[10]

We come then to a problem of interpretation in Heidegger which is not present in Arendt, due to her confidence in interpreting, in relation to the human, a clear-cut division between necessity (*oikos*) and freedom (*polis*). In her reading of Ancient Greek society, Arendt finds that only membership of the *polis* can assure that one is fully human, whereas Heidegger's reading of Aristotle suggests that one is fully human on the basis of 'dwelling' in language, and the latter is enacted in the *polis and* the *oikos* – or, to put this in more contemporary terms, whether engaged in action or labour, humans dwell in language.

Perhaps if there is an 'animal in the human', it would be manifest in a similar concern for survival and driven by events – by the past – to the exclusion of all else. While it is possible to see this occurring in the *oikos* for Arendt, so that human animal existence is played out there (cf. Arendt 1958: 24), it is more difficult to do so in Heidegger's case. For, just as the human and the word are inseparable, so, too, is the human and 'comportment'. The word and comportment make the human as such manifest. Although, historically, not every human might have been a member of the *polis*, every human *qua* human can be a member of the *polis*. Because every human has the word, no human is *essentially* excluded from the *polis* (whether Heidegger intended this or not).

If Arendt posits the realm of pre-*polis* life as one of difference and thus of the darkness of 'mere givenness', the equivalent in Heidegger is *lēthē* as the 'forgetting

---

[10] This theme will be elaborated upon in Chapter 6.

of being'. Here, a certain darkness is also implied in the sense that *a-lētheia* is the disclosedness of being in the light of the clearing, or the open. The point is that *lēthē* has its essential place in the *polis*, for there could never be a revealing and a coming into the light without a concealing – or 'oblivion': a domain of darkness. Pointedly, Heidegger says in the *Parmenides* lectures that Λιμός [Limos] – mentioned in relation to 'Lethe' as the daughter of 'Eris' (goddess of strife) – should not be translated as 'Hunger'. 'Λιμός does not mean the non-satisfaction of human desires and needs, but refers to the occurrence of the absence of a donation and distribution. Such absence is essentially characterized by falling-away, as is concealment' (Heidegger 1992: 72–73). Furthermore, it is not a matter of suffering as 'lived experience' which is at stake, but of tragedy as a force that entirely overtakes anything like a psychology. Tragedy occurs principally when the night as 'ὀλοή [*óloē*] lets all that is present disappear into concealment' (73).

Because tragedy in the *polis* is not reducible to the lived experience of a subject – because suffering cannot be explained 'psychologically', as Heidegger says – Greek tragedy is closed to modern consciousness. Indeed, the 'truth of being' as *alētheia*, transcends any biological as well as psychological determination of the human, despite modern thinking's take on this. Rather, the essence of the human as those beings for whom being is an issue is manifest through *legein* as the discourse constituting the 'being with' of beings in the *polis*, a 'being with' that is not explicable in terms of the consciousness of any given being.

The question is: Where does the *oikos* – which, as we saw, is also governed by language – figure in this? What sort of an entity is the *oikos*? Although modern thought after Arendt reduces the *oikos* to the sphere of the satisfaction of so called basic needs, Heidegger avoids all explanations of the human that evoke the physical existence of subjects, which would seem to put him at odds with the prevailing explanations of the *oikos*. But Heidegger rarely thematizes the *oikos*, preferring instead to concentrate on the *polis* and the play of *lēthe* and *alētheia*.

Oikos and economy

Oikos

In a more empirical vein, we cans see, in light of the work of the scholar of Ancient Greece, Jean-Pierre Vernant, that the *oikos* has a fundamental symbolic dimension, especially in relation to marriage alliances. The nature, for example, of the wife's dowry can be more or less prestigious. Bovine beasts, in this regard, are a sign of high prestige (Vernant 1965: 140). This implies that the *oikos* is far from lacking a public face and that symbolism and language are integral to its nature, such that it might be possible to speak of a *polis* aspect of the *oikos*, even if the tradition of Western understanding rejects this. Vernant does not hesitate either to point to the religious significance of life in the *oikos*, religion being anything but a utilitarian phenomenon – that is, one dealing with necessity (1965: 140). In sum, the *oikos*, at minimum, says Vernant, has 'a familial and territorial significance', where every effort is made to ensure the continuation of the family line and of the prestige of the family (140). Marriage, indeed, is a task of '*labour* (ἄροτος)' in the sense of working the soil to make it productive. The man is the plough who enables the woman, as the furrow of the earth, to give birth. 'Labour' in this sense is also extremely symbolic. The labour as pure pain that Arendt wants to emphasize is no doubt limited to slave labour, although we do not even know this for sure. The point is that every *oikos*-type situation has symbolic features analogous to those outlined by Vernant. It is not just limited to the Greek context. Arendt's characterization of the *oikos* is thus an oversimplification on more than one level.

Not just the *oikos*, then, but any domain of the so-called utility is never completely driven by a means–ends rationality. For reasons of hospitality alone, the *oikos* is never entirely closed. It is closed neither in its social orientation (where language is always prominent) nor in its *art* of living. What is called the 'sphere of utility' or the 'economy', in today's terms, always exudes an art of living because there is always more than one way of doing things. Three terms among others evoke an art of living here: 'cuisine', 'fashion', 'design' (as opposed to food, clothing, shelter).

Economy

Referring to the issue of the interpretation of economy deriving from Arendt's *oikos* in her study of the life and work of Hannah Arendt, Julia Kristeva notes that

> a more subtle political anthropology might however object that the 'economy' of the hearth (*oikia*) was not limited to the maintenance of survival, to a simple domain proper to the *animal laborans* and to its painful and servile work metabolising with nature in order to ensure the continuation of the body. (1999: 259–260)

Kristeva goes on to cite aspects of the etymology of the word 'economy', pointing out that it 'signified in late-Hellenism, in the Gospels and in Byzantium, "plan" ["*dessein*"]. "exemption", "transition" between the invisible (divine) and the visible (human) universe' (1999: 260). Moreover, in the work of Marie-José Mondzain, referred to by Kristeva, *oikonomia* in Christian Byzantine theology is revealed to refer to the distribution of the Holy Spirit in the Trinity, a distribution that Christ Himself incarnates: 'Christ is then economy par excellence in all senses of the term because he is the intrinsic part of the trinitarian distribution and has made manifest the union of Verbe and flesh' (Mondzain 1996: 51).

This approach leaves in abeyance the Arendtian project of retrieving the meaning of politics in the Greek sense of *polis*, although it might also be said that Agamben's approach confirms the ascendancy in politics of the domain of the utilitarian 'needs' of life over action – where, in Arendt's words, 'it was precisely life that overruled all other considerations' (Arendt 1958: 313). Or again, with Christianity, '[p]olitical activity […] sank to the low level of an activity subject to necessity' (314), so that in the modern era 'life is the highest good' (319). But if, to reiterate yet again, life always includes language, life is always a *way* – or *form* – of life. As a way of life it is always action and doing; it is never mere survival. No human exists in a state of pure survival. Agamben's reference, in his study of *oikonomia* (Agamben 2011b), to the obsolete nature of the *oikos-polis* opposition can mean, then, that the *oikos* takes on features of the *polis* – that every action manifests an element of freedom whether realized inside or outside the *polis*. But it is only possible to be receptive to this idea if the apparently ordinary actions of everyday life (actions typical of the *oikos*) become extraordinary. Is a phenomenology of the ordinary possible? Literature says: 'yes'.[11] Not only does literature make the story of 'life' irreducible to biological life but, as writing, as mediation, literature transcends the division between 'private' and 'public', *oikos* and *polis*, action and contemplation.[12]

---

[11] Arendt, in her own way, also brings literature into the political sphere when she writes in *On Violence* that 'How such a fully developed police state is established and how it works – or, rather, how nothing works where it holds sway – can now be learned in Alexandr I. Solzhenitsyn's *The First Circle*, which will probably remain one of the masterpieces of twentieth-century literature and certainly contains the best documentation on Stalin's regime in existence' (Arendt 1970 [1969]: 55). Again, in a note in *The Human Condition*, Arendt refers to William Faulkner's *A Fable* (1954), saying that it 'surpasses almost all of World War I literature in perceptiveness and clarity because its hero is the Unknown Soldier' (1958: 181n. 5). Interestingly, Faulkner's novel also won the Pulitzer Prize in 1955 for best fiction.

[12] Unfortunately, it has been all too easy to deny a form of 'literature' to certain non-Western peoples, so that such peoples would be incapable of narrating individual lives, even if they clearly have stories told at a broader community level. And yet, ironically, Arendt's description of how 'who' one is as revealed in a story could equally apply across cultures. Thus, Arendt writes: 'These stories may then be recorded in documents and monuments, they may be visible in *use objects* or art works, they may

Significantly, Arendt refers, as we know, to the *polis* as the domain of speech and action, which, for her, implies that within the human plurality men have a face-to-face – unmediated – relation among themselves. How speech can be distinctive of the *polis* alone and not of the *oikos* is entirely problematic, as we have already indicated. But with respect to Arendt's ultimate thesis that it is extraordinary feats and characters (*who* one is) that are revealed in the *polis*, speech and action become media. Even the extraordinary has its medium. Let us acknowledge that this would not, for Arendt, be like the putative saturation and technical aplomb of media that exist today. In short, while no doubt media are never entirely absent, Arendt's notion of the combined power of word and deed is light years away from the hyper-mediatized 'society of the spectacle' (Debord). In sum, as already noted, true action is 'glory': 'action needs for its full appearance the shining brightness we once called glory' (1958: 180). How ironical it is that Agamben calls media today – derivative of *oikonomia* – the source of glorifying and acclaiming power. But what is more, the origin of glory is not action in the *polis*. Rather: 'it is precisely those authors who develop the theology of the economy who also produce the elements for a theology of glory' (Agamben 2011b: 204). Overall, in the history of Western theology, '[a]ll economy must become glory, and all glory becomes economy' (210). Glory, as Arendt would have it, occurs in the *polis* which 'was supposed to multiply the occasions to win "immortal fame", that is, to multiply the chances for every *polis* member to distinguish himself, to show in deed and word who he was in his unique distinctness' (197). In short, the aim of the 'city-state' was 'from beginning to end […] to make the extraordinary an ordinary occurrence of everyday life' (197). And what is action which enables the extraordinary to emerge? – action is what 'has no end' (233).

The human

Like the action that 'has no end' the glory – the acclamation – deriving from the economy, which, according to Agamben, the media today is the animator, similarly has no end. Such is the basis of 'inoperativity'. Not the *polis*, then, but

be told and retold and worked into all kinds of material. They themselves, in their living reality, are of an altogether different nature than these reifications. They tell us more about their subjects, the "hero" in the center of each story, than any product of human hands ever tell us about the master who produced it, and yet they are not products properly speaking. Although everybody started life by inserting himself into the human world through action and speech, nobody is the author or producer of his own life story' (Arendt 1958: 184. Emphasis added). The key is that the story can be visible in 'use objects', which implies that what is being referred to are not just use objects – objects serving necessity. In this way, necessity ceases to be necessity and a large dent is put into Arendt's argument.

the *oikos* is here the basis of that which 'has no end'. Everything accompanying the ceremonial of power, all the pomp and circumstance, the display and festival, the parade and orations are the glory of power deriving from the *oikos*, from the economy. Arendt, on this basis, is apparently wide of the mark. Not only is there no *polis* today in the Greek sense, but there never was a *polis* or free acts totally separate from an *oikos* as the basis of *oikonomia*.

Once human life (and, for some, even animal life[13]) is recognized as essentially a way of life – once, in terms of our thesis, the 'ordinary' becomes 'extraordinary' – every mode of human life becomes a form of revealing. In this context it should be understood that even if the Athenian Greeks in the time of Plato and Aristotle did hold to a division between *oikos* and *polis*, however strict, this does not validate this division philosophically. It is difficult not to think that Arendt indeed thought this. Moreover, on a similar basis, a clear distinction between *oikos* and *polis* deemed to be inherited by the modern Western tradition from the Ancient Greeks does not render this distinction valid. The reason why it is necessary to overcome this distinction is because it forms the basis of declaring certain humans inhuman – those who Arendt, for instance, calls 'savages' (1968: 180). 'Savages' are those humans who would only have life and not a 'way of life', even though they presumably have language. The incoherence in thought here only confirms the strength of the tendency to exclude certain humans from humanity.

As concerns the validity of the *oikos-polis* division echoed in the *zōē-bios* opposition and taken up by Arendt and subsequently by Agamben, Finlayson, for one, disagrees and asserts that 'Contra Agamben, I think that the very idea of a single underlying paradigm of Western politics since the Greeks is ridiculous, that his [Agamben's] diagnosis of contemporary society is wholly unpersuasive, and that his social theory has no critical purchase whatsoever on the current political state of affairs' (2010: 99).[14] Let us allow this statement to give us pause and the opportunity to reflect on what Agamben has initiated with regard to understanding the tenor of contemporary political action with regard to the human and, in this light, with regard to stateless people.

Human as 'form-of-life' (first take)

As a foretaste to the analysis in Chapter 10 of Agamben's study of liturgy as a 'form-of-life', here it is a matter of underlining, in relation to Arendt's theory,

---

[13] See Merleau-Ponty (2003: 192, 198).

[14] But as indicated in Chapter 1, note 2, Finlayson assumes that there is, for the human, a level of pure biological need, a level where a way of life would not pertain.

the point that there is no bare life only ways of life. While, certainly, as far as an interpretation of *zōē* and *bios* in Aristotle is concerned, Agamben (and also Arendt) seems to be wide of the mark.[15] Does this mean that the underlying opposition of bare life and form, or way of life, is invalid? The answer, I say, is 'no'. What justification is there for this response?

To begin with, the results of Agamben's research into *oikonomia* and 'form of life' in a study of European monasticism as a 'form of life' (Agamben 2013a) provide a profound backdrop to the role of utility in modernity, so that what might be construed to support a concern for bare life, or dire poverty, actually contains the fundaments of a 'form of life' that is oriented towards freedom in the future (potentiality) and is not determined by the past. In effect, the monastic life of the Franciscans shows that the

> specific eschatological character of the Franciscan message is not proposed in a doctrine, but in a form of life through which the life of Christ is made newly present in the world to bring to completion, not the historical meaning of the 'person' in the economy of salvation, so much as his life as such. The Franciscan form of life is, in this sense, the end of all lives (*finis omnium vitarum*), the final *modus*, after which the manifold historical dispensation of *modi vevendi* is no longer possible. The 'highest poverty', with its use of things, is the form-of-life that begins when all the West's forms of life have reached their historical consummation. (2013: 143)

Thus, in the monastic context, rules form life and life takes the form of a system of rules; there is, in effect, an indistinction between life and rules. Rules, therefore, do not constitute a utilitarian backdrop enabling survival. Instead, they come to be employed for their own sake; they are the *form* life takes and can vary to infinity.

However, can monastic life be linked to modern life and, specifically, to life in the globalized world of contemporary politics? The answer is that if it can be shown that even a life of 'the highest poverty' is a 'form-of-life', the whole basis of human life as founded in the first instance on necessity is profoundly weakened. If monastic life is a form of life, then, assuredly, the very distinctions between private and public, *oikos* and *polis*, necessity and freedom break down. But these are the distinctions, I suggest, that constitute the foundation of modern political society, the society of citizenship and the 'right to have rights'. If a life of poverty is a 'form of life', there is no longer any basis for

---

[15] See Chapter 1, note 2.

a distinction between citizens who are fully human and stateless people who, following Arendt, are less so.

Illustrating life as a way of life

As a tentative step towards illustrating the notion that human life is always a way of life and to this extent based in freedom, we could point to Sarah Morris's film, *Beijing 2008* (2009), shown, in among other places, at the Whitechapel Gallery, London.[16] A substantial analysis of the film cannot be given here. But we can note that *Beijing*, the film, shot during the 2008 Olympics, brings into sharp focus the gestures and rhythms of everyday life. It shows that the repetition of actions (actions, because constantly repeated, thought to be banal) become the gestures of a way of life.[17] Here, too, the focus on the *detail* of living shows that the latter is multiplied almost to infinity and that it is this that, with sufficient attention, gives rise to experiencing a way of life.

Also worthy of attention as a presentation of gesture is Cao Fei's film *Whose Utopia?* (2006), filmed in three parts including inside an Ozram bulb factory in China.[18] While for both of these films, there is a question about the nature of the relationship between the film-maker and his or her subject (e.g., one might ask whether the 'poetry' of gesture is produced by those filmed, or by the film), we can say that, in both cases, normally unconscious, apparently repetitive gestures of life are opened up to scrutiny and the perception that there is no repetition without a certain rhythm and thus without an *art* of gesture, a gesture that is anything but simply utilitarian. Opened up here, then, is an element of transcendence.

---

[16] Seen in the context of the exhibition, 'Adventures of the Black Square: Abstract Art and Society, 1915–2015', viewed at the Whitechapel Gallery, London, on 7 March 2015.

[17] Much could be said about the relationship between the so-called everyday actions of Chinese gestures in relation to the actions related to the events of the Olympics. The speeches from the podium by the Olympics Games' organizers, for example, are events that would not pass for being banal in themselves but which are constituted by a multiplicity of repeated actions.

[18] Film viewed at the Tate Modern, London, on 1 March 2015. Available at: https://vimeo.com/76026916 Part I of Cao's film focuses on the repetition of the machinery, then on the fingers, faces, feet and then back to the faces of the workers. All stages of production are recorded. Part II includes an element of fantasy (angel among the stacked boxes of globes), with stylized gestures, including miming climbing a rope. Part III, features portraits of workers and sound track of the song, 'The Future is not a Dream'. Overall, the banality of the work gives rise to the poetry of dream through repetition, both incidental and stylized.

Conclusion

Perhaps, in an ironical way, Arendt's attempt to separate so clearly the labour of ministering to the ordinary needs of life from a life of extraordinary action has served to focus attention on the nature and validity of this distinction. Even though Arendt herself, in terms of the argument presented here, would never have agreed, we can propose that life qua life as the life of living beings is extraordinary. Living in some sense is always an *art* of living. In opposing this idea, Arendt was not going against the movement of the times but was decidedly going with it – even to the point of giving it currency. In addressing the role of the *oikos* and the *polis* in Arendt's thought what becomes abundantly clear is that we now need – even as a matter of urgency – to address the way that, in everyday life, the so-called ordinariness and its synonyms (the banal, the trivial, the repetitious, the boring, the mundane) operate. In doing so, we will come to grips with the way the artist relates to artifice and with the issue of whether there is an essential poetry in language and in living, or whether the only poetry that really exists is in the work of the poet removed from life – classically evoked in the idea of the artist or thinker's solitude. My hypothesis is that the former is true and that, consequently, it is a matter of perceiving the essential poetry of life. This is now what remains to be investigated in light of Arendt's thinking on necessity.

4

Approaching the Human and Freedom

In what follows, we investigate the notion of freedom in relation to the human as meaning that the human is *essentially* free. However, the notion of freedom, as already indicated, has been taken over by Arendt and much of political theory to mean something that can only truly be realized by individual subject-actors and become manifest in the *polis*. This view will be problematized by spelling out the fact of the human as essentially free in a 'way of life'.

In the introduction to this work (see Chapter 1), it was noted that, for Levinas, freedom was essentially equivalent to political freedom, a freedom of the self which did not necessarily include the freedom of the Other, as such freedom was also framed within the order of the Same. This did not mean that for Levinas true freedom lay elsewhere. Rather, as far as an ethics of responsibility for the other person is concerned, freedom is, perhaps paradoxically, of limited purport. Freedom nonetheless remained political freedom and was coupled with equality. In essays on Judaism, Levinas points to the limitation of freedom as freedom of the self. This is a freedom linked to a form of violence.[1] Thus, the 'violent man does not move out of himself. He takes, he possess. Possession denies independent existence' (Levinas 1990: 9). Undeniably, there is an echo here of the Hobbesian 'war of all against all' in the State of Nature. Freedom, Levinas implies, thus needs to be tempered with ethics, which in itself, is non-political.

The question to be kept in mind in the following consideration of freedom as found in a number of key texts in philosophy is: To what extent does freedom as such inevitably refer back to the Hobbesian thesis of violence in the State of Nature and to the human's putatively original animal nature?

---

[1] It is necessary to specify 'form of violence' here, for there is also violence in defence of the Other, in defence of justice. Thus: 'Violence is originally justified as the defense of the other, of the *neighbour*' (Levinas 1999: 172; Levinas's emphasis).

Freedom and constraint

A popular conception of freedom sees it as having to do with the absence of physical constraint and the potential for self-determination. Prison life thus evokes servitude compared to the freedom of life outside. Freedom, however, has many aspects. Physical constraint, for instance, usually refers to the restraint of the individual and it can be direct, as when one is in a prison cell, or it can be indirect, as when the nature of the environment becomes a force of constraint. Although free in a physical sense in the mythical State of Nature, humanity was in reality subject to the principle of 'might equals right', so that only some could be physically free; but even the strongest could be subjugated by the combined force of numbers. Moreover, as Hobbes more than anyone expressed it, in such a situation one continually fears for one's life. In such circumstances, it makes sense to give up some physical, individual freedom in order to live in a state of security called, 'society'. There is still a strong sense in many parts of the world (in the southern United States, for example) that the freedom of the State of Nature is the only true and authentic freedom and that life in society where one is subject to the strictures of government is a servile life.

Another form of indirect physical constraint has of course been seen as economic. Thus, for Marx and others, freedom does not exist unless there is a capacity to satisfy basic needs related to physical survival. Servitude in the economic sense is captured in the notions of 'subsistence', 'poverty', 'privation' and 'scarcity'. Clearly, in times of abundance, freedom would be realized as the struggle for physical survival receded into the background, while harsh economic times would bring the servitude made manifest in the effort to eke out a meagre subsistence. Without it being made explicit, there is, in the economic view, a continuity between humans and animals, the main difference being that humans in contradistinction to animals, as Marx said, have the capacity to 'produce the means of their subsistence'.

For Marx and his age, as we have already intimated, economic privation is equivalent to a form of physical constraint always present as the realm of necessity. On this basis, freedom is won to the extent that the issue of subsistence is pushed into the distance and does not impinge on life in the present. Wealth would give rise to freedom and that to the extent that the problem of necessity is well and truly solved and freedom is thereby realized. On this basis too – as with physical constraint in general – the attainment of a condition of freedom for humans would be a contingent matter: at one point, constraint imposes itself and freedom is a dream; at another, constraint is overcome and freedom is realized.

As such, freedom would be entirely historical and not as such an ontological feature of beings in general. The difficulty for the historical approach to freedom is that it leads to the filtering out of those beings that seem to be constitutionally fitted for freedom as opposed to those who are not so endowed. Aristotle's theory of slavery derives from just such a notion (see Lechte and Newman 2013: 38–41). Animals, as the most broadly held view has it, being subject to physical constraints – both biological and environmental – are thus unable to experience true freedom, and it is only in overcoming such constraints, as Hegel put it in the *Philosophy of Right* (1975), that humans assume their own freedom.[2]

Hegel on freedom

The presence or absence of physical constraint as the index of freedom has often served as a way of excluding beings from humanity proper. The slave – to take the most obvious example – can never be fully part of humanity, given that active freedom has been a necessary condition for being counted as human. In the much written-about dialectic of 'Lordship and Bondage' (or the Master and Slave), Hegel famously says: 'And it is only through staking one's life that freedom is won' (Hegel 1979: 114). And life, we find, 'is the *natural* setting of consciousness' (114; Hegel's emphasis). The fate of the 'bondsman' is, initially, simply to be alive – to be bare life, in a word. Nevertheless, through work, the bondsman can rid himself 'of his attachment to natural existence in every single detail' (117). Again: 'Through work [...] the bondsman becomes conscious of what he truly is' (118), namely, the source of the Lord's comfort, if not of his freedom, and ultimately of his own freedom, the problem being, according to Hegel in the Introduction to the *Philosophy of Right*, that, as an equivalent to the bondsman, the 'slave does not know his essence, his infinity, his freedom; he does not know himself as human essence' (Hegel 1975: 30). The slave, like the bondsman, has to recognize himself as being more than a natural being (more than an animal) concerned solely with his self - preservation. In short, the slave must transcend nature (where reason has no voice) and become a self-consciousness that frees itself from the constraints of nature (from necessity).

---

[2] In his interesting account of Hegel's philosophy of freedom, Franco notes the importance of overcoming natural drives (*triebe*) in the *Philosophy of Right* (Franco 1999: 163), but does not draw all the requisite conclusions from this observation.

For Hegel, as for so many thinkers of the Enlightenment tradition but perhaps more profoundly, it is only after the needs of nature have been satisfied that a free, truly human life can unfold. Or, to put it another way: only after nature has been mastered can thought as such make its appearance as freedom.

In the *Aesthetics*, the same argument is made about the need to transcend nature (= pure immediacy, or finitude), where the individual animal is ensconced – 'tied down', Hegel says, 'to a specific natural element, air, water, or land, and this determines its whole mode of life' (Hegel 2010: 148). Contemporary conceptions (particularly Heidegger's) of the dependence of animals on their environment have hardly progressed beyond Hegel's understanding. Freedom, then, is what the animal can never attain in the manner of human beings because its life is natural life and therefore is a life of constraint actualized within and by an environment. True freedom is the actualization of the Concept of freedom, or, 'more concretely still, the Idea', which is 'inherently *infinite* and *free*' (2010: 151. Hegel's emphasis). And, importantly, Hegel adds: 'Although animal life, as life, is Idea', such life is not the manifestation of infinity and freedom because it can never be fully permeated by the Concept. Like all natural life, animal life 'does not get beyond feeling' (151).

As a (biological) body the human also participates in nature and immediacy and as such is not free. The body is a finitude and is also rooted in feeling. Freedom can be realized, as we have seen in the *Philosophy of Right*, only by humans going beyond nature, the immediate and feeling. Here the chief defect of nature, aesthetically speaking, is that natural events are accidental, capricious, stochastic and therefore cannot qualify for inclusion in the Idea of beauty. Even regularity and symmetry in nature are 'lifeless and afford no truly actual unity' of 'ideal subjectivity which natural beauty always lacks' (2010: 142). Human art alone conforms to 'ideal subjectivity' and is therefore the only 'reality adequate to the Idea of beauty' (143). But while true beauty is 'concrete subjectivity' (144), such subjectivity is nevertheless the outcome of a dialectical process that involves going beyond or transcending nature, the latter being subjectivity's opposite. In other words, necessity is manifest in the passage through the body to the actualization of the Idea of freedom. The body as necessity is the finitude that gives rise to freedom as infinity. In sum:

> spirit cannot, in the finitude of existence [...] find [...] its true freedom, and it is compelled to satisfy the need for this freedom, therefore, on other higher ground. This ground is art, and art's actuality is the Ideal.
>
> Thus it is from the deficiencies of immediate reality that the *necessity* of the beauty of art is derived. (152; emphasis added)

Let us say that for Hegel, as for many subsequent thinkers – albeit using a different vocabulary – necessity, being prior to freedom, must be traversed or negated (= the work of negativity) if freedom is to be actualized in the Idea. In other words, there is no sense in which there can be freedom *in* necessity; were it to be thus, there could be (as with all Hegelian oppositions) no dialectical movement giving rise to the process of negativity in which, as the preface to the *Phenomenology of Spirit* says, 'The True is the whole'. Indeed, what has been recounted is the very basis of the Hegelian system where we see a movement from the primitive to the civilized, from immediacy to mediation as reason and self-consciousness, from finitude to the infinite. Just as, in the well-known simile, the acorn and the oak mark out the necessary elements in a process without in any way being identical to each other, so, in analogous fashion, human being develops out of its animal existence and an experience of pure immediacy and feeling and into a condition of self-consciousness which knows freedom as actualized in the Idea of freedom, or freedom as infinitude. Another way of summarizing this is to cite Hegel's words again from the preface, to the effect that the 'single individual must pass through the formative stages of the universal spirit' (Hegel 1979: 16). Or again:

> the *length* of this path has to be endured, because, for one thing, each moment is necessary; and further, each moment has to be *lingered* over, because each is itself a complete individual shape, and one is only viewed in absolute perspective when its determinateness is regarded as a concrete whole, or the whole is regarded as uniquely qualified by that determination. (1979: 17; Hegel's emphasis)

In Ancient Greece and Rome, Hegel points out, only some were free. Only with the rise of Christianity is the human as such free and slavery impossible (Hegel 1956: 334). However, even though such is the case, Hegel is ambivalent with regard to the elimination of slavery. For, indeed, the dialectical movement seems to entail slavery as a necessary stage to be traversed and negated before freedom can be actualized. In the more colloquial language of the *Introduction to Lectures on the Philosophy of World History* (1993), we read that although it is true that 'the essence of man is his freedom' (1993: 184), so that to be human is to be free, this does not mean that slavery everywhere can be abolished. The reason for this, according to Hegel, is that man 'must first become mature before he can be free' (1993: 184). In short, freedom is won only following the condition of un-freedom. Moreover, the dialectical movement will not allow for a simultaneity of different conditions – that, for example, freedom could be forged *in* slavery, or that, in general, infinity could be derived *in* finitude.

Even in the figure of Christ, often perceived as both God and man, and whom Hegel extols in the *Philosophy of History* (1956: 324–334), the co-presence of human finitude and divine infinity seems to be precluded, as the dialectical movement requires that only *after* finitude is sublated can a state of infinity be realized. Thus, Hegel says that the true message of Christ arrives only *after* his death: 'Christ dies; only as dead, is he exulted to Heaven and sits at the right hand of God; *only thus is he Spirit*' (1956: 325; emphasis added). It is, moreover, necessary for Christ's spiritual being to become separate from His natural body, which He is during His sojourn on earth.

Broadly, then, Hegel's philosophical position regarding freedom is that only *after* the body and basic needs have been satisfied can freedom be realized. As such, rather than being the exception in modern thought, to a certain extent Hegel sets the pattern to be followed, namely that only after experiencing the immediacy of life and satisfying basic needs can the freedom of self-consciousness and spirituality be attained. To put it another way: only after the constraints of the natural world have been overcome can freedom be actualized in the Idea of freedom.

Schelling on freedom

Although less appreciated until recently than Hegel's philosophy, Schelling's writing on freedom, within the framework of theodicy, has come to be seen as a corrective to the deterministic elements characteristic of the idealist approach to nature. In a succinct formulation that has become increasingly familiar, Schelling says: 'the real and vital concept is that freedom is the capacity for good and evil' (2006: 23). And he adds: 'This is the point of most profound difficulty in the entire doctrine of freedom' (23). The issue for theodicy, which is at issue here, turns on how to deal with the fact, as Schelling puts it, that 'God appears undeniably to share responsibility for evil in-so-far as permitting an entirely dependent being to do evil is surely not much better than to cause it to do so' (23). Again, in terms of theodicy, 'it is not comprehensible how a capacity for evil can result from God who is regarded as pure goodness' (24). It is not easy to plumb the underlying coherence of Schelling's treatise, as he has a number of balls in the air. For instance, on the one hand he seems to defend the necessity of oppositions, so that 'the essence' of good (freedom) can only reveal itself in evil; love only emerges in hate; 'unity in conflict' (41). On this basis, the darkness of nature – or, more exactly, in animals – would seem to be necessary for the light to emerge; yet, the darkness of nature is only overcome in man. Much as Schelling wants to be the opponent of Hegel in this matter, the positing of oppositions would seem to be his stumbling block. This is so, even if, at the end of his treatise, Schelling says that it is time 'to seek that which lies outside of, and beyond, all opposition' (77).

To what extent are basic needs and natural drives necessary precursors or co-presences for the realization of freedom? In this regard, the following statement by Schelling is intriguing, for it suggests that there is freedom *in* nature and not that nature must be negated in order that freedom be realized, as with Hegel: 'everywhere where there is appetite and desire, there is already in itself a sort of freedom' (43). On the other hand, it is clear that animals and man form not only an opposition, but also a hierarchy (man in the position of ascendancy), so that 'the highest summit of the revelation [of freedom] is man' (44).

Nature versus freedom – such was the way Kant proposed it. Schelling reworks this opposition, if not abolishes it, with the idea that nature is a process, a becoming, a sphere of activity and not a passive, preformed domain. More than a decade before Hegel had said in the *Philosophy of Right* that freedom is only possible after transcending 'natural existence', Schelling states in his *Philosophical Investigations* that 'we have shown that the *almost* general opinion that man only gradually raised himself up from the dullness of animal instinct to reason is not our own' (76; Schelling's emphasis).

Although there might be a sort of freedom in nature, making it irreducible to a 'struggle for existence' and even leading to it being a way of life, a different story emerges when one focuses on the notion of the will as an *act* of will. For now, nature tends to become the sphere of contingency and the irrational. Only through being separate from contingency can an act become a free act of will, one that can choose to do good *or* evil. This possibility is the key to Schelling's philosophy of freedom. Without this possibility there is no free will. Thus: 'Man is placed on that summit [i.e., away from nature – J.L.] where he has in himself the source of self-movement toward good or evil in equal portions: the bond of principles in him is not a necessary but rather a free one' (41). And again: 'free action follows immediately from the intelligible aspect of man' (49). So while Schelling's references to nature as an active, productive domain are indeed interesting, ultimately, freedom can only become manifest in the rational human will, that, as such, separates itself from the contingency of natural processes.

Hans Ruin's interpretation of Heidegger on Schelling would seem to oppose this: 'Schelling is the first to have tried to move beyond a conception of nature as that which has to be overcome in order for freedom to develop, and to try to bring freedom and nature together' (Ruin 2008: 290). Unlike Hegel – unlike Heidegger, as we shall see – Schelling does not comment on animals in relation to humans and provides only a handful of references to 'the creaturely'. It is thus not possible to place animals and humans explicitly and confidently on the same level; rather, what is more likely is that while, in principle, both humans and animals are part of nature, the human is, for Schelling, part of nature in a quite different way from the animal. Only humans, we can surmise, are possessed of reason and will, so that only humans are beings for whom freedom is the freedom to choose good or evil. Heidegger's reading of Schelling on freedom, we will see, hardly contradicts this.

If we turn for further illumination to Schelling's *The Ages of the World* (2000) fragments composed after the treatise on freedom, we find the following reference to God in relation to freedom and necessity: 'Necessity lies at the foundation of freedom and it is in God itself what is first and oldest, insofar as such a distinction can take place in God' (2000: 5). Again: 'God is a unity of freedom and necessity' (27). Necessity here is related to God's nature – to His life, to the extent that He has a life. But in order to assume His freedom God must also be able to overcome necessity: that is, He must be able to act independently of His nature, unless His nature is also freedom – which is what the following line suggests: 'Nature is not God. For nature only belongs to what is necessary in God and, strictly speaking, God is called God only in accordance with its freedom' (31). Even more explicitly from the point of view of what is considered important here, Schelling states: 'Necessity is before freedom' (44). Now it is also true that there is a sense that Schelling struggles to avoid the implicit determinism seemingly signalled here; this is why God is such an important aspect of his philosophy; for even though participating in necessity, God is never beholden to it. Perhaps more intriguingly, in *The Ages of the World*, Schelling provides some justification for calling his *Naturphilosophie* a philosophy of freedom (cf. Peterson 2004: xxxiii), even though the text of the *First Outline of a System of the Philosophy of Nature* (2004), rarely, if ever, refers explicitly to freedom – least of all to human freedom. In the *Ages* text, then, Schelling writes that the 'sight and presence of that essential purity has no other effect on nature except to posit nature in freedom' (2000: 46–47). Again: 'Nature itself, first posited in freedom, overcomes itself through the force of the summit and posits its own life, insofar as it is its own life and distinct from God, as the past' (2000: 47). Were we to follow up on this, it would imply that all of nature (animal and human) is a way of life, even if Schelling's language sometimes belies his intention. For, as we have seen, he also emphasizes the importance of human intelligence and reason when it comes to free action (Schelling 2006: 49). Nevertheless, one cannot ignore the innovative potential with regard to culture in animals of the following: 'Every animal that has such a [technical] drive steps onto the stage with its art and is born cultivated' (2004: 131). Again, Schelling hastens to add, in keeping with his era, that this does not imply that reason can be attributed to animals. As a result, although we could propose that both animal and human are essentially part of nature, the human is nonetheless above the animal in intellectual capacity and moral sensibility. In short, only humans are truly free.

After Kant saying that if everything takes place according to the laws of nature (cf. Kant 1970: 409 and 464) there is no freedom, Schelling opens up the possibility (without however clinching the argument) that there is freedom *in* nature, that nature in this sense opens the way to a radical contingency, even if, in typically contrary fashion, he denies that there can be anything like chance in nature (cf. 2004: 135). What might look like reasoning and undetermined action in animals is the result of what thought has projected onto nature, says Schelling. Thus, despite the appearance to human eyes of the hexagonal wax cells of bees, there are no hexagons in nature (2004: 134): 'everything that happens in Nature happens with blind necessity' (135).

On the other hand, against a speculative idealism, which would see the real emerging through the ideal, Schelling argues that the '*the ideal must arise out of the real*' (2004: 194; Schelling's emphasis). The task of a philosophy of nature is then to explain 'the ideal by the real' (194).

Overall, the ambivalence of Schelling's philosophy is striking. For instance, he says that Nature is '*primarily* identity' (219; Schelling's emphasis), even though antithesis is the 'dissolution of identity' (219). But again, there is no *absolute* identity in nature, as this would turn it into 'product'. Instead, Nature is productivity; it is thus dynamic and open, not closed as the notion of identity implies.

In the end Schelling's refusal to reduce Nature to something like bare life does not prevail – either in his own thought or in the thought that succeeds his. Too much comes to rest on the uniqueness of reason and language attributed to the human for it to be the case that Nature becomes truly dynamic and open to a way of life. As such, freedom also comes to be what, in a certain sense, transcends Nature. Or, let us put it this way: Schelling's thinking is irrevocably marked by idealist thought, so that it is most coherent and illuminating when it addresses issues of theodicy, the nature of eternity in relation to freedom; the ground of freedom; identity as freedom from contradiction and the assumption of an unambiguous and definite character (cf. 2000: 78). Nevertheless, idealist thought was confronted by the growing influence of the concept of Nature (hence Schelling reference to Linnaeus (2000: 92)) and the emergence of the notion of life, in the nineteenth century, as biological life. Whether it is understood as ushering in a new form of thought, as Foucault argues,[3] or whether it is seen to herald a new reality in the form of the animal, life is what most challenges nineteenth-century thought. Contrary to Hegel and Fichte, Schelling proposes that the ideal must, as we have seen, be conceived as the outcome of the real, and not the reverse. As such, it must embrace both Nature and life. It is not that such a proposal entails the diminution or the finale of idealism, but that in embracing what must now enter the philosophical agenda, thought and reason, it is proposed, can only become more resilient and versatile. Subsequently, of course, life, as a key concept in science, especially in light of the theory of evolution will come to outflank all philosophies, and the utilitarianism of the restricted economy will ensure the dominance of the concepts of need and scarcity. In the wake of this, even the subtleties of Schelling's realist idealism will stand helpless before the onslaught.

Heidegger was certainly of this opinion, even if his reading fails to take into account the complexity of Schelling's thought on this issue.

Heidegger's Idea of freedom

In his course on freedom given in Freiburg in 1930, Heidegger proposes that Dasein is founded in freedom. Or rather, freedom is the non-foundational foundation of Dasein and its instance in the human. In Heidegger's ontological approach, freedom is not a quality of man; rather, man is the outcome of freedom. In his seminar, Heidegger sees freedom as 'the' fundamental concern of philosophy. And this is so, not in the sense that freedom is an attribute of philosophy or of being human, but that philosophy and being human are attributes of freedom. Thus,

> *the essence of freedom only comes into view if we seek it as the ground of the possibility of Dasein, as something prior even to being and time.* With respect to the schema, we must effect a *complete repositioning of freedom*, so that what now emerges is that *the problem of freedom is not built into the leading and*

---

[3] Cf. 'Life is the root of all existence, and the non-living, nature in its inert form, is merely spent life; mere being is the non-being of life. For life – and this is why it has a radical value in nineteenth-century thought – is at the same time the nucleus of being and of non-being: there is being only because there is life' (Foucault 1982: 278).

> *fundamental problems of philosophy, but, on the contrary, the leading question of metaphysics is grounded in the question concerning the essence of freedom.* (Heidegger 2002b: 94; Heidegger's emphasis)

Also, to be noted is the claim that freedom is essentially *human* freedom, the freedom that at the same time makes 'man possible'. It 'is the site where beings in the whole become revealed, i.e. [man] is that particular being *through which* beings as such *announce themselves*' (94–95; Heidegger's emphasis). Rather than being a small part of being, we now see that 'man exists as the being in whom the being of beings, thus beings as a whole, are revealed' (95). The ground of man in freedom, we said above, is in effect an ungrounding, or an unconditioned cause. Also, as far as Heidegger is concerned, there is no State of Nature as the site of original freedom – a freedom that can be won or lost according to the circumstances. In other words, human freedom is essential, never contingent.[4]

For Hans Ruin, freedom is even the underlying theme of *Sein und Zeit* (SZ) of 1927:

> It is in the continued elaboration of his theme that Heidegger reaches a point where freedom is suddenly introduced as yet another name for the phenomenon of transcendence. Taken together with the previous statement, that SZ was in fact a meditation on transcendence, it implies that at least at this point he was prepared to see SZ as one long elaboration of the problem freedom. (2008: 282)

If the problem of freedom indeed underpins *Sein und Zeit*, the question of the animal also emerges, albeit in embryonic form. On the one hand, animals, as we have seen, perish while Dasein in its human incarnation dies – is a 'being-towards-death' – so that human and animal are quite distinct. On the other hand, there is a brief reference, as Brett Buchanan has noted, to the animal's relation to time (see Buchanan 2007: 61–80). Just as, in *The Fundamental Concepts*, the animal is 'poor in world' yet still has a world, so there is the possibility that, although the animal perishes, and as such is 'mere life', Buchanan argues for the possibility of the animal being *in* time, albeit minimally.[5] Given that animals reproduce, they can be related to time in an ontic but not an ontological

---

4. This is not to say, as others have noted (e.g., Nichols (2014)), that Heidegger's view on freedom remained constant but to use the notion of 'ontological freedom' as a key organizing pole in a critique of freedom understood as the work of a self-conscious subject or ego.

5. The passage Buchanan refers to is as follows: 'It remains a problem in itself to define ontologically the way in which the senses can be *stimulated* or *touched* in something that merely has life, and how and where the Being of animals, for instance, is constituted by some king of "time"' (Heidegger 1978: 396; Heidegger's emphasis).

sense, in that they live for a certain time before they perish (die). The time of clocks can then be attributed to animals, even if this is not time as such that Dasein is potentially able to comprehend in its 'being-towards-death'. The real issue of course is not what Heidegger thinks is the case but whether or not a Heideggerian phenomenology has mere or bare life as its basis, a life that cannot truly participate in existence qua the being of beings.

In this regard, animals are only in time to the extent that they are in life, which means to the extent that they are necessarily distinguished from plant and inanimate life. Nothing that Heidegger says here goes against the common-sense view. For Heideggerian phenomenology, then, animals are only in time by default. It would be totally counterintuitive to deny time to them altogether; but this in no way removes them from the having the status of bare life, to which other Heideggerian texts analysing animality and humanity bear testimony.

Heidegger's engagement with Schelling on freedom raises similar issues with regard to the animal–human distinction. Although Ruin claims that, for Heidegger, 'what Schelling is said to have rightly seen is the necessity to move beyond the separation of nature as necessity and man as freedom' (2008: 289), the question here is whether Heidegger's reading of Schelling on freedom does ultimately turn on the overcoming of this opposition. Things are complicated by Heidegger's insistence on the separation between man and animal. Indeed, freedom, like reason and language has for thinkers from Hegel to Bataille, been a key marker of the difference between the human and the animal. Heidegger hardly goes against the trend.

In his commentary on Schelling's Treatise (*Freiheit*), Heidegger, in forcing Schelling's text, divides being into the animal and the human in order to show that only man can appear as freedom. Animals might crave to be individual, but 'the animal never comes to itself' (Heidegger 1985: 140). In relation to freedom, it is proposed that man is superior to the animal. In his translation of Heidegger's German text on Schelling's treatise, Fred Dallmayr provides the following passage that refers to the animal as mere life:

> Being deserves preeminence of dignity because it occupies the highest rank before, in, and for all beings. Being is the pure air which man breathes and without which he degenerates into a mere animal and all his activity into animal husbandry. Because Schelling's treatise on human freedom is basically a metaphysics of evil; because it carries an essential new impulse into the basic philosophical question of Being; and because this impulse has so far been deprived of any effect although such effectiveness could only happen in a still further transformation – this is why we attempt here an interpretation of the

treatise. This is the real philosophical motivation for our choice. (Heidegger 1971: 118. (cited in Dallmayr 1984: 222)

Here 'being' is given the highest accolade, with man being its custodian through language, while animality is ultimately, 'mere' life. This, however, is not in keeping with the letter or the spirit of Schelling's text.[6] For as was seen, Schelling strives to show that man and animal are part of nature as productivity, and that nature as such opens the way to freedom. According to Heidegger, by contrast, only man, not the animal, can 'become present in language' (Heidegger 1985: 141). As such, man transcends nature as he must in order to confirm his freedom. The structure of the arguments on freedom in relation to nature put forward by Heidegger and Hegel are thus identical. From this we can only conclude that Heidegger's humanism is further demonstrated.[7]

When Heidegger comments on Kant's idea of freedom in relation to personality, the nature of animality again arises:

> For Kant, the personality is that which constitutes the essence of the person as person, the *being a person*. This essence can be referred to only in the singular. In corresponding fashion, animality refers to what is specific to animals, and humanity refers to what is specific to human beings rather than to all humans taken collectively.
>
> In what does the personality of a person consist? We can understand this if we consider the personality as distinct from the humanity and animality of man. All these elements go together to define the full essence of man. To be sure, the traditional definition of man recognizes only two elements: *homo animal rationale*, man as the animal endowed with reason. It is thus animality which characterizes man as a *living* being. Reason is the second moment, but this does not make up the content of what Kant calls humanity. It is, rather, *humanity* that characterizes man as both a living and a rational being. The relation to animality is contained in the concept of humanity. (Heidegger 2002b: 179; Heidegger's 's emphasis)

Again, Heidegger says of Kant: 'Personality is the proper essence of man. Experience of the person is at the same time the essential experience of man, the mode of knowing that reveals man in his proper actuality' (2002b: 186).

---

[6] Heidegger is forced to admit at the end of his commentary that the treatise 'only speaks explicitly of man in a few passages. We do not find a self-contained analysis of human being at all' (Heidegger 1985: 162).

[7] In relation to Heidegger's view of the animal and man, see also the *The Fundamental Concepts of Metaphysics* (1995: 201–212) and the *Parmenides* seminars (Heidegger 1992: 80, 107), where the animal is placed in a deficit situation by comparison with man as Dasein. More will be said about these texts in Chapter 6.

Indeed, for his part, Kant proposes that man *could* be driven by his animality, but that this is not the case. The essence of humanity resides in the person as the bearer of the moral law. It is the latter which, 'infinitely', Kant says, 'raises my worth as an *intelligence* by my personality in which the moral law reveals to me a life *independent of animality* and even of the whole sensible world' (Kant 1997: 133–134; emphasis added). Personality, in sum, goes beyond animality. Heidegger thus notes the freedom of the person in the context of the animal nature of man: in Kant, he says, 'the possibility of the freedom of the person in the context of the animal nature of man is also demonstrated [in cosmological freedom]' (Heidegger 2002b: 182).

Even though Heidegger has reservations about the importance Kant attributes to the human will in relation to freedom, his view of the animal as being outside freedom brings him closer to Kant than is often supposed. Even though man may be formed in freedom rather than have freedom as an attribute, the fact that the animal lacks language and reason firmly differentiates man from the animal. Here it is almost impossible *not* to think that, in the end, it *is* a question of attributes.

Nancy on freedom

In the case of Jean-Luc Nancy's influential treatise on freedom, common views of freedom as free will are an obstacle to thinking freedom (Nancy 1993: 3). 'Freedom is everything except an "Idea"' (11), says our author. Again, as if alluding to Schelling and Levinas, Nancy states:

> Evil and good are correlative possibilities here, not in the sense that one or the other would first be offered to the choice of freedom – there is not *first* evil and good, and *then* freedom with its choice – but in the sense that the possibility of evil (which proves to be, in the last instance, the devastation of freedom) is correlative to the introduction of freedom. This means that freedom cannot present itself without presenting the possibility, inscribed in its essence, of a *free renunciation of freedom*. (1993: 16; Nancy's emphasis)

In clearly rejecting a subjectivist (read: liberal) approach, Nancy confirms that 'Freedom cannot be presented as the autonomy of subjectivity in charge of itself and of its decisions, evolving freely and in perfect independence of every obstacle' (66). Nancy leans towards what he perceives to be an ontological, if not a Heideggerian, approach to freedom. The sharing of being as being-in-common:

freedom belongs to this (73). 'Freedom' Nancy continues in evoking Kant's argument in 'What is Enlightenment', 'cannot be awarded, granted, or conceded according to a degree of maturity or some prior aptitude that would receive it' (77). Human or animal with regard to freedom is not, it would seem, the issue but rather the implications for freedom that stem from the positing of existence. If existence is posited, is freedom also included in this positing; or is freedom the act of positing itself? Existence evokes, to be sure, the Heideggerian Dasein. And Nancy cites the following passage from *Being and Time*: 'The "essence" of Dasein lies in its existence' (Heidegger 1978: 67). The point, however, is to know – as Nancy's questioning indicates – whether the 'being-thereness' of Dasein implies an essential freedom. The issue concerns the limitation to freedom that occurs in designating it as an essence. What is essential and what is limited would seem to undermine freedom. Nancy's way out is to argue that freedom cannot be thought as such (it is not an idea or a concept) but has to be appreciated as a fact and an experience. In this sense, freedom could be the fact of existence; existence could be the fact of freedom. But, again, this seems to lead to the paradox that freedom *necessarily* pertains to existence. And here the question for the ontologist of freedom is: Does freedom exist? Freedom is not a 'property' and yet freedom is the freedom of a finite being. For Nancy, there is no freedom in infinity, so that there is no issue as to whether freedom pertains to God. Nancy is not like Schelling in this; it is not a matter of theodicy.

Significantly, Nancy begins to render his notion of freedom more coherently when he refers to 'sharing freedom' and thus evokes political community in the manner of Arendt. Whether Nancy also accepts the baggage the notion of *oikos* brings with it in Arendt's approach is unclear. Freedom is relation in the ontological sense that enables relation (and therefore sharing) to be present. Nancy at one point appears to concede that being must incorporate more than human being (73), but, for the most part, like Heidegger, being is related most profoundly to human being. That is, freedom belongs essentially to human being more than to being writ large. Nancy does not ask whether animals have an existence that is also ontological.

When he discusses Arendt's view of freedom, it is hard to believe that Nancy could situate freedom in the 'anteriority' of the public sphere. Precisely the opposite is the case, as we have been at pains to demonstrate. It is as though the world of animality would, in Arendt, *succeed* the *polis*. The public space is also the political space for Nancy, just as for Arendt, albeit with the reservation that it is also the space of freedom: 'we will call this space the public or political space, as does Hannah Arendt, though ours may not exactly be in accordance with her perspective' (1993: 75). The political space is also 'the originary space of freedom' (75). Does this not mean that this is also, and necessarily, a space of exclusions (of animals, of humans made to be like animals, of the stateless)? Indeed, how would Nancy respond to Heidegger's claim that the *polis* is 'essentially related to the Being of beings' (1992: 90)? – a statement that fits well with Nancy's notion of freedom as the sharing of being. Here, animals are forever excluded because the *polis* is the place where the hand of man appears to the extent that 'beings as such appear in unconcealedness and man comports himself in a disclosing way toward beings' (Heidegger 1992: 84). Importantly, we recall Heidegger's view: 'The hand sprang forth only out of the word and together with the word' (80). And he adds that the hand and language as writing are essentially linked and that 'the hand and the word [are] the distinguishing mark of man' (84). The hand–language duality marks out the essence of man in the *polis* and thereby results in the exclusion of the animal from both the *polis* and from Being. Thus: 'No animal has a hand' (80) and, moreover: 'Being only reveals itself in the word' (99). Philosophically, the key here is that there is no *polis* without exclusion; exclusion is integral to the very nature of the *polis*, and exclusion that is also an exclusion from truth (*alētheia*).

Nancy could of course point out that Heidegger claims that the *polis* is an exclusively Greek reality and has nothing to do with the modern notion of politics. No one today thinks that politics opens the way to truth or to 'beings in their Being'. Indeed, '[n]o modern concept of "the political" will ever permit anyone to grasp the essence of the πόλίς' (91). But this claim is implausible to the extent that the lack of connection between the πόλίς and the modern political is based on the concealedness, oblivion (*lēthē*) or withdrawal of Being. In other words, the disconnection (concealedness) is a kind of connection. We are, in effect, still in the same philosophical zone. Hannah Arendt's approach, which posits freedom in the modern incarnation of the *polis*, would, as it were, be a confirmation of the Greek connection. For Arendt, word and deed, freedom and human artifice enacted in common are no longer visible in the modern political scene. For Heidegger, instead of the unconcealedness of Being as *alētheia* appearing in the *polis* there is uniquely concealedness of beings, but equally, it should be noted, there is here manifest in a certain sense the 'conflictual essence' of ἀλήθεία (90).

Like Heidegger, but even more abstractly, Nancy endeavours, as we have said, to separate freedom from the 'metaphysics of subjectivity' (Nancy 1993: 144). The 'me' who decides in freedom is also the 'you' and the 'us' in freedom as relation and as sharing. Schelling's freedom, if not Kant's, thus becomes too egotistical. For now it is a matter of saying that freedom itself acts; it is itself a *praxis* and not a *poeisis* (production). Freedom becomes, in light of Heidegger, the freedom of Being. That is, 'being-free' becomes the freedom of Being (106). Thus understood, it is impossible to *think* freedom, so habituated are we in the modern era to assuming that freedom is a property or in assuming that one arrives at freedom after a period of maturation or consolidation, as seen in Hegel. Similarly, it is not possible to experience freedom because 'freedom itself is experience' (169).

As a final point, let it be noted that for Nancy freedom is the 'space of freedom', but this is not an institutionalized free space, but rather freedom 'gives itself space' (like the nomad). It is also the 'free space of thinking' (145) to the extent that freedom is existence as the surprise of being (147).

Overall, Nancy's approach does not privilege anything like the *oikos* in Arendt's sense and even birth, death and the body are integrated into an experience of freedom. Birth and death are the ruptures in existence that constitute the 'surprise' of freedom, making it open to thought. Indeed, if there is a term that might encapsulate the whole of Nancy's approach to freedom, it is 'openness'.

Equaliberty

While the question of the relation of animality to humanity is not immediately explicit in contemporary political theory when it addresses the question of freedom in relation to citizenship, the terms 'exclusion' and 'inclusion' – whereby those who are excluded from any political community are stateless – evoke the fact that stateless people are often deemed to be living an animal existence, given that a truly human existence is deemed to be a political existence. Etienne Balibar has addressed the issue of the relation of inclusion to exclusion in some detail, and so it is worth evaluating Balibar's approach to freedom in his concept of 'equaliberty'.

According to Balibar, 'What is distinctly characteristic of modern citizenship, at least by right or in principle, is the universalization of the status of the citizen. In other words, this status ceases to be a privilege and instead comes to be conceived in terms of universal access, or a universal right to politics: a right not only to political rights (a "right to have rights," as Arendt said)' (Balibar 2004: 312). As if to anticipate the objection that exclusion is still part of the presumed universalization of citizenship, Balibar says: 'This intensive universality excludes exclusion, forbids the denial of citizenship in the name of determinations of condition, status, or nature. We should take note of the element of negativity or "negation of the negation" that is, of course, inherent in the conceptualization of the universal' (2004: 312). Thus, we have the formula that: 'equality requires liberty and liberty requires equality' (313). It is the call for equality, then, that prompts the activation of freedom. Furthermore 'equaliberty' 'equates in principle generic humanity and citizenship, implying a juridical adequation of the "rights of man" and the "rights of the citizen"' (313). With regard to the exclusions that might occur, Balibar says that he is also 'thinking of the fact that universalization as such appears to be inseparable from procedures of exclusion and, I would even say, of inner exclusion' (314). This is why, 'Equaliberty is nothing other than the demand for a popular sovereignty and autonomy *without exclusions*, which implies that it occurs in conformity with the rules or principles of universal reciprocity' (318–319; Balibar's emphasis). Moreover: 'the *forms of exclusion* (exclusion from citizenship, even exclusion from the "human condition" itself) that are inherent in every procedure of definition of the intrinsically political import of the universalism of human rights' (320; Balibar's emphasis). Equaliberty is thus the invocation of freedom to demand equality when the latter does not exist. This is why there is, for Balibar, an 'insurrectional' element in equaliberty.

Balibar endorses Arendt's view that the key political right for every human being is the 'right to have rights'. Most often, as we know, this means the right to citizenship, given that the status of being nothing but human does not – for both Balibar and Arendt – give access to rights, even if Balibar also argues that being human – or the 'Man' of the French Declaration – becomes inseparable from the status of citizen. Thus, in commenting on Arendt's work, Balibar writes: 'If the abolition of civic rights is also the destruction of human rights, it is because in reality the latter rest on the former and not the reverse' (2014: 171). If this is so, the question of the plight of stateless people still remains. For, indeed, how can stateless people make a claim for the 'right to have rights' (this is Rancière's question[8]) – which is also the claim to be recognized as a legitimate political actor – when such a claim is only possible (or at least only effective) within a political community? Arendt's point is that actions outside a political community are destined to be futile, it being more to the point, as we saw in Chapter 1, for a stateless person to commit a crime within a nation state; for then at least such a person will benefit from the rights to accorded under the law, even if only temporarily.

From Balibar's position, the problem seems to be equally intractable. While equaliberty is realizable in civil society, or within the type of constitutional

---

[8] See Rancière (2004: 306), where he refers to the 'vicious circle' inherent in Arendt's argument.

republic inaugurated by the French Revolution, it is unclear as to how freedom can be enacted from outside the political processes of a state, or, as Balibar puts it: 'without a political system of institutions and actions, not only is there no implementation of human rights, but there is also no "right" within these "rights"' (Balibar 2013: 18). In short, Balibar is saying, along with Arendt, that *human* rights can be recognized and fulfilled only within a political community. The question then becomes one of working out how, if at all, political community can exist free of exclusions, both positive and negative. Overall, freedom comes into play as a form of insurrection, if not of revolution, when the battle begins to eliminate inequalities, including the inequality of some being outside any form of political community, which thus excludes them from the 'rights to have rights'. But in what sense can such an unsurrection be a *political* act? Or, indeed, what kind of insurrectional act can it be that demands inclusion in political community? Balibar does not really say, as we shall see.

The question still remains, therefore, as to how exactly insurrection, civil disobedience or indeed, revolution, can be inaugurated in the name of freedom by those who are yet to be accorded the 'right to have rights' (and indeed, it would seem impossible to avoid the need to *accord* rights here). In other words: What precisely is the status of the stateless person in light of equaliberty? One can only conclude that it is one of exclusion. When Balibar does address the issue of exclusion at some length, it is in order to discuss exclusions *within* a European context (2014: 199–207). Things are not clarified by Balibar's reference to Marx's call for self-determination: 'Remember the formula coined by Marx in the Provisional Statutes of the International Working Men's Association: "the emancipation of the working classes must be conquered by the working classes themselves," which I take to be a perfect illustration of the insurrectional aspect of the "right to have rights"' (2013: 22). Such a formulation does not address the dilemma of statelessness; it is only concerned with emancipation *within* an existing state or society. In other words, there is a huge element of voluntarism here which presupposes that, apparently at their own volition (for how else could it be that emancipation could be achieved by the 'working classes themselves'?), those who are unfree, so to speak, can indeed throw off the yolk of oppression and liberate themselves. This is not just a form of voluntarism but equally a form of political romanticism.

As a result, Balibar in no way demonstrates how stateless people (qua human) could possibly enter into a political community (*polis*) or create their own. In short, the path from exclusion to inclusion remains opaque.

Foucault and freedom

The interest of Michel Foucault's approach to freedom – an approach that is refreshingly free of the presuppositions of political theory – is that it variously takes place *within* a pattern of constraint: 'Liberty', Foucault says in an interview, 'is the ontological condition of ethics. But ethics is the deliberate form assumed by liberty' (1987: 115). Ethics is thus the *form* taken by liberty. Foucault also sees power and freedom as not necessarily antithetical. Such a conception opens the way to freedom being understood as a 'way' or 'form of life' – freedom here being a way of ethical life. As we saw, Heidegger's approach differs from this, in that the connection between freedom and action is rendered tenuous. In other words, the ontological approach to freedom is not necessarily – in Nancy's words – an 'experience of freedom'.

In contrast to Foucault's underlying ontology, few humanist accounts of freedom in modernity neglect to mention that a key starting point is biological – the satisfaction of basic needs. Foucault is even misunderstood as participating in the biologism that sets up basic needs as the point of departure for numerous analyses. Charles Taylor's analysis of Foucault's conception of freedom and truth is exemplary in this regard – to the point indeed of setting up humanism as deriving from the separation of *zōē* as bare biological life and *bios* as qualified life. Thus, Taylor writes:

> What lies behind this modern humanitarianism? This is a big and deep story. No one can claim to understand it fully. But I have to go into it a little, because his interpretation of it is central to Foucault's position. I think one of the important factors that underlies it is the modern sense of the significance of what I want to call 'ordinary life'. I use this as a term of art for that ensemble of activities that are concerned with the *sustaining of life, its continuation, and its reproduction: the activities of producing and consuming*, or marriage, love, and the family. While in the traditional ethics that came to us from the ancients, this had merely infrastructural significance (it was the first term in Aristotle's duo of ends: 'life and the good life' [zen kai euzen]; a career [bios] concerned with it alone put us on a level with animals and slaves); in modern times it becomes the prime locus of significance. (Taylor 1984: 155; emphasis added)

In this way, Taylor almost immediately places himself in opposition to Foucault; for 'ordinary life' can never be a 'way of life' (*bios* in Aristotle's sense), can never be a source of freedom, as it is for Foucault. While for Taylor and a certain conception of modernity, it is only after the needs of 'ordinary life' have been satisfied that freedom can be realized. Foucault, especially in *L'Usage des plaisirs* (*The Use of*

Pleasure) and *Le Souci de soi* (*The Care of the Self*), shows that what has hitherto been deemed to be the most intimate forms of life for human beings (diet, sexual relations, medical procedures, care of the body, etc.) is in fact a 'way of life' ('*manière de vivre*' – Foucault 1984a: 113[9]). Consequently, the key difference between Foucault and Taylor on freedom is less to do with differing notions of power (e.g., in relation to positive and negative freedom), as Paul Patton suggests (Patton 1989: 260–276[10]) and more to do with bodily and other activities carried out in such a way as to take on a form. Here, the form constitutes uniqueness, and not arbitrary, uninhibited impulsive acts that would be permitted to take place outside any kind of law or order. Foucault's approach shows that such a notion of freedom – in keeping with the freedom of the State of Nature – is trivial and incapable of doing justice to the complexity of human (and no doubt animal) freedom.

What of relativism with regard to ways of life? Taylor argues that, for Foucault,

> there is no order of human life or way we are or of human nature that one can appeal to in order to judge or evaluate between ways of life. There are only different orders imposed by men on primal chaos, following their will to power. Foucault espouses both the relativistic thesis from this view, that one cannot judge between forms of life/thought/valuation, and also the notion that these different forms involve the imposition of power. (Taylor 1984: 175)

This passage shows that Taylor, like a number of commentators, misconstrues a key element of Foucault's thought, and, no doubt, the thought of post-humanism. For there are no 'men', subjects or individuals prior to socio-cultural relations, as it is the latter that are constitutive of and not prior to already constituted beings – whether human or even animal.

The work of Gilbert Simondon extends this idea in the study of individuation (see Simondon 2013).

The human, if not being in general, would thus be the outcome of a way of life – of a *bios*, in short. The notion of '*manière de vivre*' is where Foucault takes

---

[9] The phrase 'manière de vivre' recurs throughout the volumes *L'Usage des plaisirs* and *Le Souci de soi*. Cf. 'À ce titre la médicine n'était pas conçue simplement comme une technique d'intervention, faisant appel, dans les cas de maladie, aux remèdes ou aux opérations. Elle devait aussi, sous la forme d'un corpus de savoir et de règles, définir *une manière de vivre*, un mode de rapport réfléchi à soi, à son corps, à la nourriture, à la veille et au sommeil, au différentes activités et à l'environnement' (Foucault 1984b: 122; emphasis added). [Trans: 'In this way, medicine was not conceived simply as a technical procedure, relying, in the case of illness, on remedies or operations. It had, as a corpus of knowledge and rules, also to be defined as *a way of living*, a mode of a reflective relation to the self, to the body, to food, to wakefulness or to sleep, to various activities and to the environment'.]

[10] Significantly, while Patton does refer, in his analysis, to Volume 2 of Foucault's *Histoire de la sexualité* (1984a), where it is a matter, as in Volume 3 (1984b), of a meticulous delineation of the Greek 'manière de vivre' as a mode of freedom, his primary emphasis is on the relation between truth, power and sexuality rather than on a way of living.

us in relation to freedom; this is what freedom is. This means that a *manière de vivre* is open to change or, even more fundamentally, that it *is* change. But, to repeat: it is not change brought about, as Taylor implies, by pre-existing beings. Rather, things are more complex. It means, in the first place, that there is no essential foundation determining the nature of the socio-cultural domain. Every socio-cultural domain could have been otherwise. Does it follow from this that every socio-cultural regime is equivalent to every other? Does relativism prevail? A full answer to such questions goes beyond the scope of the theme of freedom that is the concern of this chapter. Suffice it to say, however, that working with the notion of a *manière de vivre* does not entail relativism at least for two key reasons.

First, relativism with regard to socio-cultural relations is not a position that could ever be effectively sustained because, qua self-conscious action, it implies that there is a non-relative position of enunciation from which relativism could be proclaimed. In other words, the claim that there are only relative positions cannot itself be relativist. A similar paradox exists with regard to a Nietzschian-style perspectivism.

Secondly, to work with the principle of *manière de vivre* does not assume that the totality of any socio-cultural formation can ever be known in its entirety, or therefore judged in its entirety. As Foucault says, at best, 'the archive of a society, a culture, or a civilization cannot be described exhaustively, or even, no doubt, the archive of a whole period' (Foucault 1974: 130). The argument that there are 'progressive', 'decadent', 'enlightened' or 'evil' socio-cultural formations is thus based on a fictitious totalization, not to say, homogenization. But, in addition, it is not possible to be a self-proclaimed relativist because, to use Foucault's words, 'it is not possible for us to describe our own archive, since it is within these rules that we speak' (1974: 130). Like the archive, then, a socio-cultural system of relations can never be described in its totality. They can only be described, via an archive, in 'fragments, regions, and levels' (130). Understood in this vein, freedom becomes entirely contextual – that is why it is, for Foucault, essentially ethical.

Conclusion

When one considers freedom as generally understood in contemporary Western society, it is evident that the approach proposed by Hannah Arendt is extraordinarily influential. At least this is so, in that the most commonly held view is that human freedom can only be won after the call of necessity has been satisfied. Not only this, but whole societies can be deemed to be beholden to necessity and thus still in a position of having to anticipate a freedom that still remains on the horizon. Only those in a political community (as typified by the Greed *polis*) can realize freedom. Jacques Rancière, we noted, has recognized the deadening effect of the vicious circle implicit in Hannah Arendt's and similar arguments – for instance, those proposed by Balibar and his defence of 'equaliberty'. What Rancière rightly shows is that if one follows the Arendtian position, freedom, human rights, justice, etc., are necessarily unavailable precisely to those who should be the recipients of them because they are not part of a political community. There is no political position external to the *polis* from which an effective call for, and implementation of freedom and justice could be made. Rancière, however, is primarily concerned with the so-called political sphere in Western societies. He is less concerned with the implications of Arendtian and Hegelian necessity. It is only when this is addressed that the truly deleterious nature of the current notion of the 'right to have rights' can be appreciated. It is thus necessary to complete Rancière's project.

Certainly, the ontological approach to freedom, where the latter ceases to be an attribute of the human, is a clear progression. And in this regard the work of Jean-Luc Nancy is exemplary, especially in the emphasis placed on freedom as an experience. On the other hand, Heidegger's ontological approach to freedom is hampered by the philosopher's distinction between human and animal, a distinction that makes it impossible not to think of the human as possessing certain attributes (language, reason) by comparison with the animal. For Heidegger, the animal being 'poor in world' can never arrive at the philosophical 'as such' of the human even while freedom is deemed to give rise to the human and to philosophy.

Foucault's notion of *manière de vivre* can be seen to be an approach worth pursuing in that it does not presuppose a separation between economy, culture or power. Acts of living beings are is not essentially inscribed within a *polis* or its equivalent. In principle, therefore, stateless people can be politically effective in so far as they, too, are the products of a *way* of life. Indeed, truly political action always takes place within, or in relation to a way of life, of which no human – and maybe no animal – as a living being can be deprived; for it is what constitutes living beings, 'as such'. To sum up: not action in a political community, then, but acts done as part of a '*manière de vivre*' is where freedom lies.

5

Sovereignty and Heterology in Georges Bataille's Version of Necessity and Freedom

Introduction

This chapter explores Bataille's conception of sovereignty, eroticism and heterology. These domains cross over with the notions of the servile life in sovereignty, violence in relation to the sacred, and otherness in heterology, and they intersect with Bataille's notions of the general economy of expenditure and the restricted economy of utility. How does all of this connect with a vision of the human? And what is the human in relation to animality? Such are the questions to be addressed in what follows.

While it is reasonably well understood within Bataille scholarship that the general economy refers to all those forms of activity that do not have any obvious utilitarian end – such as eroticism, festivals, sacred rituals that involve sacrifice and conspicuous consumption – what is less appreciated is that animality underpins a number of Bataille's key notions, such as eroticism. This fact will entail a consideration of the extent to which there is a separation between life as the satisfaction of needs and life as a *way* of life. It is likely, in this regard, that Bataille himself was not fully cognizant of all the ramifications of his theorizing. The notion of death as a continuity of being will be crucial here, as well as the fact that it is supposed to constitute a rupture in discontinuous existence, the latter being the normal form of human individuality. Also of significance is rethinking the implications in relation to sovereignty of the notion of the restricted economy. We recall that it is the latter that embodies the Enlightenment concern, consolidated in the nineteenth century, for human biological survival and is ultimately based on the notion of bare life. To the extent that the general economy exhibits an obliviousness to the possible consequences of action, it can be said to contain an impulse towards destruction (hence the importance of considering death here).

More broadly, the chapter will look at the extent to which Bataille's thinking does or does not correspond to a restatement of the opposition between 'necessity' and 'freedom', so important for Arendt.

If, for Bataille, death implies that the human is an essentially tragic being (Bataille 1970b: 239), what might the implications of this be? This is considered to be more significant than the idea that only the one who does not die (e.g., the sacrificer in human sacrifice) can have an experience of death. While one can acknowledge that this idea has a certain plausibility (because, obviously, to die is to cease experiencing, *tout court*), it is necessary to show that there is much more to this, in particular, with regard to the notion of identification which Bataille relies upon from time to time to make his point. What indeed would one be identifying with when identifying with the death of the other and manifesting anguish as the sign of this identification? For it is anguish, or anxiety,[1] that is also indicative of a relation to death as a future event in time that is opposed to the sovereign moment of sovereignty. The possibility is that, in terms of sovereignty, anguish becomes an indicator of servile existence.

Bataille's materialist approach to death needs to be reconsidered. For how can a materialist approach avoid falling into the biopolitical mode of bare life? In other words, how can a materialist approach avoid reducing life to biological life (to mere 'perishing', in Heidegger's terms) and thus reducing death to a biological event, and, what is more, to everyday dying? How can there be any allowance for transcendence in such an approach? It will be a matter of determining the nature of Bataille's materialist approach in relation to the human as a tragic figure whose – to use Heidegger's terms – 'being-towards-death', and for whom death is its 'ownmost' possibility (Heidegger 1978: 294), seems to mean that it does live on the basis of the call of the future.

Death, for Bataille, is also part of the structure of being as continuity. In this regard, sacrifice and the framework of the sacred within which it is inscribed could not be more crucial. But it needs to be determined whether sacrifice as Bataille presents it is part of the structure of being and not reducible to biological death or to everyday dying, or whether he falters and conflates death in sacrifice with everyday, biological death. Bataille, we know, calls human sacrifice, 'the key to the whole of human existence' (Bataille 1976: 264). And he adds, by way

---

[1] The term Bataille always uses is 'anguish' (angoisse) rather than 'anxiety' (anxiété), which may connote for him the difference between immediate distress and unease (anguish) in relation to something in the present, as opposed to a fear of something in the future (anxiety). However, a slippage between the two terms cannot be denied, and indeed Bataille himself links anguish to anticipation: 'Man is always more or less in a state of anguish, because he is always in a state of anticipation, an anticipation that must be called anticipation of oneself' (Bataille 1997: 316).

of stressing the link to the human as such, 'A discourse on being, a metaphysic makes no sense if it ignores the play that life was obliged to play with death' (264). It thus becomes essential to determine exactly what is meant by sacrificial death. Certainly, in saying that sacrifice occurs apart from animal needs, Bataille opens the way for sacrificial death to assume a certain transcendence. However, Bataille's view of the human as such is not reducible to sacrifice, but includes the so-called 'animal needs' (Bataille 1990a: 25), so that, to this extent, there would seem to be in Bataille a conventional understanding of the human, where, as we have seen, bare life is set apart from a way of life. In this sense, Bataille does not take account of his own insight that human destiny is tragic, necessarily encompassing all aspects of life. It will be necessary to show that as far as the human and tragedy is concerned, there are no half measures.

If, as has been suggested up until now, bare life has an ever – increasing hold on what is thought to be the human, the question is to know whether Bataille's work also succumbs to its determining influence. Given that bare life is absolutely devoid of transcendence – at least according to the meaning I attribute to it – how does Bataille's theory of the sacred measure up in this regard? The theme of sovereignty becomes an important barometer of the role of bare life in Bataille's thought to the extent that sovereignty is possible only through transcending animality.

Sovereignty

Unique as Bataille's theory of sovereignty[2] might be – because not limited to institutions or relations between states – it has to be understood in the first instance as the transcendence of necessity. Only after the needs of necessity have been met can full sovereignty be realized. Or it could be that if a certain disdain with regard to necessity is also the mark of sovereignty, such as when the wine brings the 'miracle' of intoxication for the worker, it is still necessity that gives meaning to intoxication. Bataille's reading of Hegel does not contradict this.

We are not, however, just interested in the way Hegel figures in Bataille's *oeuvre*, but also in illuminating the way that Hegel allows Bataille to argue that sovereignty is a way of challenging a certain style of servile philosophy – a philosophy that would retain too strong an echo of necessity as utility.

Let us, then, note the following: 'In a world of failed sovereignty, imagination alone enables moments of sovereignty' (Bataille 1976: 300). This can be

---

[2] A summary of Bataille's 'vision' of sovereignty in relation to sovereign power is available in Lechte and Newman (2013: 165–169).

interpreted to mean that the only escape from a world now dominated by utility (i.e., by the restricted economy) is through imagination. Today, necessity (utility) can only be thwarted through imagination.

Sovereignty in Bataille's original version, however, concerns the moment in which an individual actually escapes the servitude of work and the servile nature (as Bataille has it) of knowledge. A deeper appreciation of sovereignty here requires us to move away from the dynamic of the Master–Slave dialectic that offers such a tantalizing vocabulary for thinking sovereignty, given that, there, work that ultimately enables the slave to assume mastery is entirely caught up in the play of necessity, or in the struggle to take care of basic needs. Moreover, if the slave works to produce what he does not consume, he is not sovereign. Work qua work can never lead to sovereignty. Only the one who consumes free of necessity can experience sovereignty. Thus, only beyond work – or more correctly, beyond labour – can sovereignty be realized: 'Let us say that the sovereign (or the sovereign life) begins when, with the necessities ensured (*sic*), the possibility of life opens up without limit' (Bataille 1997: 302). Again: 'Life *beyond utility* is the domain of sovereignty' (302; Bataille's emphasis). Death as 'the impossible coming true' (309). 'What is sovereign in fact is to enjoy the present time without having anything else in view but this present time' (302).

Notably, Bataille does not see work or labour in any Rousseauian sense, where labour would remain internal to the one who labours in the original State of Nature and where production (= gathering) and consumption would be indistinct from one another. Instead, he follows Marx and views labour in industrial society as externalization, as alienation. This is labour as pure production cut off from consumption. The one who labours is indeed cut off from sovereignty: sovereign is he who consumes the surplus product (beyond utility) of labour – who consumes wealth without producing it (302).

For Bataille, there is not just a blindness in idealist philosophy concerning its supposed materialist base. Nor does he think of inner experience – in which are included eroticism and transgression – as being a simple opposition to idealist thought. Although Derrida observed in his early study of Bataille and Hegel on sovereignty (Derrida 1978), that Hegel, for Bataille, sets out the key terms of the debate (as we shall see below), Derrida does not take full cognizance of the implications of the title of his study: '*From* [my emphasis – JL] Restricted to General Economy', which might be transposed into Bataille's argument to signify the equivalent of the movement *from* servility or the satisfaction of 'animal need' *to* sovereignty. This is also Hegel's position, as we saw from the *Philosophy of Right*. That Hegel's Master or Lord does not follow through on sovereignty as the *continual* encounter with death and therefore is not fully sovereign is another question.

The approach of Bataille prompts us to avoid being prisoner of oppositions, even if oppositions also figure in his own approach. Through Bataille, Hegel becomes a model of a fundamental tendency in Western thought. This tendency, summarized by the notion of absolute knowledge (spirit), is amplified by the following series of terms: 'work' (labour), 'project', 'production', 'knowledge', 'mastery', 'mediation', 'reason', 'recognition', 'discourse', 'meaning' and 'identity'. This series, which is not necessarily exhaustive, evokes the parameters of Hegel's system, a system which may also be encapsulated in Bataille's concept of the 'restricted economy' – the economy of balanced books, exchange value, utility in the satisfaction of needs and the striving for equilibrium. Absolute knowledge is quite possibly the telos of the developed market and money economy. This is the end of history as a project, after all. In Bataille's reading: work is equivalent to knowledge, and is essentially part of the restricted economy, because, initially, knowledge arises from 'know-how'. The telos of knowledge is thus knowing how to realize something. Knowledge, as a result, is related to 'project' and to 'production', and it accumulates over time. It is here that Hegel's Master–Slave dialectic adds a further dimension to the whole situation. For, the tension between work (of the slave) and recognition (of the Master by the Slave, and, ultimately, the Slave by the Master) is supplemented by the enigmas of meaning and discourse. Discourse – or the Symbolic – is the means through which recognition can be realized once the risk of death has been placed to one side. The Master is master above all, then, of discursivity. Or, at least, the one who would cast himself as master casts himself essentially as the master of discourse, the discourse through which knowledge is articulated. Such a reliance on the word – such an externalization – on the part of the Master in the dialectic is required by the exigencies of (mutual) recognition, even if, in the last analysis, the recognition of the Master by the Slave through knowledge and the mediation of the word is to be the source of the Master's eventual loss of sovereignty as well as of mastery due to his dependence on work.

Knowledge and discursivity are in time as duration, are opposed to the instant and are thus servile. They are part of the restricted economy and do not contribute to sovereignty. They have a utilitarian character or use value. As such, they are clearly connected to necessity. Would sovereignty then be connected to freedom, even if Bataille does not make this explicit? The answer is, yes. Like sovereignty, the *enactment* of freedom, too, is about the risk of death. With necessity, every effort is made to avoid death. The animal is in man at the level of necessity: 'We must satisfy our needs, and we suffer if we fail, but where the necessities are at stake we are only obeying the animal injunction within us' (Bataille 1997: 302). To live a truly sovereign life means putting the anxiety of future death to one side, of living in the moment: 'If we live sovereignly, the representation of death is impossible, for the present is not subject to the demands of the future. That is why, in a fundamental sense, to live sovereignly is to escape, if not death, at least the anguish of death' (1997: 317).

Freedom, then, is also about risking death, but not in the sense of fighting *for* freedom, but in the sense of a 'breaking loose' as the enactment of freedom. This is why freedom is on the side of evil rather than of good. The latter entails the fight *for* freedom (Bataille 1992: xxvii).

Thus, it is the animal in man that wants to live and to care about self preservation. It is the animal in man, indeed, which opens onto a servile existence. The enactment of freedom, like sovereignty, is the risk of death and the transcendence of animal immanence.

In summary, Bataille sets out his interpretation of Alexandre Kojève's interpretation of Hegel's *Phenomenology of Spirit*. It is clear that the human is equivalent to its separation – even in sacrifice – from the animal existence, which it also is:

> I have linked the meaning of sacrifice to man's behaviour *once his animal needs have been satisfied*: man differs from the natural being which he also is; the sacrificial gesture is what he humanly is, and the spectacle of sacrifice then makes his humanity manifest. Freed from animal need, man is sovereign: he does what he pleases – his pleasure. Under these conditions he is finally able to make a rigorously autonomous gesture. So long as he needed to satisfy animal needs, he had to act with an end in view (he had to secure food, protect himself from the cold). This supposes a servitude, a series of acts subordinated to a final result: the natural, animal satisfaction without which man properly speaking, sovereign man, could not subsist. (Bataille 1990a: 25; emphasis added)

Clearly, 'man' is not identical to himself precisely because he *is* the animal existence that he must transcend to become human. Sacrifice marks the passage to this point of transcendence. Animal existence also marks the domain in which there is no way of life. Ultimately, therefore, animal existence is, as for Hegel, bare life.

The positions of Master and Slave might change, but this makes no difference to the status of sovereignty. Sovereignty is not equivalent to mastery, as we have said, unless it is continually tested against death. In fact, true sovereignty escapes the whole milieu of dialectical thought in which oppositions take root. Sovereignty is so far removed from dialectical thought, and thus from mastery and slavery, that it throws the true logic of Hegel's enterprise into sharp relief. 'As a manifestation of meaning', Derrida writes, 'discourse is thus the loss of sovereignty itself. Servility is therefore only the desire for meaning' (Derrida 1978: 262). In this way, sovereignty emerges as another instance of inner experience, while the dialectic, as science, is revealed essentially as a pure externality based in the sign system in time as duration.

If sovereignty is ultimately lost in discourse, does true sovereignty arise in an experience of silence? Although Bataille was certainly fascinated by the word, 'silence', silence as such is only one aspect of an inner experience which includes poetry, laughter and the sacred as sacrifice. To know poetry, sacrifice and laughter, as in a dramatization of them – that is to say, in a conscious presentation of them – is also at stake in Bataille's thought. But, it must never be forgotten, poetry here is only possible *after* the satisfaction of natural animal needs.

Sovereign consciousness, for its part, is consciousness of the instant, not of duration. But the instant as sovereign is a *non-savoir* (un-knowledge). The instance can only appear indirectly in tears, laughter, poetry and music. Non-savoir undermines consciousness so that there can be no consciousness of death as such because death, for Bataille, to speak in Husserlian terms, is the ultimate intentionality, hence the difficulty of believing in it. If there is a consciousness of death, this does not stem from any natural predisposition. Animals do not have a consciousness of death. Human consciousness is thus transcendent vis-à-vis natural life:

> what is certain is that the consciousness of death has moved far away from the natural given. Not only do animals not have this consciousness, they can't even recognize the difference between the fellow creature that is dead and the one that is alive [this is evocative of Heidegger's view – J.L]. Death, in the disorder which, owing to its irruption, succeeds the idea of an individual regarded as part of the coherence of things, is the appearance that the whole natural given assumes insofar as it cannot be assimilated, cannot be incorporated into the coherent and clear world. (Bataille 1997: 315)

The tension between the natural scheme of things, which the human also inhabits, and what escapes this (sovereignty, the sacred, poetry, etc.) induces a disabling confusion: 'From the very beginning, as a result of an immense confusion in which the consciousness of death takes hold, men have placed the beyond at a safe and distant remove from this undefinable menace, but their effort is futile' (Bataille 1997: 316). The sovereign gesture is to throw oneself into the midst of the 'undefinable menace'. But, more frequently, no doubt, humans exist in fear and trembling – in anguish as the fear of death.

Anxiety, or anguish, we have said already, is equivalent to a knowledge of death in the future, or a knowledge that the future, for the human, is death. Sovereignty is the erasure of anguish: 'in a fundamental sense, to live sovereignly is to escape, if not death, at least the anguish of death' (317). Horror and anguish are features of the practical world of work. Lucidity, coherence, rationality and enlightenment are the characteristics of modern consciousness. As such, sovereignty is rendered invisible. Sovereignty is the instant for 'nothing'. This is an instant which has no practical, utilitarian import.

Again, in Bataille's approach sovereignty will be manifest in chance and in what is arbitrary – in that which is not the result of the forward planning typical of a concern with utility in the restricted economy. There is thus no becoming in sovereignty even if, given the dominance of the restricted economy in modernity, imagination is crucial to the domain of sovereignty. But, for Bataille, this is an imagination that takes shape because it is the incarnation of an unreal world, a world exemplified by Sade writing in solitude in the Bastille. Sovereignty here is the sovereignty of profound subjectivity. As such, it can only appear in relatively marginal contexts: in art, in laughter and tears, in poetry, music and dance. Yet sovereignty as a form of inner experience does not manifest itself in forms of consciousness. Although sovereignty is a communication and the most profound form of subjectivity, the supposed immediacy of animal existence (think of the privilege of the instant), ironically, seems to fit well with most of its key features.

But both delirium and autoeroticism – because, by implication, they are removed from animality – are also the basis of the imaginary and evoke sovereignty. It is plausible, therefore, to consider intoxication in terms of the imaginary. What is troubling about certain of Bataille's propositions regarding sovereignty is, as we have already had cause to mention, the fact that the ideal moment of sovereignty is also a supposedly animal-like state of pure immediacy. Thus, Bataille says, 'The *sovereign* man lives and dies like an animal. But he is a man nevertheless' (Bataille 1997: 317; emphasis added).

What we have to deal with here is the fact – reiterated in Bataille's theoretical introduction to sovereignty – that sovereignty and the instant are one. Crucially, it is possible not to become embroiled in this dilemma of the instant as destructive of the imaginary. Eroticism throws more light in the notion of the instant.

Eroticism

Bataille contrasts eroticism with sexuality uniquely centred on reproduction. Eroticism is specifically human, while reproductive sexuality is characteristic of animal behaviour. Humans also participate in reproductive sexuality confirming the link between human and animal. In other words, to be fully human is to be capable of engaging in eroticism, where sexual activity is done for its own sake. To be noted, therefore, is the fact that sexuality, like all key aspects of human comportment for Bataille, takes place within the opposition of human and animal. Thus, Bataille remarks: 'The eroticism of humans [de l'homme] differs from animal sexuality precisely in the fact that it puts inner life in question' (Bataille 1957: 35). And again: 'if eroticism is the sexual activity of man, it is in the sense that it differs from that of animals' (35).

As background to his study, Bataille points out that work, too, can be understood most profoundly when compared with animal activity. Like Marx, Bataille says that the first humans made tools which they used to assure their subsistence (36). Like many others so for Bataille, the human initially emerged from a condition of animality. Thus, in the mid-Palaeolithic period, 'man separated himself from a primal animality' (37). Furthermore, when discussing the origin of hunting, Bataille says: 'Initially, man is taken to be similar to an animal' (81). And still further, when referring to nature of war engaged in by humans, it is a matter of pointing out that the cruelty in war is something of which 'animals are incapable' (87).

What is more, however, animals and humans were initially indistinguishable with animals being 'more *sacred*, more divine' (91; Bataille's emphasis) than humans because they were bereft of any form of prohibition. This is why ancient divinities were animals. Strictly speaking, then, it is the prohibition, along with other markers of discontinuity, such as language, that enabled humans to separate themselves from animals. And yet the animal can only be fully inscribed in the sacred and in continuity in light of the prohibition. Otherwise, as we have already seen, it is simply a matter of pure immanence where the animal is in the world 'like water in water'. No doubt this is why Bataille explains that '[f]rom the moment that humans [les hommes] attribute a meaning to animality, we enter the world of transgression, forming, in the maintenance of the prohibition, a synthesis of animal and human; we enter, in fact, the *divine* world (the *sacred* world)' (94; Bataille's emphasis). Meaning makes the animal part of the human world. As such, it can participate in the world of transgression that presupposes the prohibition. It would be as though the animal could potentially assume the status of discontinuity, where it would have an individual identity. In fact, prohibitions do not concern the real animal world, but only the animal world as grasped symbolically, mythically – a world, no doubt, where animals could speak.

Continuity–discontinuity and animality

The important opposition for Bataille of continuity and discontinuity is situated within eroticism. As an identity, the human is a discontinuous being – a being that is so in contradistinction with, and separation from, other beings. All the things that have already been noted, such as work, knowledge and language, are constitutive of discontinuous being. Eroticism introduces violation and the transgression of the prohibition (of what is forbidden), which effectively means the transgression of boundaries. Violence is a violation. It leads to a loss of self in eroticism and is also typical of sacrifice and the sacred, both of which are founded in violence. Nudity begins to dissolve the boundaries of the body that clothing institutes. Transgression, or violence, however, does not erase the interdictive boundaries, but confirms them. Similarly, the extreme violence that results in death in sacrifice does not expunge life, but confirms it. Continuity, then, involves the dissolution and dispossession of the self and a 'fusion' with the other. While in sum, the profane world is one of prohibitions, the sacred world is one of transgression. Freedom here has nothing to do with the primal freedom of animals (76). Rather, transgression always entails a way back to the profane world, even if the sacred emerges with the death of a discontinuous and thus profane being. Death confirms continuity.

Clearly, within Bataille's theory of eroticism animality, in terms of the aspects addressed above, is a crucial element. It is not as if Bataille himself did not recognize this. For he says explicitly that animality is the foundation of eroticism: 'whether [eroticism] begins or ends with the animal, animality is no less its foundation' (104). Eroticism would be the state in which the human rediscovers its animal origins but at the same time is able – and necessarily so – to return to the human state of discontinuity and all that this implies: prohibitions, work, knowledge, individuality, reason and language. Like Hegel before him, Bataille signals through his theory that although the human is born in animality it is also destined to transcend it and is only *truly* human in transcending its animality.

Rupture, discontinuity and continuity

Rupture as inner experience, as loss of self bordering on mysticism, occurs within discontinuity (the knowing subject). This is odd. For if rupture leading ultimately to death inaugurates continuity within a discontinuous being, rupture itself can be seen as the vehicle of discontinuity, and especially in relation to community. Community as inner experience – thus, community which is ultimately founded on the union in death – is a continuity which may be ruptured, as Jean-Luc Nancy says (Nancy 1990: 29), by the discontinuity of society, in particular, by the world of work. Bataille, however, steadfastly characterizes the discontinuous as equivalent, as we have seen, to language and individuality, that is, to identity. The latter, as a principle, has an air of homogeneity, if not of continuity, about it. The principle of identity (A = A), it is true, is what is identical with itself, whereas continuity leads to a situation where the being is no longer identical with itself: it is life *and* death.

The continuity of being in death, and of the discontinuity, in relation to work, etc., of beings in life is entirely implausible if the actual relation – or non-relation – between discontinuity and continuity is not addressed. The continuity of death is clearly discontinuous with the discontinuity of life – paradoxical as this might seem[3] – just as knowledge (work) is discontinuous with non-knowledge. The worlds of discontinuity and continuity are, then, absolutely separate from one another.

But let us assume that the much – vaunted miracle induced by wine and intoxication and experienced by the worker when he is not working were indicative of something else, namely, of the intoxication of work. Or that there is drinking on the job! How many executives (i.e., those in the higher echelons of business and bureaucracy) keep a ready stock of alcohol for enhancing conviviality, a conviviality deemed to be necessary for achieving management goals. The supposedly irrevocable separation of 'sacred' from 'profane' – alternative terms for 'continuity' and 'discontinuity' – means that, ultimately, within the profane world there can be a domain of pure subsistence and thus of bare life. But Agamben apparently shows that bare life can indeed be sacred and that it is just this sacredness which leads to the exclusion of *homo sacer* from profane society. By comparison, it has been argued in this study that bare life is to be understood in a strictly secular sense. It remains to be seen if this is still plausible.

---

[3] It is paradoxical in the sense that if continuity is discontinuous with discontinuity, its status as continuity is brought into question.

Heterology

The force of another argument concerning the sacred resides in the notion – with regard to *what* is sacred – of its extreme ambivalence: at one moment the sacred entity is pure and to be venerated, and at another it is inseparable from violence and the lowest of the low – sacred, yet low. Bataille's reference to spit comes to mind. Dirt (or what is perceived to be so) and the sacred are thus not foreign to each other.

To confirm the point about the ambivalence of the sacred, we can (like Agamben) refer both to Benveniste's entry on the sacred in his *European Language and Society* (1973) and to ethnographic data on the nature of the sacred in non-European cultures, particularly as presented by the nineteenth-century anthropologist, Robertson-Smith. Thus, for Benveniste as for Robertson-Smith the sacred is entirely paradoxical, evoking ambivalent meanings and often composed of heterogeneous elements. What at one time can be clean and subject to a taboo can at another be unclean and escape any taboo. Thus, the nature of the thing is not what makes it sacred; rather, the sacred is in the thing's location or in its relation to other things. For his part, Benveniste indicates that the Latin origin of the word, sacred, refers both to what is 'consecrated to god and affected with ineradicable pollution, august and accursed, worthy of veneration and evoking horror' (1973: 452).

Bare life has set the scene in addressing Bataille's approach to sovereignty and sacrifice and the sacred. Now I want to show the significance of the element of bare life in Bataille's theory of heterology. With each investigation, bare life becomes still more deep-seated in Bataille's thought. But heterology, one might think, is just what is geared to make the ambivalence of bare life apparent. For if it is true that, currently, power makes sacred life its plaything, reducing it to bare life (stateless people, politically speaking, have nothing but their humanness to fall back on), is it still true that there is no bare life that is not at the same time touched by transcendence?

As noted in Chapter 1, Bataille addresses the theme of the sacred in terms of immanence and transcendence in his *Theory of Religion* (1994). The life of the animal (or of animals) is exemplary of immanence in that the animal 'is in the world like water in water' (1994: 24). The immanence of animal life returns for the human at level of intimacy. Originally, human life probably approximated animal life, and was thus dominated by immanence rather than transcendence. We could also say that the time when human and animal life coincided was also understood as the time of bare life as a struggle for survival, as a battle between the 'eater and the eaten' (1994: 17).

In pursuing the relation of the animal to the sacred, Bataille addresses the way that the full impact of the sacred is revealed in sacrifice and the festival. If the principle of sacrifice is destruction, it is essentially the destruction of utility, which, in Bataille's terms, is also the destruction of the profane world; for the latter arises on the back of utility. With sacrifice the sacrificer becomes separated from the world of things, and there is, ironically, a return to continuity, immanence and the intimacy of the divine world (which begins to resemble the animal world). Identification, anguish and intimacy come together at the moment of sacrifice and the sacrificed is restored to a moment of lost immanence. 'But', says Bataille, 'if man surrendered unreservedly to immanence, he would fall short of humanity; he would achieve it only to lose it and eventually life would return to the unconscious intimacy of animals' (1994: 53). The festival 'drowns everything in immanence' and thus needs to be controlled.

Clearly, this is a sacred world shrouded in immanence, whereas the profane world exhibits a certain transcendence: 'the profane world', Bataille confirms, 'is predicated on the transcendence of the object' (1994: 71). The object appears only in the profane world, the world of consciousness.

A high and a low sacred?

For Denis Hollier, referring to Bataille's early work, the sacred, 'is itself split into a *high sacred* and a *low sacred*: the low sacred is produced by scatology (the bit (*sic*) toe, base materialism, low social strata), whereas the high sacred is only the ideal image that the profane projects of itself'[4] (Hollier 1989: 132; Hollier's emphasis). The low sacred is, in part, a weapon in Bataille's polemic with Breton. As such, it is set to oppose any idealist, abstract or ontological approach to materialism, where matter is not to be thought of as the 'thing-in-itself', as Bataille says in 'Base Materialism and Gnosticism' (1986: 49). Notable here is the link between the search for knowledge (whether or not this be self-knowledge), in Gnosticism (cf. Gk, 'gnosis' = knowledge) and the materialism that Bataille is anxious to promote. This is yet to become the 'un-knowledge' of Bataille's philosophy and so still evokes transcendence. In all his efforts to valorize, in one way or another, the lowest of the low, there is transcendence even if only by virtue of the action

---

[4] In a posthumously published text that challenges Hollier's reading collected under the title 'Dossier "Hétérologie"', Bataille, strikingly, notes that the term 'sacred' is itself polarized into 'pure and impure'. And he adds: 'It thus appears that the sacred is at the very least neither high nor low' (see Bataille 1970b, 167). Here, Bataille seems to signal the sacred's ambivalence even if he tends not to draw the full implications of this in his published work. This point will be further addressed later in the chapter.

of 'valorising' itself. But there would also be a transcendent quality if the sacred is as ambivalent as the anthropological view claims it to be. On this basis, there is nothing so low that it cannot be sacred. Conversely, what is elevated often hides a hideous face of baseness and violence.

On the face of it, then, Bataille's '*Documents*' period (1929–1930), where lowness is in vogue, seems to exhibit a different approach to the sacred than that found in *Theory of Religion*. On the other hand, one is pulled up short by a footnote that, like the passage cited in note 3, points precisely to the ambivalent nature of the sacred. The note occurs in the essay (the full title is significant, as it evokes the polemic with Surrealism), 'The Use Value of D. A. F. de Sade (An Open Letters to my Comrades)' and refers to heterology as the 'science of what is completely other' (Bataille 1986: 102 n2). In speculating that the term '*agiology* would perhaps be more precise', Bataille points out that *agio*, like *sacer*, has the double meaning of '*soiled* as well as *holy*' (1986: 102 n2[5]), only to opt, under the circumstances, for *scatology* as a more appropriate synonym for heterology. All of which suggests that Bataille wants to hold onto the autonomy of a 'base materialism', a materialism without transcendence.

The sacred and the 'excluded part'

Although not explicitly related to the sacred, there are, in Bataille's articles in *Documents*, examples which evoke the nothingness (*néant*) of what are effectively non-objects. These non-objects without definite form become, for that very reason, abject. Examples would include: the 'formless' itself, exemplified by, among other things, spit or saliva, sperm, blood or urine; then there is dust, along with random or arbitrary formations, like people in queues, or people walking across a concourse (matter (people) out of place).[6] If we add to this, examples, such as 'the big toe', where the border of the body is evoked, activities, such as 'shaving, tidying-up, cutting one's nails',[7] we have a series of things which become the basis of the sacred as ambivalence. For the sacred, banality, materiality and arbitrariness are no obstacle, as it were, to a certain consecration,

---

[5] Hollier also cites this note (1989: 98), but rather uses it to emphasize the implications of the lowness of the content of scatology.

[6] In his article in *Documents*, 'Musée', Bataille writes, 'A museum is like the lung of a big city: the crowd like blood flows into the museum each Sunday and it leaves purified and refreshed' (Bataille 1970a: 239). Similarly, in *Inner Experience*, Bataille writes, in talking of idleness or *désoeuvrement*, of crowds on the boulevards on Sundays that evoke 'the character of ancient festivals, the forgetting of all project, consummation beyond measure' (Bataille 1988a: 48).

[7] These activities are referred to in the *Documents* article, 'Lieux de pèlerinage: Hollywood' (Bataille 1970a: 198).

or to a making sacred of such objects. On this basis, even a base materialism will not escape the path to transcendence.

While it is true that the ambivalence of the sacred has difficulty in being accepted into a Western and European vision – while, for example, saliva or nail clippings might, in certain non-Western societies, be ritually excluded from the socio-cultural world and thus still remain in it in a sense as sacred – it is a matter, in the West, not just of excluding, but of attempting to entirely eliminate the objects in question so that they cease to have any existence or meaning. Another way of putting this, one which resonates with Levinas's notion of transcendence, is to say that the attempted exclusion of the ambivalence of the sacred from Western culture corresponds to the exclusion of the other *tout court*. Otherness as such can now be understood as that which is unable to enter into the realm of Western culture *as* sacred. Would it be this and not the arbitrary exclusions connected to a 'base materialism' that heterology is called upon to make manifest? This question remains at large as we venture to address those aspects of Bataille's thought that evoke the issue of transcendence, an issue that has in the past seemed to be what Bataille had set himself against – at least when it was a question of materialism. Bataille's invocation of the myth of Icarus is a partial confirmation of this.

Consequently, it is important to examine closely both materialism and the notion of the 'act of exclusion' as these connect with Bataille's concept of community as the 'union of those who have no community' – or again, as the union of those among whom there is only a negative relation. This is a kind of non-group, thoroughly heterogeneous to all forms of society, as conventionally understood, and even to the human (recall *homo sacer*). Could such a union of those without a community be constituted by the ambivalence of the sacred and does Bataille's work make it any easier to break down such an exclusion or does it, on the contrary, confirm it? This is what remains to be seen.

Heterology, then, as the 'science of the excluded part',[8] points to a domain that is entirely other and foreign to identity and to the order of the Same. More literally, though, heterology is the discourse on the other (from the Gk, *heteros* = other). And it is this which requires scrutiny and interpretation. Accordingly, the following is a key passage: 'L'hétérologie recevant ainsi au début une définition minimum – en tant que science de ce qui apparaît *tout autre*' ('Heterology receives therefore from the start a minimum definition – as the knowledge of what appears as *entirely other*').[9]

---

[8] This 'excluded part' is also the heterogeneous, which Bataille designates as the 'sacred' (see Bataille 1970b: 61 and 167). Thus, science cannot study the sacred with any degree of comfort.

[9] This definition echoes that of the article by Bataille, 'The Use Value of D.A.F de Sade' (see Bataille 1986:102 n2) and Bataille (1970b, 61)

Unlike Bataille, Levinas would consider the excluded part (excluded from the Same) as entirely beyond the reach of any science or philosophy. Would this imply that Bataille was overly optimistic in thinking that the excluded part could be an object of science, as the term *hetero*-logy implies – despite the precautions he takes in pointing out that, strictly speaking, a science can deal with only what is homogeneous? – or, is it that, for his part, Levinas underestimates the power of materiality when it comes to the sacred and the absolute other? Is it not true that, despite the connotations of the term 'heterology' (its evocation of difference, for example), Bataille's strategy is more that of recuperation (i.e., ultimately, of inclusion) within the same than it is a path to gaining access to the excluded part as radical difference? This is suggested by Bataille's failure to carry through the implication that heterology is as riven with ambivalence as the sacred it seeks to make extant. In other words, heterology is inherently unstable and unsusceptible to being lashed to the mast of conventional science. Bataille knows this, but seems bent on creating a new science just the same, one that would be distinguished more by the object it seeks to know than by any scientific method. Or might it be that, through his approach, Bataille stretches the resources of language to their limit and so reveals its underside – its excluded part as the practice or performance (cf. performative) of language?[10] As a way of responding to these questions, we consider some aspects of Bataille's approach to the theme of the human and bare life.

Bare life and heterology

It is important to recall again that the idea that we are dealing with an essentially materialist philosophy might be the result of a superficial reading of Bataille's encounter with surrealism, an encounter which appears to be based on the participation of Bataille in the 'idealist-materialist' debate, and which would see him take up the cudgels for a radical base materialism, as opposed to the putatively Icarian stance of Breton and those of the surrealist entourage closest to him. To take this at face value, however, implies reducing the issue of materialism and the sacred to an ideological battle, when, ultimately, it is anything but this.[11] Within the ideological interpretation, Bataille would stand for the assertion of

---

[10] In this respect, note the subheading of 'Principles of Practical Heterology' in 'The Use Value of D.A.F. de Sade' (see Bataille 1986: 99).

[11] Consequently, Bataille's position on materialism cannot be seen to be captured in his complaint that every materialism hitherto has turned out to be an idealism (see Bataille 1986: 15).

a base materialism incarnate in the objects of a scatology (*'ordures'* – faeces, urine, sperm, dirt) that Surrealism represses, but which evoke an essential truth about the world. The difficulty is that, like the objects of heterology, scatological objects still signify. This means that there is transcendence even in the midst of this base materialism. But, in any case, it is a matter of determining whether repression of the scatological object in modernity is what explains the attraction of base materialism, or whether the latter is instead an evocation of the ambivalence of the sacred that is the subject of exclusion, one constitutive of the very condition of possibility of modernity.[12] This exclusion is central to (the constitution of) modernity and results in the opposition, not just between the sacred and the profane, but more profoundly, between bare life – which would be assimilated in base materialism – and life as transcendent, as based in the Other as Infinity and signification, to use Levinas's terminology. Bare life becomes the means of dividing the world into – as has been said – the people and culture of a non-ambivalent sacred and those for whom life lacks any transcendence – those who, in the recent past, have been defined as living nothing but a subsistence existence, an existence of pure (albeit minimal) utility in the 'struggle for existence'. Does Bataille's thought contribute to this division, formative of modernity, or does he, perhaps despite appearances, found a kind of 'transcendental empiricism'.[13]

Reconsidering animality

When reduced to bare life in modernity (or is it *by* modernity?), the human is also reduced to animality as the satisfaction or otherwise – as has been repeatedly noted – of basic biological or 'natural' needs.

Bataille's numismatic studies are also significant for understanding his approach to the human–animal distinction. There are two important reasons for this. First, these studies again raise the question of the relation of the human to the animal and vice versa. Or rather, the medals of interest to Bataille are those fabricated at a time when a clear division between human and animal was yet to

---

[12] Such a thesis would also imply that Bataille's base materialism is not simply the result of a lapsed Catholic's reaction to the puritanism of the church.

[13] The phrase, evocative as we have seen, of this theme in Deleuze's philosophy, has been taken up by Kane X. Faucher (2005) in relation to Bataille, in a manner, unfortunately, that strikes me as too limited. For a start, Faucher bases his reading of Bataille almost entirely on *Inner Experience*, and so neglects the issue of base materialism.

be firmly established. This also implies that the distinction between 'necessity' (satisfaction of needs) and 'freedom', or between the restricted and general economy had yet to be established. As Elisabeth Arnould-Bloomfield (2012) has noted, there is a distinction that can be observed between Bataille's early writing featuring animals in the surrealist inspired *Documents* and the more abstract animal (or animality) in his later writings, such as *Theory of Religion* (1994) and *The Tears of Eros* (1990b). Certainly, in saying that sacrifice occurs apart from animal needs, Bataille opens the way for transcendence in sacrificial death. However, Bataille's view of the human as such is not reducible to sacrifice, but includes, as we have seen the so-called 'animal needs', so that, to this extent, there is in Bataille – apart from the animal as immanence in relation to the sacred – a conventional, Enlightenment understanding of the human, where, as we have seen, bare life is set apart from a *way* of life. Bataille does not, in effect, take account of his own insight that human destiny is tragic (Bataille 1970b: 239) because played out in an awareness of death, and that this necessarily encompasses all aspects of life.

If, in the end, heterology's task is to bring to the fore 'animal needs' as made manifest in the human by scatology – if actions satisfying 'animal needs' are the excluded part par excellence – this implies that, indeed, bare life is the excluded part – the question being: If these animal needs are the excluded part, do they potentially become sacred? And, to be sure, bare life *is* the excluded part; but bare life does *not exist* in the sense that all human life is a *way* of life. This is why, bare life, even if it called 'sacred', is an instrument of power and not an instance of the human qua human's existence. Heterology thus pivots around two types of exclusion: the first, as we saw earlier, is based around the ambivalence of the sacred, where the abject, as incarnate in ambivalent threshold states, is ritually kept at bay, and the second is based around the so-called animal needs and would include the need for food, shelter, reproduction and the evacuation of waste, including, most of all, human waste. Here, the notion dominant in modernity, but apparently deriving from Aristotle, that culture and freedom are only possible after basic needs have been satisfied provides the precondition for the prevalence of bare life. In his effort to bring into focus the elements of base materialism, Bataille brings bare life into presence – that is, he shows it to be part of culture and thus to have a degree of transcendence. Heterology would, on this basis, break with the notion of repression found in Freud. On this basis, too, the abject would cease to be the object of an absolute exclusion and would have instead a certain conceptual status, which might imply that there is nothing that is absolutely abject.

Death, anguish and sacrifice

The theme of death as sacrifice in relation to Bataille's notion of the general economy and difference is no doubt the most difficult and sensitive part of the relation between the human and transcendence. For it raises the question, with regard to transcendence, as to whether there can be any form of human death that, for Bataille, is not, in some sense, sacrificial. In other words, while Heidegger distinguishes, more or less without a backward glance, between 'everyday dying' and 'being-towards-death', and while Agamben seems to agree that the original *homo sacer* was killed as bare life and not sacrificed, and while, more poignantly, there is a strong feeling of revulsion in referring to death in the Nazi camps of 'extermination' as sacrificial, we have to try to go still further than has been done in establishing just how bare life works in the play of power. For were one to concede – despite my remark in Chapter 1 concerning 'veridiction' – that there are instances where bare life is objectively true, how is it then possible to support a notion of the essential transcendence of the human? Indeed, it might mean that a huge concession has to be made to the 'necessity-freedom' thesis and the consequent recognition that there *is* bare human life – that there is such a thing as 'perishing', which even the human can fall into, and there is *also* human sacrificial death, even if its underside is extermination.

We can note, however, that aspects which take Bataille's approach to death beyond the immanent moment are, firstly, that sacrifice (source of anguish) requires the field of the sacred for it to have meaning and for its effect to emerge. It is, then, mediated, not immediate, as it would be as the pure 'present-at-hand'. As such, anguish becomes revelatory of the sacred as an existential structure in the world. Secondly, death, according to Bataille, reveals, as we have already noted, the human's essentially tragic destiny (Bataille 1970b: 239). The human becomes that being for whom death as such, and not simply individual dying, is the basis of a way life that is lived, a point evocative of Heidegger's 'being-towards-death'. In this sense, the *tragedy* of human death – the human whose destiny is its finitude – would transcend a materialist explanation of the human. Death for Bataille is not simply reducible to biological death, as Paul Hegarty (2000: 177) notes. What, then, would life be exactly? If human life – but maybe the life of all living beings – is never reducible to biological life, this is because there is always a *way*, or *ways* of life – or the *love* and *enjoyment* of life, as Levinas proposes (see Chapter 9)? This has implications for any materialist approach that would transform all entities into (material) objects – entities such as the human body, for example.

Conclusion: Heterology, sovereignty and transcendence

As proposed by Bataille, heterology, aspires to do justice to the excluded part of human existence. And in posing its questions it opens up a crucial domain of thought in relation to the human. In doing so, however, this discourse, or semblance of discursivity, embraces certain presuppositions concretized by modernity – such as the idea of a clear distinction and separation (confirmed by Durkheim, as Bataille shows[14]) between the sacred and the profane, that profane life is essentially animated by the restricted economy of work, utility and project. Here, transcendence is referred to, but it is implausible to think of full transcendence in such a context of utility and means–ends rationality. Moreover, there is, in Bataille, little recognition that base materialism can also evoke the sphere of what has here been referred to as the ambivalence of the sacred. Base materialism can be understood in a manner analogous to the term 'proper' or 'clean' when it crosses the boundaries of culture. For European modernity, 'clean' – especially in relation to waste products – means antiseptically clean, or clean in a medical sense. Or, we could say, a notion of clean circulates in the supposedly profane and secular domain of modern Western culture.

The other meaning of 'clean' relates, of course, to the idea of ritually clean, or being cleansed in a religious sense, as is echoed in the opposition of 'purity and danger' made famous by Mary Douglas. Thus, a 'base materialism', similarly, can refer to 'actual' material objects that are only seen as being worthy of destruction, or it can interpret such objects in light of an evocation of the ambivalence of the sacred, opening them to an aura of transcendence, an idea foreign to Bataille because, for him, what is evoked is immanence. These objects can also be understood to play a part in the satisfaction of 'animal needs', as Bataille expresses it, where the material, biological existence of the human would be at stake. A key strand in the tradition of Western thought sees the satisfaction of 'animal needs' as the precursor to the rise of authentic culture. And in this regard certain cultures and/or societies are viewed from a Western perspective as destined to remain at subsistence level where humans merely survive in the 'struggle for existence'.

Is what has just been said here not incompatible with any transcendence and in favour of a radical immanence? Such would indeed appear to be the case, so

---

[14] '[Durkheim] faced the impossibility of providing it [the sacred] with a positive scientific definition: he settled for characterizing the sacred world negatively as being absolutely heterogeous with the profane' (Bataille 1986: 142).

that 'communication' would ultimately consummate a vertiginous adventure of the self in what would be its effective erasure of the other. How a heterology that proclaims its allegiance to heterogeneity and otherness could operate in such circumstances can only be wondered at. It might of course be that for Bataille otherness can never truly pertain to the human, that the human is, above all, an identity and an essence (in being), and that true otherness is irreducibly material in the basest sense. Yet, inner experience is an 'un-knowledge' – an 'ecstasy' – with no other end than itself; this would supposedly make possible access to another's interiority through dramatization and a transgression of boundaries, such as might be initiated in nudity and orgasm. At the same time, inner experience is a unity that makes it (a form of) communication (Bataille 1988a: 13).

In *Guilty* (1988b) (second volume of *Somme Athéologique*), Bataille writes: 'I say: communication is a sin. But the opposite is evident! Only egoism would be a sin!' (1988b: 66; trans. modified). More important than the sentiment expressed here is Bataille's terminology: communication, sin, ego. These would confirm the notion of interiority, which in turn calls up essence, being, the same. This introduces the question as to whether or not *'expérience intérieure'* (inner experience) is inscribed in the order of the same to the exclusion of the other. Indeed, to what extent does otherness really intrude into Bataille's *expérience intérieure*? To what extent can it give access to exteriority?

When it comes to sovereignty, it has been shown that animality is at its foundation. In speaking in such terms, Bataille wipes away any possibility that the domain of utility could be inscribed in a way of life. Instead, poetry, art, music and dance emerge only *after* human animality has been transcended. But tears, laughter, chance and eroticism are also part of sovereignty. They initially occur in the instant not in a duration of time; they do not give rise to servility. Manifesting laughter and tears, dealing with chance, displaying eroticism – such would be acts that occur, not after the satisfaction of basic needs, but within the way of life that also embraces the restricted economy of utility.

Despite this, the conclusion that cannot be avoided is that, in the end, Bataille and Hegel on human animality are as one; for they both presuppose that bare life in animality must be overcome before human life can be marked by poetry. The contrary thesis is of course possible: poetry (let this word stand for all that it gives form to a way of life) is in the 'everyday' – in the actions of the restricted economy where utility supposedly has free reign.

6

Humans and Animals: Way of Life as Transcendence

Prologue

Animals[1] and animality – the focus of this chapter – clearly have implications for understanding the situation of particular humans, as it is in relation to the animal that the human has often been defined and understood.[2] While a great deal of work in the ever-expanding field of animal studies has endeavoured to counteract the anthropocentrism seemingly inherent in human conceptions of animality, my concern is to counteract a particular *animalization* of the human. By this I do not mean that there is an essential animality to which sectors of humanity have been reduced. For, indeed, the aim is to question this essential animality. Rather, I mean that the view of the animal as mere life or nothing but a struggle for survival (the view of the *doxa*) has been applied, as others have noted (cf. Agamben, Calarco, Oliver), to designated sectors of humanity.

Philosopher and critical animal activist[3] Matthew Calarco has recently offered an overview of theoretical and philosophical approaches in animal studies while at the same time coming out in support of a version of what he calls 'indistinction' to describe the human–animal relation. Interesting as it is as a counterfoil to anthropocentrism, it is precisely the way that Calarco presents indistinction that I believe is problematic. Indistinction is contrasted with approaches to the

---

[1]   Every effort will be made to avoid reference to 'the' animal, as this has the effect of totalizing, if not homogenizing, what is in fact a highly differentiated collectivity. The same applies to 'the' human.

[2]   Here, however, Andrew Benjamin's argument should be noted that, in fact, animal to human is characterized by a '*without relation*'; for the animal in philosophy cannot appear as other to the human (see Benjamin 2011: 95–98; 106–112). My approach is to suggest that, nevertheless, there is an original natural, biologistic dimension which leads to the human being as constituted as *both* animal *and* not animal, so that, in a sense, the human has, and does not have, a relation to animality.

[3]   'Critical animal studies' are those studies aiming to make a political impact on human–animal relations in favour of the animal.

animal designated as 'identity' (represented by the approach, among others, of Peter Singer) and 'difference' (particularly as presented by Jacques Derrida) and presents the relation between human and the animal as continuous, not discontinuous. For Calarco, both entities are united in the struggle for survival, a struggle in which they would both show their joint biological heritage, where the human body, like the animal body represented in the paintings of Francis Bacon, is also 'fundamentally and essentially meat' (Calarco 2011: 57). A more nuanced interpretation of Calarco's argument would be that our author wants to avoid reductionism. It is thus more the case that both animal and human have a biological component without either being reducible to this. And, indeed, it will be argued that 'indistinction' together with 'indiscernibility', as presented by Brian Massumi (2014), are *not* essentially reductive, but indeed offer the possibility of revolutionizing thinking about the animal–human relation. The problem here has been that, for many, the most felicitous way to unite animal and human is at the biological level, hence the prevalence of biological language in discussions of the human–animal relation. Calarco's words cited above are a case in point.

As a reminder of what has gone before in philosophy regarding animals, I will look at the way that the animal and the human appear in the philosophy of Descartes and Heidegger with reference to Bataille. With Descartes and Heidegger, albeit in different ways, the human and the animal are irrevocably estranged from one another. For Bataille, the human, even though it can also rise above it, originates in animality. For Bataille, the myth of Icarus was a warning as to what can happen if humanity strays too far from its material, animal roots. Such an approach echoes Alexandre Kojève's interpretation of Hegel, where being fully human entails going beyond the human's animal origins signified by an overriding concern for self-preservation. In his characteristically astute way, Roberto Esposito pinpoints what is at stake:

> Only when the law becomes more and more 'human' – in other words less and less influenced by the original biological ground – will its confines be expanded to include a growing number of individuals. Only when freed from the animal compulsion for survival will law restore to life its most authentically human dimension. (Esposito 2014: 112–113)

Thus, the human's animal origins – where the struggle for physical survival supposedly pertains to the full – is, as has already been argued, the level of necessity, while freedom can be defined as the human's 'detachment from its own animal support' (Esposito 2014: 113). This is a position that we have already encountered in Arendt in relation to the *polis*; in Hegel in relation to freedom and in Bataille in relation to sovereignty. It remains now to further investigate the animal–human relation.

Thinking the human-animal relation

More than half a decade ago, Kelly Oliver pointed out:

> With the exception of a few continental philosophers, most philosophers discussing animals today still do so in terms of animal suffering or animal intelligence, which in turn lead to discussions of animal rights or animal welfare. Most of these discussions revolve around the ways in which animals are – or are not – like us and therefore should – or should not – be treated like us. (Oliver 2009: 25)

Oliver's description fits in with that domain of writing on the animal that Matthew Calarco names as an 'identity' approach, where the human is the basis for understanding and defining the animal. Thus, without philosophical rigor, what passes for the support of animals ends up being another version of the human's relation to animals. In particular the human becomes animal and vice versa (cf. 'human and non-human animals').[4] We already know that a residual neo-Darwinian discourse emphasizing survival reduces both animal and human to bare life, something evoked by Darwin's phrase 'struggle for existence'. The idea that the human, like the animal, is essentially engaged in the struggle for biological existence is implied by David Wood's statement made in the context of a discussion about over-population and finite resources, which is, effectively, a restatement of orthodox economic theory's notion of scarcity as driver of human life on the planet:

> The threat of violence-upon-violence both for humans and other animals, comes largely from increasing competition for scarce resources, driven by our own unprecedented expansion of numbers. There are optimists who argue that the human population will level off – the affluent want fewer children. But affluence currently construed would put greater pressure than ever on the planet's limited resources. (2004: 143)

---

[4] Calarco's view is that philosophy for the animal activist consists in resting from activism and taking stock of the situation (Calarco 2015: 3). The question is to know whether one can have a philosophical activism or an activist philosophy where there is no separation of the two. If philosophy is defined as contemplation, it is difficult to see how activism and philosophy can be reconciled.

                                    The Human

And Wood continues: 'we need to come to recognize that our inter-est, our inter-esse, our being-connected, being related, is in need of enlightenment even for the sake of *our survival*' (143; emphasis added). Wood's point is that until the problem of physical survival for both human and animal is solved, everything else is of secondary importance.

Despite all the problems that are integral to the human–animal relation, my aim – as should now be clear – is to set the scene for both human and animal to be part of a certain transcendence, the opposite of solving the problem of survival, or of dividing history into a dialectic of necessity and freedom, or of reducing existence to the problem of bare life. The notion of indistinction can in fact reveal the place of transcendence.

Let us, to begin our study, consider the following:

1. The term 'animal' originates from the Latin *animalis*, meaning 'having breath', from *anima* 'breath' or 'air' (OED).[5] It is no doubt possible to interpret *anima* as the breath of life in a physical, biological sense, but it is also often translated as soul or spirit.[6] While the Latin, *spiritus*, also means spirit and the Greek, *pneuma*, also means breath, the terms all derive from the same Indo-(or proto-) European root. Hence the irony of the Latin translation of Aristotle's Greek title (*Περί Ψυχῆς* – *Peri Psūchēs* lit: On the Psyche) as *De Anima* or, 'On the Soul', for it means that 'animal' evokes breath as life as spirit – as transcendence – at least as much as it evokes biological or purely bodily existence, even if the latter has been, since the nineteenth century, usual way of characterizing animality.

Commenting on Hegel's discussion of nonphonetic writing, Derrida says: 'What writing itself, in its nonphonetic moment, betrays, is life' (1976: 25). If writing is then a threat to life, this means that it 'menaces at once the breath, the spirit, and history as the spirit's relationship with itself' (1976: 25).[7] The breath of life – is it spiritual or physical? No doubt it is impossible to decide. Or rather, it is both spiritual in the sense of the soul *and* physical. We could let the term 'animal', evoke this double movement instead of it being reduced to purely biological traits. This will be further clarified in a reading of Calarco on 'indistinction' (2011, 2014 and 2015) and Massumi (2014) on animal 'play'.

---

[5] Karen Raber (2015) also notes the origin of 'animal' in 'anima' and adds that as a result, 'animal studies encompass more than merely mammalian or avian life' (287).

[6] Richard Onians says: 'In *anima* there is apparent confusion. In surviving literature it means "breath" and it means life-soul; but the life-soul originally was not in the chest, where breath as ordinarily conceived was, but was in the head, the *genius*. Whether it was also called *anima* by the early Latins we cannot tell. If it was, the explanation appears to be that the word *anima* was generic' (2011: 169).

[7] Suzanne Guerlac claims that in his early work, Derrida counterposes writing as information to the notion of life as the living, or to what in his later work Derrida claims has always been his concern (See Guerlac 2012: 697).

Let us recognize, too, as Simondon does (see below), that for Aristotle there is no Cartesian separation of body and soul. Rather, the soul *is* the body as life. A certain neo-Darwinian discourse has blotted out this connection, so that both human and animal, as Wood's remark illustrates, are deemed to be biological entities before they are transcendent entities.

2. Human and animal are fused symbolically and linguistically, as is evoked by the following passage from Lautréamont cited by Julia Kristeva: 'A regal soul, inadvertently surrendering to the *crab* of lust, the *octopus* of weakmindedness, the *shark* of individual abjection, the *boa* of absent morality, and the monstrous *snail* of idiocy!' (Kristeva cited by Oliver (2009: 32); emphasis added). Illustrated here is the fact that animal names and what they evoke are part of human thinking, so that it is not just a matter of thinking the animal or animality, but of thinking *by way of* animality. As Lévi-Strauss observes in his book on totemism: 'natural species are chosen [as totems] not because they are "good to eat" but because they are "good to think"' (1973: 162). As such, human and the animal are irrevocably entwined.

A little reflection reveals that human language is riddled – both at the conscious and unconscious levels – with animal references, both positive and negative:[8] cf. asinine, as the crow flies, aviation (from Latin *avis* for 'bird'), to badger; to beef up; to clam up; cash cow; bull market/bear market, to lionize, elephantine, caterpillar tractor, to be a 'dove' (for peace) or a 'hawk' (for war), to be a mole (a spy), to get on someone's goat, to play at cat and mouse, to pussyfoot around, to worm one's way in, book worm, to pursue a goal doggedly, the world is one's oyster, loan shark, to squirrel away, wise as an owl, monkey business, snail mail, stupid cow, straight from the horse's mouth, like a bull at a gate, to chicken out, to ferret out, to strut like a peacock, a bird's-eye view, eagle eye, to rabbit on, blind as a bat, a silly goat, a snake in the grass, greedy pig, chirpy as a cricket, and so on.

The most significant instances, however, are those derived from animals without this being obviously the case. For example, in his dictionary of animal metaphors, Robert Palmatier cites the word 'alphabet' as not only deriving from the first two letters of the 'Greek ordered set: *alpha* and *beta*', but these in turn are derived from the Phoenician, *aleph* meaning 'ox' and *beth* meaning 'house'. An '*alphabet* is literally an "ox house"' (Palmatier 1995: 4). Also, *porcelain* can be shown to derive from the Latin, *porcellus*, the diminutive of *porcus* meaning

---

[8] Indeed, to quote Kovecses, 'much of human behavior seems to be metaphorically understood in terms of animal behavior' (2002: 124, cited in Talebinejad and Dasterjerdi 2005: 133).

'pig' (Palmatier 1995: 30?). We can also note the prevalence of animal genus and animal species as human family or surnames in English – names such as: Aardvark, Bear, Bird, Bull, Dove, Fish, Fox, Crane, Crow, Drake, Gecko, Hare, Hawk, Heron, Lamb, Lory, Mallard, Otter, Partridge, Peacock, Pike, Raven, Salmon, Sparrow, Seal, Swallow, Swan, Swift, Teal, Tern, Weaver, Wolf, etc. The origin of such last or family names is predominantly inheritance (changing one's name by deed poll notwithstanding). This means that in human existence animal evocations are present today, whatever position is taken regarding animals. Equally, of course, humans name animals, so, to this extent, animals have been humanized. Naming animals marks their importance in human cultures.[9]

Significantly, too, 'sheep' and 'lamb' as word and image figure strongly in Christian theology, especially in the pre-Byzantine period. As is well known, before being represented in human form, Christ is depicted in the early church as a lamb (Belting 1996: 155).

Stibbe (2001) argues that the more negative animal references in language occur, the closer an animal is deemed to be to the human. Thus, in relation to dogs: '*sick as a dog, dying like a dog, a dog's dinner, it's a dog's life, working like a dog, going to the dogs*' (2001: 150; Stibbe's emphasis). Although Stibbe rightly documents the ways that language is used euphemistically to hide animal suffering, it is also important to note that the fusion of animality and language renders all the more problematic the attempt to identify the animal, in contradistinction to humans, as being essentially part of nature and as such open to objectification. For, as has been pointed out, animals can only be thought – at least in part – by way of animality. There is no clear-cut position, exterior to the human–animal nexus from which animality in itself could be contemplated.

Equally problematic is the objectifying homogenization that occurs in employing the category 'the animal' to cover all animals,[10] as Wood, Derrida and Calarco note. 'The animal', in blotting out differences between animals, makes them part of the order of the same. Calarco says that this homogenization of 'the animal' is characteristic of what he calls an 'identity-based approach' to animal welfare (Calarco 2011: 42). Derrida refers to this homogenization as 'symbolic sacrifice' (Derrida 1991a). Every possible animal taxonomy would be a sacrifice on the altar of identity.

---

[9]   Andrew Benjamin points out that the act of naming and acting 'in the name of' are also important in coming to terms with the human–animal couple. The human naming of the animal inevitably entails the human naming itself in some way (see Benjamin 2011: 77).

[10]   See note 2 regarding the term 'the' animal.

Although Emmanuel Levinas's own conception of animality has been open to question (see Derrida (2008b: 105–218); Calarco (2004: 188)), the Other (*Autrui*) as the other person is already an externality constitutive of the self that is unavailable to objectifying thought. The same may apply to an animal Other so that I am responsible for an animal prior to my conceptualization of it or of animals in general. However, the criticism of Levinas is that ethics is, in the first instance, always *human* ethics, where the human person would be both subject and object of ethical comportment. As such, Levinas's approach would fail to escape a certain anthropocentrism. The question is whether this is also the case in principle – whether, in other words, Levinasian ethics only makes sense and can have an impact if the human is given pride of place in it. If, on the other hand, it is living beings that are at issue, a different set of implications would seem to follow.

Peter Atterton addresses the issues involved here and concludes that certain animals (those which have a 'face' and the capacity through signs to evoke compassion and empathy) do in principle form part of Levinasian ethics, even if Levinas himself is extremely ambivalent about this (see Atterton 2011). We will return to Levinas in Chapter 9 in order to develop this point. It is a matter of showing that the psyche and ultimately the self is irreducible to the ego and consciousness, or to what Levinas equates with the order of the Same.

3. Still, it is necessary to consider whether the imbrication of animal and human in language and, more broadly, in the symbolic, means encountering the animal as it appears in a uniquely human frame. Reference to Levinas leads us to suggest that it is possible to discern the reverse of this, with animals taking note of the human. Thus, when I reflect on the animal–human imbrications in the symbolic this reflection is equivalent to a certain hylomorphism, where a philosophical or theoretical frame is imposed, at the level of the *énoncé*, on the world of animals. On the other hand, if we consider the situation at the level of the *énonciation* (the *performance* of the utterance), animality is present existentially before any reflection. Indeed, animals are present in the sense of that which captivates, just as Narcissus, captivated by his image, is unable to reflect on what is happening to him. What is thus rendered problematic is the possibility of a reflection *about* the animal unhindered by captivation.

A key point made by Derrida in this regard is that the human world is unimaginable without animals. To be human is thus to be in an animal–human world. However, animals are rarely, if ever, viewed as responding to the human (cf. Derrida 2008: 119–140). An animal, unlike a human, is therefore always perceived as lacking a sense of responsibility. Derrida's engagement with his cat is part of an attempt to problematize the one-way conception of the human–animal relation in symbolic terms. The real question we want to answer is: When are humans enfolded in an animal world?

In this regard let us consider the possibility that even an approach like that of indistinction is only able to describe and to think about the world within what would have to be called the human world. To do so, however, is to assume that there *is* a singular human world within which description and thought can take place. Rather, it is a matter of problematizing this.

In his study (to which we shall return) of what animals can teach us about politics, Brian Massumi uses the term 'indiscernibility' (in light of Bateson's work) to indicate that instinct and play in animal behaviour merge into each other. In effect, animals are not limited to mere utility activities, including combat that would enhance their physical survival (cf. Massumi 2014). As such, it is possible to speak about a certain animal autonomy as against human intentions. In the end, humans, captivated by animal play, come to act in accordance with animal autonomy rather than the reverse.

4. The image and animality are, apart from stories such as Tarzan and the Jungle Book, also inextricably linked. Not only have animals often assumed human form – and vice versa – but, the human, conceived as an essentially biological being, has, particularly in the nineteenth century, been portrayed as 'animalistic'. Lévi-Strauss draws attention to a series of famous drawings of 'Naturalised Man' by Charles Le Brun (1619–1690), where the faces of an owl and a fox take on human form; or, we could say, where the human face takes on animal features (Lévi-Strauss 1974: Image 3, between 148 and 149). In an article on Le Brun's lectures on the face, Line Cottegnies writes, 'his physiognomic sketches all go to show that some faces are innately similar to animal heads, and that the individuals with these faces share certain characteristics with the animals they look like' (2002: 150). Whether these 'characteristics' are deemed to be positive or negative is less important than the fact that animals become a key and almost automatic reference for interpreting human features. The use by sporting teams of animal 'mascots' can be seen as an extension of this 'human like animal' phenomenon. Nerissa Russell refers to this in terms of the opposition between wild and domestic animals: 'We do not have to look far for this in our own society, whether it is the nobility and ferocity of wild animals invoked as team mascots or the denigration of other humans as living like wild animals. The classic works of Leach (1964) and Tambiah (1969) demonstrate that other cultures have made similar symbolic use of the wild and domestic' (2002: 295). The nature–culture opposition, so prevalent in science and much

philosophical thinking, merely reinforces the idea that animals are on the side of nature, while humans are on the side of culture. However, as Russell remarks, nature only comes into view once there exists a culture – or, in the case of the animal, domestication – against which a domain can be conceived as nature. In effect, before the domestication of animals, there were just animals. As there is a diversity of human cultures, Kelly Oliver asks: 'Which human culture will be the standard for considering whether or not animals are like "us" and deserve rights?' (2009: 30).

5. In light of Derrida's meditation on the animal, other questions arise, questions which call for a response: Can a sacrificial culture (a culture characterized by the non-criminal killing of life) ever avoid being carnivorous? The implication here is that one never simply eats in order to live or to survive, but eats either 'well' or 'badly' (even if Derrida's sentence, '*Il faut bien manger*', can be translated as 'we have to eat', as Wood says (Wood 1999: 30), or as 'one should eat well'). Wood, in taking up the question of a carnivorous culture, has claimed that vegetarianism is possible, but only at the price, it would seem, of reinforcing a utilitarian attitude towards animals and culture. In other words, the question for Wood ultimately is: *what* can we eat to survive? – whereas, the import of the approach I take here is that there is never a 'what' as such in relation to eating and much else besides, but only a 'how' one lives, or a *way* of life. This is what gives life its transcendence. The utilitarian argument about survival is thus mistaken.

*

I turn now to a discussion of the work of Simondon, Heidegger, Agamben and Calarco with regard to the animal–human relation, in order to consider how, in particular in light of Agamben's thinking, a way of life – life as breath (*anima*), as spirit, as transcendence – should take precedence in thinking this relation.

Aspects of Simondon's genealogy of the human–animal relation

Gilbert Simondon's little book of two lectures on the relation between the human and the animal (Simondon 2011) offers a brief historical account. The lectures are embedded in the teaching of psychology, but Simondon was no ordinary psychologist. He does, however, paint in broad brush strokes as an aid to his teaching. It is an approach that no doubt needs nuancing but, nevertheless, it serves to alert us to the fact that the animal–human opposition is of recent date. Thus, in the following passage, our author highlights the way that the ancients blurred the distinction between animal and human:

> In Antiquity, the first notion that emerged is neither that of instinct nor that of intelligence in opposition to instinct, but rather more generally that of human life, animal life, and plant life. What appears to be quite clear, or clear at least for the Presocratics is that the human soul – and this has really surprised the historians of thought – is not considered as different in nature from the animal soul or the vegetal soul. Everything that lives is provided with a vital principle, the great dividing line passes between the reign of the living and the non-living much more so than between plants, animals, and man. It is a relatively recent idea to contrast animal and human life, and to see human functions as fundamentally different from animal functions. (Simondon 2011: 32)

Animal and human can then be brought into proximity with one another because it is here a matter of the existence or non-existence of a soul, not a matter of language, reason or intelligence. But what of Aristotle's philosophy on this point? For here is the thinker who claimed that slaves are born, not made, and that the difference between those who are slaves and those who are free turns on the difference between the soul of a free person and the soul of a slave (Aristotle 1995: 1254b33–4). What we want to know is whether, for Aristotle, the fact that the slave labours is indicative of the nature of a slave's soul. Or, more pointedly (because free men also engaged in certain kinds of labour), whether the fact that slaves were supposedly exclusively involved in ensuring that basic needs were satisfied led to them manifesting a different soul. In fact, Hannah Arendt cites Aristotle as saying that 'slaves and tame animals with their bodies minister to the necessities of life' (Arendt 1958: 80 citing Aristotle *Politics* 1254b25).

Simondon bypasses this aspect of Aristotle's philosophy and instead sees Aristotle as the one who essentially draws conclusions from careful observations of the world. This gives him the status of scientist: '[h]e is indeed,' says Simondon, 'the father of biology' (2011: 52). It is, then, life – human, animal and vegetal – that the Greek philosopher excels in distilling as far as Simondon is concerned. In Aristotle's theorizing, our author writes, there is 'an invariant, and this invariant is life; the functions of life; the means used to fulfil these functions change with species, but the functions remain, life is an invariant' (2011: 52). Not addressed here is whether life is essentially 'psyche' (Ψυχῆς) or something else. But, in any case, if 'life is an invariant', it is not reducible to a body as inert matter. Rather, life, as was indicated above, is the 'breath' of life – *pneuma* and *anima/spiritus*.

As Bergson showed, to spatialize life in a representation is to falsify it (Bergson 1993: 235–251) because life is essentially *lived* in time; it cannot be represented because representation, so dear to perception, relies on spatialization and the infinite divisibility of the continuum.

The much-discussed (if ill-defined) notion of life also includes, as we know, the relationship between *zōē* and *bios* and interpreting the significance of the elements of this duality. It is unclear as to how Simondon's reading can be reconciled with one that takes its cue from the idea of *zōē* as the realm of necessity and *bios* as the realm of freedom, to which only certain human beings may aspire.

Descartes

Descartes's thinking on the animal is largely determinant for modernity, and for this reason, beginning with Simondon's reading, we look now at the philosopher of the *cogito*. For Descartes, says Simondon, the animal is a complete automaton. Not only is it incapable of reasoning, but it is not even driven by instinct. It is but a tool. Consequently, when the mole digs out the earth to make its hill, it does so with an efficiency that can only be compared to a mechanical device. An animal cannot do other than what it does. At least this is the way Descartes has most often been understood and Simondon hardly contradicts this picture. However, if, in light of Jean-Yves Chateau's Introduction to Simondon's lectures (2011: 17–18 n7), we delve a bit deeper, a more nuanced picture emerges, even if this is one where the animal is still inherently subordinate to man. Animals indeed have passions, like humans, even if from this it cannot be concluded that animals have thoughts (Descartes. 2010: 694). For, only man has the word (695), which is not to deny that the expression of an animal's passions can reach sophisticated levels allowing it to mimic certain parts of human speech. The issue, though, as Ferdinand Alquié notes (Descartes 2010: 695 n2.), is that while attributing feelings to animals (such as fear, sadness, hope and joy) might not imply a capacity for thought or for the acquisition of language, it makes the animal more than a mere automaton; for it suggests that animals have a certain level of consciousness.[11] Although Descartes remains absolutely firm

---

[11] For his part, Andrew Benjamin sees a much more radical approach to the animal by Descartes, namely that it is about doing 'without animals', akin in the human with doing without the body (Benjamin 2011: 26). Life and thought do not coincide in Descartes (2010: 29), which implies that life is 'bare life'. Crucially, Benjamin summarizes what is at issue by pointing out that '[P]hilosophy's traditional concern with the animal was to specify that which is proper to human being' (Benjamin 2011: 75).

in claiming that the animal and the human cannot be equated because the latter has language and reason and the former does not (2010: 695), it is nevertheless clear that, whether he intended it or not, Descartes's characterization of the animal makes of it a sentient being and no mere machine. Indeed, here, we are reminded of Bentham's question as to whether or not animals can suffer.[12] Even though the very basis of the distinction between animal and human is blurred by Descartes and Bentham, we know that for the purposes of the practices of industrial farming so evident in modernity, the animal–human distinction is made as sharp as possible.

The sharpness of this distinction remains true too for Descartes himself; for he claims that if an animal does not have thought in the manner of humans, it must, consequently, act automatically. Just as movements can be the outcome of automata built by men, so too is this the case with animals. To define animals as automata, Descartes thinks, is not at all to preclude any of the activities in which animals engage. The creation of automata by humans is an instance, Descartes tells us, of art imitating nature; for 'nature can, for its part, produce automata, that are more excellent – such as the brutes – than those which derive from the hand of man' (2010: 886). Above all, animals are deemed to lack a capacity for thought because they lack a capacity for language, language being the sign of this capacity.

This, then, is the Descartes who resonates with Heidegger, where it will be found that 'the' animal is subject to a 'poverty of world' and cannot engage in language, or, therefore, in 'being'. Such a view sets the scene for the 'anthropological machine'.

The human–animal conceptual couple: An 'anthropological machine'

'Human' and 'animal', then, seem to invite efforts to attribute to each a content. Both Aristotle and Descartes say, in this regard, that reason and language define the human, while Descartes says that the animal is, in a certain sense, an automaton (by comparison with the human). Rejecting the content so defined does not entail the abandonment of the conceptual couple itself. And

---

[12] This question has been seen, incorrectly, in my view, to imply another, namely: Can animals feel pain in a contingent sense, that is, as opposed to conforming to fixed patterns of behaviour? See Harrison (1991) and a response by House (1991).

no doubt it is not possible to dispense with it by an act of fiat. Calarco (2010), in accepting the inevitability of the human–animal couple, nonetheless pushes for an agnosticism as to what the animal might be, just as Heidegger and Agamben after him refuse to provide any content for the notion of the human. The advantage of Agamben's notion of the 'anthropological machine' is that it brings to the fore the inclusionary-exclusionary logic in relation to the human in all its paradoxical perversity. Thus, in defining the human as part animal, science has to determine exactly what aspect of the human corresponds to animality. An attempt has to be made to determine what part of the human is non-human, if not inhuman, so as to exclude it from humanity proper. The animal part of the human which is not human is revealed when human beings exhibiting certain behaviours are pejoratively classified as animals. In Agamben's words:

> the anthropological machine [...] functions by excluding as not (yet) human an already human being from itself, that is, by animalizing the human, by isolating the nonhuman within humanity: *Homo alalus*, or the ape-man. And it is enough to move our field of research ahead a few decades, and instead of this innocuous paleontological find we will have the Jew, that is the non-man produced within the man. (Agamben 2004: 37)

And, crucially, from a political perspective, Agamben adds that latterly, it is a matter of the humanization of an animal (an 'inside obtained through inclusion of an outside'), and we have 'the ape-man, the *enfant sauvage* or *Homo ferrus*, but above all the slave, the barbarian, and the foreigner, as figures of an animal in human form' (2004: 37). Humans that are like – or are – animals (Jews) and animals that are like – or are – humans, such would be the way the anthropological machine plays itself out, with murderous consequences.

If the slave, whose labour preserves biological life, is in fact an animal in human form, it is pertinent to speculate whether the peoples of the so-called subsistence economies also fit the description of being animals in human form.[13] Certainly, early accounts of Indigenous Australians correspond to this characterization. For example, art historian Bernard Smith cites Sir John Barrow (1764–1848) as describing the Australian Aborigine as 'an animal of prey ... more ferocious than the lynx, the leopard or the hyena' (see Smith 1983: 322).

Through understanding how the anthropological machine works, Agamben says, we might be better able to stop it. One of the difficulties at this conjuncture

---

[13] On this, Hannah Arendt reiterates a prevalent view of subsistence societies. Thus, in 'Politics and Freedom' (1960) Arendt says: 'Where men live together but do not form a body politic – as, for example, in tribal societies or in the privacy of the household – the factor ruling their actions and behavior is not freedom but the necessities of life and concern for its preservation' (1960: 30).

(2014), as Calarco and others have noted, is to know how give an account of the animal '*on its own terms*' (Calarco 2007: 166; Calarco's emphasis.), that is, without making the animal a means of explaining the nature of the human. But if it is still up to humans to give an account of animals, however sympathetic, the animal–human distinction is still retained – which is the core of the problem. To take a stand as a human on behalf of the animal clearly presupposes that animals cannot take a stand on their own behalf. A paternalistic politics, which also exists in other spheres, is not overcome. No doubt something like the animal putting the human in question, as is exemplified in Jacques Derrida's relation to his cat, needs to happen. Thus, Derrida remarks: 'Before the cat that looks at me, would I be ashamed *like* a beast that no longer has the sense of its nudity? Or, on the contrary, *like* a man who retains the sense of his nudity? Who am I, therefore? Who is it that I am following? Whom should this be asked of if not the other? And perhaps of the cat itself?' (Derrida 2008: 5–6; Derrida's emphasis). Perhaps like the Other for Levinas, the animal – *an* animal – puts one in question, undermines one's agency as a human, forces one to confront one's vulnerability. Gradually, it dawns that we do not know what we are dealing with in our individual and quite specific relations with an animal. There is no doubt much here that remains to be thought through, even if Derrida has made a promising start. Suffice it to say now with Calarco that: 'Anyone who argues that existing forms of politics can be reformed or radicalised so as to do justice to the multiplicity of forms of non-human life is clearly the unrealistic and utopian thinker' (Calarco 2007: 175).

Heidegger, Bataille and animality

Because his thought is so significant for the European tradition of philosophy, it is important to understand Heidegger's thinking on the animal–human distinction, a mode of thinking, I suggest, which has political ramifications. To be sure, others have already begun to interpret Heidegger on the animal and to test the extent that his might be an anthropocentric approach.[14] My interest is rather in the characterization of the *polis* – already touched upon in Chapter 3 – that Heidegger's characterization of the animal facilitates.

---

[14]　A recent account is Tanzer (2016) where consideration is given to Heidegger's approach to the animal in terms of a comparative view with the human as opposed to an the animal as having an absolute, ontological status. What Tanzer does not discuss in any detail, like a number of commentators, are the implications of Heidegger's view of the animal for his view of the human.

We note Heidegger's reliance on the work of Jacob von Uexküll and the notion of *Umwelt* (environment), where species other than the human are constrained by a 'world'. This is the idea Heidegger takes up in defining the animal as having 'poverty in world'. Environment is always an environment for … never an objective environment. There is a continuity between the animal and its environment, whereas man, by contrast, is distinct from his environment. In a nutshell, this thesis from Uexküll is also Heidegger's.

Heidegger and the *Polis.*

Emphasis in the following analysis will be on the way that Heidegger's conception of the animal highlights the nature of the human in relation to the *polis*.

As Agamben (2004) points out, it is the *polis* that provides the place for the taking place, as it were, of unconcealedness, or of αλήθεια (*alētheia*). The *polis* would be the place where the Being of beings comes into the light of the Clearing or the Open. It is this domain – and this domain only – where the human as such shows itself and can be comprehended by those beings gathered together (recall the human as '*mitsein*' – 'being with'; also *koinonia* – 'being with another or others'[15]) in the *polis*. It is precisely the human, then, that, according to Heidegger, can appear in the *polis*, while the animal is condemned to remain within the domain of unconcealedness (*lēthē*). Let us see how Heidegger proceeds to articulate this key idea.

In a determining statement, Heidegger says that 'Being manifests itself in the word' (Heidegger 1992: 76). The word becomes manifest in its most essential form in the *polis*, and the word is, as we know from the *Letter on Humanism*, the 'house of being'. Even when considering the fact that sculpture, architecture and poetry are of equal importance in terms of presence with the word in the Ancient Greek world, Heidegger says that in the silence of these things the word is enacted. There is no discourse of 'aesthetics' to confuse the matter. Thus: 'how could there ever be temples or statues, existing for what they are, without the word?' (116) Indeed:

> The statue and the temple stand in silent dialogue with man in the unconcealed. If there were not the *silent word*, then the looking god as sight of the statue and of the features of its figure could never appear. (1992: 116; Heidegger's emphasis)

---

[15] But these 'others' are not animals, as Andrew Benjamin has pointed out (cf. Benjamin 2011: 39). No community can be formed with animals.

The absence of any aesthetic discourse 'bears witness to the fact that these works stood well secured in the clarity of the word' (116). Together with monumental art, the word lets Being appear and 'brings Being into unconcealedness' (115), and this appearing as unconcealedness (as *alētheia*) essentially takes place in the *polis*. What gives this pertinence with regard to the animal, as we are aware after Derrida's reading (Derrida 1987), is that the human hand is bound to the word and the animal does not have the equivalent of a hand: 'Man himself acts [*handelt*] through the hand [*Hand*]; for the hand is, together with the word, the essential distinction of man' (Heidegger 1992: 80). The hand is inseparable from the word and reveals the Being of beings, a revelation or disclosure that can only take place in the *polis* (not a city-state or a republic (too Roman!)) as the place of '*politeia*' (the place – often confused with a 'space' – of politics). The word and the hand inseparable from it ('the hand sprang forth only out of the word' (80)) distinguish humanity from animality: 'No animal has a hand, and a hand never originates from a paw or a claw or a talon' (80). The animal, as Agamben notes, can never be part of the *polis* – can never enter the open of unconcealedness, of *alētheia*. In this regard, Heidegger says, in an crucially revealing statement: 'There is a "hand" only where beings as such appear in unconcealedness and man comports [animals can only "behave" – J.L.] himself in a disclosing way toward beings' (84).

Clearly, the *polis* becomes the domain of the intricate relation between 'hand' and 'word'. It is in the *polis* where disclosure takes place so that, broadly speaking, what is essentially human unfolds in the *polis*, the place from which the animal is essentially excluded. For man, 'dwelling in the πόλις is a sojourn here on earth' (93). Even though Heidegger claims that '[n]o modern concept of the "the political" will ever permit anyone to grasp the essence of the πόλις' (91), it is, I think, worthy of note that the *polis* is of such inordinate importance for Heidegger, given that it evokes the political today, particularly in the work of Arendt. This is despite the further claim that the Greek term *politeia* is 'unpolitical' '[b]ecause the Greeks are the utterly unpolitical people, unpolitical by essence' (96). Heidegger could not be clearer, however, about the significance of the *polis* for thinking; for: 'the essence of the Greek πόλις [*polis*] is grounded in the essence of αλήθεια [*alētheia*]' (89). He elaborates on this as follows:

> That is, if αλήθεια as unconcealedness determines all beings in their presence (and that means, for the Greeks, precisely in their Being), then certainly the πόλις too, and it above all, has to stand within the domain of this determination by αλήθεια, provided the πόλις does indeed name that in which the humanity of the Greeks has the centre of its Being. (1992: 89)

The 'humanity of the Greeks' is the only form of humanity that really counts. In their broadest aspect the entirety of the lectures on *Parmenides* are ultimately geared to make this point. The whole of Western historiography is constitutionally unable to grasp the significance of the Greek relation to Being, so focused is it on 'lived experience', where 'forgetting' is equivalent to the faulty memory of a subject or a psychological being and not the 'oblivion' of '*lethe*'. The modern concern for 'subjectivity' has thus been projected back onto Greek thought and culture. Epochs are mixed up – the modern and the Roman with the Greek, etc. – so that what is produced is a 'historiographical mash' (1992: 96).

Even though the *polis* is firmly distinguished from the play of power, Heidegger acknowledges that 'strife' is its essential characteristic. For aletheia 'possesses a conflictual essence' (90). Here, we have strife as a kind of struggle between '*lēthē*' and '*a-lētheia*', between oblivion and disclosure or unconcealedness. Unconcealedness is also called the 'Open' in which Being appears to the extent that the word is manifest. No animal has the word, therefore no animal can appear in the Open, which ultimately means that no animal can appear in the *polis*, paradoxical as that might sound to modern ears.[16] The modern is where subjectivity abounds and where the only valid experience is the lived experience of the subject-self. Here, man – the human – is a mere object of representation, which means, in effect, that he is 'animal', albeit a 'rational animal'.

We have referred here principally to Heidegger's remarks in his *Parmenides* lecture series, which illuminates the nature of the *polis*. A more extensive meditation on the animal as such is contained in the 1929–1930 lecture course entitled *Fundamental Concepts of Metaphysics* (1995). There, Heidegger, with reference, as mentioned, to research in biology (particularly the work of von Uexküll (1921) on the *Umwelt* and the *Innewelt*), presents his thesis that the animal has 'poverty in world', which means it is subject to a 'captivation' which it cannot transcend. There is an echo here of Bataille's view that the animal is 'immediacy and immanence'. The animal engages in 'behaviour', which implies that it cannot do other than what it does. It is determined in its 'way of being' (Heidegger 1995: 198) (it lives, but does not exist) by drives and instinct. Thus, Heidegger says by way of illustration: '[t]he blade of grass is simply a beetle-path on which the beetle specifically seeks beetle-nourishment, and not just any

---

[16] The question that Derrida's thought raises concerns language. Is it so certain that animals are excluded from langage? – or is it not rather a matter of the way that language is defined and what it circumscribes? In the most prevalent cases, it is a matter of excluding from consideration non-human aspects of language from an understanding of language, aspects such as: 'the mark in general', 'the trace', 'iterability', '*différance*' (Derrida 1991: 116). The exclusion of the animal from language may not be as radical as Heidegger claims in light of these aspects.

edible matter in general' (198). And then follows a particularly revealing passage: 'Every animal [i.e. '*all* animals, *every* animal' (Heidegger 1995: 186; Heidegger's emphasis), unicellular as well as multicellular, insects as well as mammals] as animal has a specific set of relationships to its sources of nourishment, its prey, its enemies [because it can be prey to other animals], its sexual mates and so on' (1995: 198). In other words, every animal's living is a mere surviving: it is eating, reproducing, perishing (not dying). The life of the animal is a mere surviving because it does not have the word. Only through the word can life be existence, can comportment take the place of behaviour, and death take the place of perishing. All of this stems from the animal's captivation and its consequent inability to know the world *as* world. In large measure, therefore, the human and the animal in Heidegger cannot be reconciled.[17]

As already noted above, humans exhibit traits of captivation similar to those of animals, but only up to a point. Thus, in analysing different 'moods', or *stimmungen* (cf., 'attunement', 'tuning (of the piano))', morals, tonality, atmosphere, as well as 'frame of mind'), Heidegger argues that whereas the animal's captivation is interminable, 'man's' captivation is transitory and gives rise to thinking, that is, to the appearance of Being in beings. Boredom, for instance, is always only ever periodic, never permanent. It is on this basis that 'man is world-forming'. Man is world-forming because his destiny is not just to survive and perish. Even though Heidegger pays lip service to the idea that both man and the animal 'have world', the separation between the human and the animal could not be wider. For the animal's eternal captivation is, as we saw, confirmed by the fact that it has neither word nor hand. Only humans, therefore, can exist in the *polis* as the place of unconcealedness, where beings can come to know things, *as such*. The animal, precisely, is excluded from this 'as such', even though there seems to be no reason as why *Dasein* as 'being there' could not refer to the living rather than just to 'man'. Be this as it may, it is only through the *polis* and through it alone that Being is revealed, is dis-closed or emerges in unconcealedness.

---

[17] Despite an extremely illuminating commentary on Heidegger and the animal and despite pointing to the 'dead end', we find in Heidegger's 'discussion of animality in *The Fundamental Concepts of Metaphysics*', Matthew Calarco fails, it seems to me, to appreciate the full implications for a conception of the human contained in Heidegger's conception of the *polis* (see Calarco 2004: 28). For even if in principle, as Calarco recognizes, the human for Heidegger is a question and that, consequently, he is no naive humanist, and even though it seems that only animals are essentially excluded from the *polis*, the exclusion of a figure like *homo sacer*, not to mention slaves, from the *polis* are yet to be acknowledged. Or, to put it more bluntly, could a Roman or a modern social scientist ever be fully accepted into Heidegger's *polis*?

Bataille and animality

We recall that continuity (overflowing of boundaries, particularly that between self and other) in communication is also important for Bataille's understanding of eroticism and other states of what Bataille, in *Inner Experience*, calls 'rapture' (*ravissement*), or intoxication, states, such as anguish, ecstasy, laughter, horror and repulsion, silence, poetry, sovereignty, sacredness and death. Heidegger would not disagree with this assessment and would probably add 'boredom', 'captivation', 'absorption', 'transposition'/'transposibility' [*versetbarkeit*], melancholy and indeed, 'moods', 'tonalities' or *stimmungen* in general. But the difference between the human and the animal, Heidegger says, is that the animal never comes out of its state of captivation, while the human never remains in moods for more than a given period – or at least the human has the potential to cease being in a mood. This is why human activity is a comportment that is 'world forming', while that of animals is 'behaviour' and exemplifies a 'poverty in world'.

For Bataille, communication is also comportment rather than behaviour. For, with the exception of death, it is possible and necessary to waken oneself from it.

We saw in Chapter 5 that Bataille's later theory of animaltiy to be found at the beginning of his *Theory of Religion* (1994) posits animal life as one of 'immediacy or immanence' (1994: 17), so that 'the animal is in the world life water in water' (24). Ultimately, then, Bataille's view does not escape the 'anthropological machine' that Agamben speaks of, where the human–animal and animal–human couple participates in the play of power. Nor does he differ from thinkers from Descartes to Heidegger with his notion of immanence and the animal as continuous with its environment and without language or reason.

For Heidegger, the animal can never effectively and in its own right participate in politics, while for Bataille, political engagement can take the human back to its original animality through transgression, a transgression perhaps manifest in revolution.

Indistinction of the human–animal relation

Recently, Matthew Calarco has extended his meditation on the human–animal relation. His goal, as we have noted, is to challenge all aspects of anthropocentrism through both philosophical debate and activist politics. In *Thinking Through*

Animals: Identity, Difference, Indistinction (2015), Calarco provides an overview of recent philosophical trends in animal studies, which he summarizes under the three terms in the subtitle of his book, namely identity, difference and indistinction.

Animal rights and animal liberation philosophers such Peter Singer and Tom Regan propose that there is a strong philosophical case for certain animals like the primates to be treated, from an ethical point of view, like humans. In other words, certain animals, at least, should have extended to them the same consideration in terms of moral and legal status that have hitherto only been attributed to human beings. To withhold rights to animals, to refuse them an ethical status, these philosophers argue, is to bolster human exceptionalism and, thus, 'speciesism'.

The problem with this position for Calarco is that it still uses a conception of the human as a basis for judging or dealing with the non-human animals. As our theorist recognizes, the term 'speciesism' is a gross overgeneralization, for not all humans have related and do relate to animals in the same way. Indeed, certain categories of humanity (women, slaves, indigenous peoples) have also been deprived of rights and of moral worth: '[E]ven the most liberal and progressive forms of humanism have openly excluded large swathes of humanity from their scope and concern' (2015: 26). Identity approaches to animality, however, tend to treat not only humans in an undifferentiated manner, but animals also. Even though it is proposed that all animals (or 'the animal') should be treated ethically on a par with humans, in fact, only those animals deemed to most closely resemble the human are awarded equal status with the human. A much more nuanced approach is required.

Such a nuanced approach might be said to be provided by 'difference theorists', first among the latter being Jacques Derrida. Derrida and others emphasize, says Calarco, the differences existing in both animal and human societies while at the same time maintaining the difference between animals and humans. Derrida has questioned claims about animals that consign them to a radically inferior position in relation to humans – such as the notion that only humans have language and can respond to others, or that animals cannot be relational as human can, or that only humans can have individuality, or that only humans die, while animals, by contrast, perish, or that animals are only automata (Descartes) in contrast to human purposiveness. Views like these, held by the vast majority of thinkers in the philosophical canon, Derrida demonstrates to be based on anthropocentrism and not on rigorous thinking or evidence. And this, for Calarco, certainly represents a progression in animal studies.

The weaknesses of difference theory and philosophy in Calarco's view, however, and the basis for his move to what he calls the approach of 'indistinction' is, first, that it still holds to the idea of a fundamental difference between animals and humans and does not accept that there is an essential continuity between animal and human, even if it recognizes that that there is no such thing as 'the' animal, or 'the' human. Derrida's aim here is to show the enormous complexity of this difference rather than to paper over it.

The second problem that Calarco finds with the difference approach as it is practised is that it 'unable to generate much that is novel in terms of strategy and policy' (2015: 45). For these reasons, then, Calarco proceeds to outline the approach he calls 'indistinction', one that is inspired by already-existing philosophies in the work of Agamben (2004), Esposito (2012), Grosz (2008), Haraway (2003 and 2008), Massumi (2014) and Plumwood (2002), among others.

Rather than applying existing forms of human ethics to animals, as the identity approach does, and rather than retaining a complex version of the human/ animal opposition, as the difference approach does, indistinction emphasizes fundamental features that are common to all living beings, features such as agency, creativity and play, as well as biological necessity. The latter is illustrated for Calarco in the work of the painter Francis Bacon and the philosopher Val Plumwood, who both draw attention to the fact that to be human or animal is also to be meat – Plumwood having narrowly escaped being eaten by a crocodile and Bacon painting (a point highlighted by Deleuze's reading) sides of meat, about which the artist says that he, too, felt like meat. To sum up this point, Calarco approvingly cites the following passage from Deleuze: 'every man who suffers is a piece of meat. Meat is the common zone of man and beast' (Deleuze 2003: 23 in Calarco 2015: 58) By making commonalities between humans and animals evident to an ever-widening body of people throughout the world the hope is that, difficult as it might be to realize, it may be possible to live alternative ways of life, to the benefit of both humans and animals.

Perhaps the most intense affirmation of the indistinction approach is to be found less in Calarco's overview and more in Brian Massumi's already cited book *What Animals Teach Us About Politics* (2014). Beginning with an evocation of Gregory Bateson's discussion of animal play in *Steps to an Ecology of the Mind* (1972: 177–193), Massumi, systematically, begins to break down the barrier between humans and animals. Clearly, although indistinction could well be brought to bear in reaffirming a general biologism – something which certain neo-Darwinists are only too happy to do – Massumi's aim is to demonstrate that play and creativity (among other things) are common to humans and animals, even in the context of instinctual behaviour. For within the context of the latter, not only are there numerous activities which do not simply follow the script of 'normal' behaviour as it endeavours to satisfy need and nothing else, but, our author says, 'Play and nonplay are not mutually exclusive' (2014: 28). This idea is the springboard in which Massumi is able to demonstrate that there is no pure and simple biologically oriented behaviour whether the reference point is animal or human. Each individual act harbours the potential to be both utilitarian and ludic, both instrumental and creative. Even actions driven by fear, such as combat, carry a ludic element: 'Combat, to the extent that it is improvisational, carries a ludic element' (2014: 24) even if 'there is no combat without fear' (26). Play, Massumi recognizes, is not necessarily 'happy' or 'fun'. The politics which can be derived from this emphasis on play is one 'that re-establishes ties with *our* animality' (38; emphasis added). I return to the phrase, 'our animality' in a moment. But now it is important to complete the point as it is a question of a politics that downplays utility: 'Such a politics does not recognise the wisdom of utility as the criterion of good conduct. Rather, it affirms a ludic excess' (39). Thus, at the risk of overemphasizing the human, we can say that, if the animal actions always contain a ludic dimension against any purely utilitarian concern, how much more is this the case for the human? It is as though (and Massumi recognizes this) it has taken a detailed reflection on animality to arrive at a truth about humanity.

Despite Massumi's willing acknowledgement of his debt to Deleuze and Guattari, I have played down this aspect of his book the better to make the main thesis explicit. There are, however, aspects that bear further consideration. First among these is the fact that at certain points Massumi seems to privilege survival as the driving force of action. Thus, Massumi writes of the 'adaptive pressures that make the final irrevocable selection in accordance with the necessities of survival' (2014: 18). And he continues by saying that there 'is no question that the environment exerts selective pressure. Adaptation is indeed the law of the external milieu' (18). Again, our author affirms, 'Evolution, of course, never escapes adaptive selection' (18). Even though 'they do not tell the whole story' (19), there are, indeed, 'hard necessities of life' (19). The question is: To what extent can a necessity be truly harsh if it is mediated by ludic excess? Here, Massumi situates the ludic/creative/inventive side as being absolutely distinct from the ludic side. But surely his argument is to the contrary of this. Surely, the argument is that not only is there an indistinction between animal and human, but also between play and necessity. Only through indistinction – or indiscernibility – can a reductive element be avoided. That Massumi is pressing in this direction is suggested by this statement early in the book in question, where 'indiscernibility' is initially announced: 'Where the immanent modulation and stylistic deformation overlap – that is to say, in the gesture itself – the arena of combat and that of play enter into a *zone of indiscernibility*, without their difference being erased' (2014: 6). Again, in the event of play, animal and human come together without merging into one another: 'In play the human enters a zone of indiscernibility with the animal. When humans say "this is play", we are assuming our animality. Play dramatizes the reciprocal participation of the human and the animal, from both sides. For when animals play, they are preparatorily enacting human capacities' (8). Overall, at issue is a 'mutually exclusive zone of indiscernibility' (24).

At this point, one is reminded of the indiscernible nature in practice of Julia Kristeva's theory of the semiotic (or poetic drive/affective, 'material' element) and the symbolic (or articulated language as meaning and as a social phenomenon). Language enacts both dimensions simultaneously; the difference between them, Kristeva says, is 'only a *theoretical presupposition* justified by the need of description. It exists in practice only within the symbolic' (1984: 68; Kristeva's emphasis). Just as meaning is derived through semiotic and affective processes that form the basis of the symbolic (the latter being equivalent to the formal organization of these), so play is discerned in the putatively utilitarian activities that aim to satisfy basic needs, or, more broadly, to fulfil a definite purpose. A totally purposeless act, like an entirely poetic utterance that would refer to nothing but itself, is difficult, if not impossible, to discern.

Consequently, we arrive at the point where neither human nor animal can be reduced to a biological substratum and a struggle for survival – that is, for life, where the latter would be nothing other than aliveness. Even though the language of the proponents of indistinction or indiscernibility might at times appear to privilege the biological domain, in principle the terms in question are not inherently reductive, but give rise to transcendence as purposelessness, or, as 'inoperativity' (see Agamben 2011b: 239 and *passim*).

Epilogue

A consideration of the evolution of the notions of natural life and 'biopower' shows that, today, the truly human is reduced to biology (satisfaction of needs). (Is not the 'end of history' in Hegel as the moment when all needs have been satisfied – satisfied universally and without exception – the realization of true communism?) There is an echo here of Nietzsche's 'Last Men' (*'letzten Menschen'*) who invented happiness, a happiness derived from solving of the problem of the satisfaction of basic needs. From a modernist perspective, the aim of humanity is to universalize happiness, to reduce the human to its natural and self-contained immanence, where transcendence becomes a matter of choice not an imperative of human or animal potential. In short, everything points to the idea that a way of life, too, qua *way* of life, is a matter of choice; it is not essential to 'being-in-the-world'. Or at least, all one can do for certain peoples, it is implied, is to ensure that they can have a chance to obtain happiness; if they also go on to create a political community and its attendant freedom and creativity, along with a realm of art, a respected domain of education and scholarship and an environment of cultivated living, so much the better. But first and foremost the task is the preservation of physical life for its own sake – or, in Arendt's terms (but aren't these now everyone's?), the solving of the problem of necessity so that it does not have to figure anymore as an obstacle of the human *vita activa*.

The point is that there is a continual oscillation between defining the human as distinct from animality and then defining it, ultimately, in terms of 'animality' (the anthropological machine as biopower), so that, at stake, is the definition of life (albeit mostly by default) as nothing but the preservation of life, and where the distinction between human and animal would only be incidental.

It might be objected that within modern global politics where the fate of asylum seekers and refugees – in short, the fate of stateless peoples – is at stake, Arendt's necessity–freedom opposition, or Aristotle's *zōē-bios* distinction is no longer current. In Paul Patton's words:

> What then would [Agamben] make of the Draft Declaration of the Rights of Indigenous Peoples currently (in 2006) under review by the UN Commission on Human Rights? This document was drafted over a long period in explicit challenge to the authority of nation-states over colonised Indigenous Peoples. It is not founded on an appeal to their bare natural life (although in many cases this is also at stake), but on their commitment to a distinctive *bios* or way of life that is all too often not recognised in the conditions of citizenship in the colonial societies in which they now find themselves. (Patton 2007: 211–212)

The problem with this presentation and assessment of the *zōē–bios* distinction is that it misses the point that the distinction itself (like necessity–freedom) is what is pernicious, not whether or not, finally, indigenous peoples now have attributed to them, a *way* of life, after being for so long defined as subsistence peoples. Every so-called '*zōē*' mode of mere life – even possibly in the animal realm[18] – is a *way* of life. There is no *bare* life other than what is manipulated within the sphere of power – the sphere Agamben calls after Foucault, 'biopolitics'. Biopolitics, in other words, is more politics as power than it is biology, more power than truth. But, furthermore, just as it is inappropriate to bring peoples into the fold of 'political community' in Arendt's sense, where such peoples are deemed to be bereft of politics, so it is inappropriate, I would say, to *attribute* 'a distinctive *bios*' to indigenous peoples, as Patton implies the Draft Declaration does.

Agamben, in fact, rails against the caesura – the break between human and animal, where animality is invoked to define the human and reference to the human explains animality (this is Heidegger's strategy, for example). By contrast, Merleau-Ponty argues that even animal behaviour is often 'the manifestation of a certain style' (2003: 192). 'In brief', the philosopher concludes, 'we can speak in a valid way of an animal culture' (2003: 198). To speak of 'animal culture' is a crucial gesture in the effort to show that bare life – life as a struggle for mere existence, as mere utility – must be rejected as part of the play of power. And this may well imply that another investigation is now required, one that seeks to establish that power opposes a way of life – opposes any form of the living as transcendent.

---

[18] Merleau-Ponty makes the point that behaviour in the animal world cannot be explained reductively by a struggle for survival or in terms of utility. Thus, he says: 'We must grasp the mystery of life in the way that animals show themselves to each other. In this way, in the twenty-seven species of crab in the Barnave Islands, there are twenty-seven types of sexual display. [...] Sexuality, if it aims only at utility, could manifest itself by more economic paths. [...] We must criticize the assimilation of the notion of life to the pursuit of utility' (Merleau-Ponty 2003: 188).

7

The Moment of Death

In discussing the paradoxes arising from attempting to pinpoint the very moment of death in carrying out the death sentence – which, in the United States, has to be put into effect without being a 'cruel or unusual punishment' – Kelly Oliver puts forward an illuminating and engaging view of the relation between death, the human and representation (Oliver 2012).

With human execution the problem (if the precept specified in the United States is to be followed) is to know precisely when actual death has ensued, for only then is it possible to judge whether suffering and thus cruelty have been prevented or whether, on the other hand, there has been a failure in this regard. A first-hand witness has the task of verifying the instantaneity of death. But, in her fascinating commentary on Jacques Derrida's seminar, *La bête et le souverain* (2008a) (The Beast and the Sovereign), where discussion turns around the paradox of the impossibility of being a first-hand witness to death, Oliver contends that testimony, based in perception, can never capture the moment of death, even when instruments to monitor it are in use.

'Authentic death', moreover, 'is produced through technologies of representation that augment the real event of death and make the image of death more real than death itself, precisely through its reproduction' (2012: 88). To overcome the problem here, Oliver implies that all the resources of indexicality must be brought to bear to give the impression that there can be an event/image of death as such, much as one has to speak of the indexical signs of time, or, for that matter, of the indexicality of the photograph.

Part of what follows, then, will involve an investigation of the relationship between death, indexicality and the image in order to determine the variables in play. The execution of a human being must not be cruel – must not lead to suffering. Yet, it seems that it is never death as such that one perceives, but only signs as the index of death. Moreover, our era is one where the instant or moment of death prevails. The implications of this for bare life will also be addressed.

The instant of death

Given that to consider the moment or instant of death is to consider, in this day and age, what it means for death to become implicated in technologies that seek to record it, how is it that death has become equivalent to a 'moment' and that it has become so important to establish when this moment occurs? As will become clear, the argument to be presented is that the punctual nature of death is linked to the reduction of life to bare life. And it is as bare life that the moment of death connects with modernity's approach to (or is it management of?) death. As Benjamin Noys writes: 'What is the time of death? Perhaps this fundamental question has undergone a modification in "modernity"' (2002: 51). In response to this, we can say that, indeed, compared to the so-called traditional socio-cultural formations, death in modernity has undergone modification in the direction of becoming entwined in bare life and the power, wrought by technology, to continue or terminate life in certain cases almost at will. Defining death today means defining the moment when the biological organism in a condition of mere aliveness can be said to have ceased to function in a particular way, giving rise to the moment of brain death, or to the moment when death supervenes because the heart has stopped beating (cf. the straight line of the encephalograph). In a word, there is death at the moment when vital functions cease. The issue, however, is still about how one knows that vital functions have ceased working. There is, today, a veritable epistemology of death, with human perception as such in question. In effect, the issue of subjectivity – if not subjectivism – is raised by the question of perception. At the level of consciousness, however, the dying man does not, as Merleau-Ponty pointed out, have a consciousness that, in itself, registers the dying: 'Until the final coma, the dying man is inhabited by a consciousness, he is all that he sees, and enjoys this much of an outlet. Consciousness can never objectify itself into invalid-consciousness' (Merleau-Ponty 1992: 434). This, of course, is to take things from the 'inside' of another's consciousness – something, admittedly Merleau-Ponty said was perfectly possible if we inhabit the world as truly social beings. The world is what we perceive, are conscious of and can communicate. Such is Mereleau-Ponty's wager.

With the medicalization of death, however, it is no longer possible to gel with the consciousness of the other to the extent that the passage to death takes place at the level of bare life, at the level of life that has left the realms of consciousness and communication only to become a remnant in the purely physical struggle for survival. A strictly phenomenological approach à la Merleau-Ponty could detect no authentic human life in bare life. Indeed, the phenomenologist says that the scientific view of the body as a collection of body parts is not the 'true version of the phenomenal body, that is, the body we live by' (1992: 432). The body we 'live by' is a body that is so only within a way of life.

The moment of death, for its part, has been understood at both macro and micro levels. At the macro level is the question of what it means for death to occur when the possibility of an organ transplant depends on the certification of the death of an organ donor. Does brain death suffice, or should other signs of death (cessation of heart beat) be taken into account? Here it transpires that an unambiguous definition of death is essential and yet such a definition is difficult, if not impossible, to arrive at, given the range of variables in play in relation to biological death, a key variable being the life support technology now available to maintain signs of life. In this context Agamben has argued that bare life has become central to sovereign power and its incarnation in biopolitics (see Agamben 1998 and Noys 2002). For instead of being a matter of concern for an individual and medical ethics, the moment of death now has ramifications for politics and society at large. Organ transplants are now accepted as part of medical science and medical practice, so that it becomes imperative, and yet impossible, to define definitively the moment of death. Patients can, indeed, live (in a physical sense) on life support for very considerable lengths of time, thus rendering problematic the whole idea of natural death.

Most people know that Agamben cites the case of American woman Karen Quinlan, kept on a life support respirator in 1975 after suffering irreversible brain damage. It was thought that the patient would not survive without life support, which her parents asked to be withdrawn, a request that was granted on appeal to the New Jersey Supreme Court in 1976. As it turned out, the comatose patient lived for another nine years without life support.

Agamben shows that even though Karen Quinlan became an instance of 'pure *zōē*' (1998: 186), or bare life, the case raises issues of a medical, legal, ethical, religious and social nature. As such, bare life, in the context of the debate about what constitutes biological death, moves to the centre of biopolitical practice after being for so long the quintessential element excluded from politics. Similarly, the whole of the private sphere – or what the Greeks called the *oikos* – now becomes, our author argues, swallowed up within the domain of biopolitics, to the point where '*zōē*' itself becomes mode of *bios*, or form or way of life.

The problem with this view, as we shall see, is that it proposes that there is a domain of purely biological existence, separate from a way of life, a proposition that goes against the tenor of Agamben's position as presented in other contexts, such as in the essay 'Form-of-Life' (Agamben 2000: 2–12), initially published in 1993.

Before returning to the argument about the current centrality of bare life in politics as illustrated by the moment of death more broadly defined, we turn now to the moment of death as a problem to be solved, in particular in the context of capital punishment.

Capital punishment and death that is not cruel

As mentioned, Kelly Oliver has drawn attention to the paradoxes of witnessing the moment of death in capital punishment in the United States, where the Eighth Amendment to the American constitution is in force, one which prohibits 'cruel and unusual punishment' in capital punishment. Executions in the electric chair and lethal injection have raised issues about victims' suffering before the moment of biological death. The question is: Did the process of execution involve cruelty in contravention of the Eighth Amendment? Here, Oliver points out, a witness to an execution is struck by the 'look of pain' or the 'look of death', which may or may not correspond to actual pain or actual death. While botched electrocutions have in the past produced 'wracked and bleeding bodies aflame' (Oliver 2012: 87), the fully perfected lethal injection is designed to cover all angles:

> The Supreme Court's decision upholding the use of tripartite lethal injection – the first rendering unconscious, the second paralyzing the muscles, and the third stopping the heart – ruled that there is no cruelty in execution as long as the prisoner is unconscious while being killed. But why that second injection to paralyze the muscles? This supplement to rendering unconscious and stopping the heart is for the sake of the witnesses who want to see an inert body devoid of movement. (Oliver 2012: 86–87)

For Oliver, at issue is the fact that there is an appearance and a reality of death – and appearance or 'look' of death that would conform to the general stereotype of death (what we see in films, as Oliver notes), rather than real death, where a variety of bodily spasms and contortions often occur. Death as witnessed almost invariably evokes a certain verisimilitude, where the *look* of death conforms to the expectations of witnesses to an execution, just as reality in feature film has often fed into audience expectations rather being equivalent to reality 'as such'. There is then a clear tension between the look of death that, in terms of verisimilitude seems – due to the manifestation of a calm and inert body – to imply no cruelty and the real death throes indicated by postmortem. As Oliver reports:

> A study of postmortem examinations on prisoners executed by lethal injection and summarized in *New Scientist* maintains that given blood levels of anesthetic, 'prisoners may have been capable of feeling pain in almost 90% of cases and may have actually been conscious when they were put to death in over 40% of cases ... 43 of the 49 inmates studied were probably sentient, and 21 may have been "fully aware"' (Motluk 2005). The article continues, 'Because a muscle relaxant was used to paralyze them, however, inmates would have been unable to indicate any pain'. (2012: 90)

The desire to witness actual death is then complicated by a prior expectation as to what actual death looks like, a 'look' that most often conforms to the sanitized representation, rather than to the real thing. Along with official witnesses, a number of state administrations in the United States require members of the public to witness executions. Witnessing is a key element in the process of capital punishment. However, to witness what is effectively a representation raises doubts as to whether the biological death of a human being – or, perhaps of an animal[1] – has truly been witnessed. The real moment of death thus becomes hypothetical. Indeed, Oliver contends that testimony, based in perception, can never capture the moment of death, even the encephalo-cardiogram and other instruments are in use. Death, says Oliver,

> is always beyond sovereignty, beyond knowledge, beyond the visual realm upon which we rely to confirm its existence. The same could be said of consciousness, which, as we will see, necessarily troubles the fantasy of an instant 'clean' death imagined in the latest death penalty protocols involving lethal injection as a humane way to kill. (Oliver 2012: 88)

As a matter of fact, '[a]uthentic death is produced through technologies of representation that augment the real event of death and make the image of death more real than death itself, precisely through its reproduction' (2012: 88). However, the image of death is not the same as the 'look of death' (the still body, for example). For as Oliver acknowledges in a referring to Louis Marin's *Portrait of the King* (1988): 'The image appears as the real thing, even more powerful than the thing itself insofar as it shows or tells the truth about it' (2012: 80). The

---

[1] Oliver comments at length on the execution of animals in light of the opening of Session Ten and Session Eleven in *La bête et le souverain* which, as we shall see, introduces the scene of a seventeenth-century elephant autopsy at the time of Louis XIV (Oliver 2012: 76).

image of death, then, would be the appearing of death as such, while the 'look of death' and its equivalents we could say is an index of death. On this basis, what Oliver is in fact invoking is an index, not an image. Oliver implies, then, that all the resources of the image are brought to bear to give the impression that there can be an event/image of death as such, much as one can speak of an image of time with reference to Father Time with his scythe. The latter, however, is an index, not an image of time. There can be no image of time as such, and neither can there be an image of death, only indices of death. This is what the technology that monitors vital signs gives us.

Again, in distinguishing index and image, smoke is not an *image* of fire, even if there can indeed be an image of smoke. Smoke, as an index of fire, is not an image. Many (like Rosalind Krauss) in calling a photograph an indexical sign confuse index and image. An image is the presence of the thing in its absence.

What the photograph brings to the fore is the issue of the instant as such and the question, in particular, as to whether time is a series of instants, or frozen moments or is something else.

A post-Heideggerian, not to say, post-Bergsonian notion of time of course refuses the idea of time as a series of 'now' moments, and sees it instead as 'ex-static' (Heidegger) or as a duration (Bergson). As I have said elsewhere (Lechte 2012), one can only say that the photograph is a static instant if one identifies the photo with the material that is the necessary bearer of the of the image's incarnation. As an image, the photograph can communicate whatever is there to be communicated or presented, whether this be a static object, such as a statue, or something in movement, like the photographic sequences of Mary or Muybridge. Despite the opposite being inscribed within the modern imaginary, there is no *instance* of time (rather, the instant is timeless) and thus it is only problematically that one can speak of the instant or the moment of death.

The implications of the opposition: Life–death

Although the moment of death cannot be either predicted or observed, it might nonetheless be argued that there is, after all, a moment of death, just as there is a moment of birth. Despite the apparently self-evident nature of this statement, one can invoke a number of reservations that begin to problematize the self-evident status of life and death as 'moments'. Here, we set aside some obvious points – such as the idea that we begin to die the moment we are born, or that, à la Zeno's paradox, that every hypothetical moment is in fact infinitely divisible so that the actual moment of death never arrives, or that death is simply a kind of life, or 'after–life', or that death is in fact part of life, or that – accepting a mind/body distinction – death is only ever a biological, material affair, while, spiritually, life is eternal.

Instead of all this, at issue is the role of death as punctual, as a moment that can be circumscribed, and therefore as one part of the opposition: life–death. At stake here is the question of how actual death, instead of being the punctual moment of the end of biological functioning and therefore integral to bare life, could be part of a way of life. How, in effect, could a vegetative, comatose state that seemingly comes to an end at an exact moment (Karen Quinlan is reported to have died at 7:01 pm on 11 June 1985) be part of a way of life? Not only is death most frequently assumed to be purely punctual, but is referred to in a punctual manner: death comes to us all. It is hardly ever necessary to explain or interpret the word, 'death'. Rather, death comes – what then? We all know what death is.

Death for Dasein, we know, is 'being-towards -death'. But Heidegger also proposes that my death is what is essentially mine. No one can die in my place and I cannot take another's dying from them.[2] Even if I sacrifice myself for another, I do not thereby save the other from death. In his reading of Heidegger on this point, Derrida says that if, of all things, my death is essentially mine this implies the 'sameness of the self' (1995: 45). And he continues: 'what remains irreplaceable in dying, only becomes what it is, in the sense of an identity as a relation of the self to itself, by means of this idea of mortality as irreplaceability' (1995: 45).

Maybe Plato began evoke a different path in relation to death, when he described the philosopher's life as a preparation for, or the 'practice of death'.[3] Even more than Plato, Bataille, as we have seen, problematizes the punctual nature of death when he refers to it as 'the continuity of being'. Life is beings in their discontinuity (i.e., in their discrete identities), where the maintenance of borders is pursued, while death is equivalent to the dissolution of all borders. The problem raised in Chapter 5 when discussing Bataille on the relation between continuity and discontinuity concerns the relationship between life and death. Surely it has to be concluded that life is discontinuous with death. But this is to infer, however obliquely, that life is dominant over death. For Bataille is the

---

[2]   Heidegger does not consider the status of Christ here, but it is interesting that Christ, precisely, is He who *can* die in my place.
[3]   On this, see Derrida (1995: 14).

first to concede that death cannot be conceived of as a kind of life – perhaps as the being of non-being. And, as a consequence, it is never possible to have an experience of death. The closest one can get is to identify with the other's dying – an identification manifested in anguish – thus transforming the other's dying into *my* dying. But this can only be vicariously, by proxy, as it were. The other's dying as my own dying is still only available to me in a quasi-hypothetical mode.

The death of being becomes caught up in the paradox – already evoked – of the being of non-being. Such a paradox is not necessarily illuminating, as Heidegger suggests when he, too, places death, or the Nothing, within being (Heidegger 1993b: 45–47). The Nothing, like Being, is not a being. It is not a separate entity existing in the world. It is a continuity rather than a discrete something that exists. Being, too, in Heidegger's terms, is a continuity.

Death as continuity and the dissolution of identity undermines the whole idea of a punctual, or instant, death. An instant death, like clock time – time as a series 'nows' – would be part of the sphere of discontinuity and identity, given that discreteness is part and parcel of the instant. Bataille considers the instant, as we saw, in relation to sovereignty. Work takes place in duration – in time – and work is servile. Only the instant – living for the moment – gives rise to sovereignty. This is an instant, as we have already noted, which necessarily represses any hint of the future.

How ironic is it, then, that the instant of death in the context of execution or in relation to bare life in the medicalization of death has become anything but a manifestation of sovereignty. Indeed, in the context of medicalization, it is precisely the possibility of sovereignty that it removed from the patient. In no sense can the one on life support embrace the moment of death as the affirmation of the sovereign moment. The same pertains to death by lethal injection in as far as the first step to execution in certain states in the United States is the cancelling out of any possibility of consciousness. In both contexts, it is impossible to ask about how one *faced* one's death.

Of course, given other more traditional forms of execution, such as the firing squad, or hanging, it is perfectly possible to imagine asking about how the prisoner faced death. To embrace death here can be the basis of a sovereign moment in Bataille's sense.

Sovereignty – in Bataille's sense – is also the repression of (a fear of) death, where one lives as though one were immortal – where, in short, death is of no consequence. This does not mean that when it does come, it is not, at some level, instantaneous. The instant, or moment, of death is tied so firmly to the conceptual opposition, life–death that it becomes impossible not to think of death as the instant of death. This instant, however – as has been said – cannot be sovereign in relation to bare life

If life is *haunted*[4] by death, this applies to the repression of death referred to earlier. To repress death does not mean that it will not appear in many symptomatic ways, as Freud indicated. The very absence of (references to, or indications of, or silence about) death in relation to sovereignty does not mean that sovereignty is the less haunted by death. There is also mourning and funeral rites that make death – albeit at one remove – a cultural phenomenon, or part of a way of life. In this way death ceases to be an instant. Or rather, the instant of death becomes endlessly extended in as far as it is the absolutely present moment that is haunted or has its identity as a moment undermined.

Biological and non-biological death and mediation

Jean Baudrillard's commentary on death in Bataille's work takes us back to the point, moment or instant of death where we began this chapter. In particular, Baudrillard notes that '[f]inality belongs in the discontinuous order, where discontinuous beings secrete finality, all sorts of finalities, which amount to only one: their *own* death' (Baudrillard 1993: 156; Baudrillard's emphasis). From the notion of finality, Baudrillard can raise the issue of 'punctual' death. In an important passage that repeats part of the argument being presented here, he says: 'The irreversibility of biological death, its objective punctual character, is a modern fact of science. *It is specific to our culture*' (158; emphasis added). The idea of punctual death can be compared to a situation where 'life goes on after life' (158) and even where life and death merge into one another.

Thus, anthropologist Katie Glaskin (2006) points out in her study of death in the Bardi Aboriginal group in north-west Australia that ritual mortuary practices are geared to ensure the transition of the deceased between life and death. This particularly entails a prohibition on speaking the name of the deceased, or in invoking the deceased's totem or image including, in recent times, a prohibition on photographs of the departed. The point is that the recently deceased is not fully dead and could, during the transition phase, return to harm the living (2006: 113). Persons and names are intrinsically connected, so that a name is not simply a symbolic form evoking the person. Rather, the person *is* their name. The name is also evocative of the fact that, as regards mourning rituals, death

---

[4] On haunting, see Derrida (1993: 31, 255 and *passim*).

is an intrinsically mediated phase. There is nothing punctual here. Indeed, the immediacy of trauma is obviated by every possible means. Not punctuality, then, but mediality characterizes death for the Bardi and Aboriginal people more generally.

Furthermore, as the one who dies in this Aboriginal community is a fragmented, divided entity, parts might not die simultaneously. As Glaskin explains, place, bones, flesh, blood and hair are the elements that not only make up the person, but which have a significance in their own right (2006: 112 and note 23, which refers to 'inherent powers of parts of the body'). The low viscosity of a corpse's blood can indicate the extent the deceased 'obeyed the Law' (114). Hair, for its part, can become a relic and thus stand in for the deceased person (120).

The ghost in *Hamlet* can also be seen as a mediating figure in relation to death. Hamlet's father is between life and death, still able to trouble the living as a force to be reckoned with. Time is out of joint. Hamlet's father is neither dead nor alive because there is no *moment* of death. This, in Baudrillard's terms, would mean that the ghost subverts punctual death; it subverts the 'irreversibility of biological death' (1993: 158).

Death as a moment, point or instant is a cultural phenomenon, one that combines two aspects: first, the biologization of death, where death is nothing other than the death of a living body – the death, to be more precise, of bare life – and, secondly, a preference for the objectification characteristic of empirical science and for theory as a spectacle, where the researcher takes up a position to view death as the object (cf. *theoria*) – something that belies the fact that death is essentially an *experience* of death.[5] Moreover, as with clock time that proposes time as a series of 'nows', the moment of death becomes death viewed at a distance, death that is intellectualized. The reason as to why thinkers such as Bergson, Heidegger and Deleuze refuse to equate time with clock time is that the latter is the objectivist or intellectualist view of time, whereas beings are *in* time, not exterior to it, as the time as 'now' moments implies.

In this light, what is one to make of the present moment in Bataille's notion of sovereignty? Is this also a 'now' moment? Here, we note that the 'present' in sovereignty can be anything but a 'now' moment. Rather, the present here is not at all opposed to duration and could, hypothetically, last forever, the point being that there is no anticipation or a turning towards the future. Moreover, such a

---

[5] This can be compared to Nancy's notion of freedom as an experience of freedom in the sense that true freedom has no concept (see Chapter 4).

moment is a pure experience, just the opposite of the intellectualist approach characteristic of theorizations of punctual death.

Thus, do we arrive back at the themes in relation to the moment of death, of bare life and indexicality introduced earlier. Kelly Oliver's problematization of the representation of the moment of death clearly brings the latter into a socio-cultural frame in the sense that the possibility of any representation of death must invoke the means a given socio-cultural milieu makes available.

Death and the image

As Kelly Oliver's analysis makes clear, it is the supposedly punctual nature of death that renders the representation of the dead body so problematic. Punctuality is, as we have implied, unrepresentable. While there may be indexical signs of death, there can never be an *image* of death, however much common parlance suggests the contrary. In everyday terms, the '*dance macbre*', a skull or the Grim Reaper become images of death. But if – and I believe that this is doubly relevant when talking about death and time – an image is not an object but is the presence of the thing in its absence (a principle illustrated, for instance, by the photograph), it will always be a matter of indexical signs when death is at issue.

In what might seem to be a contrary view, Maurice Blanchot proposes that there is an intimate rapport between death and the image to the extent that death is circumscribed by the cadaver. The 'cadaveresque strangeness', says Blanchot, 'is also that of the image' (Blanchot 1955: 344). This is because the cadavre 'is' the person who has died. The cadavre of my friend Pierre 'is' Pierre and no one else. If I hold Pierre's dead body in my arms, I hold Pierre in my arms. In other words, I cannot not believe that the cadavre in my arms 'is' Pierre. When I look at the cadavre of Pierre, I do not see a cadavre; I only see Pierre, if not as he was when he was alive, then in a new state. The cadavre, in short, has all the ambiguity of the image as being the presence of the thing in its absence. It has all the transparency and thus invisibility of the image that brings Pierre to me. Because this is Pierre, all the rituals of mourning must be done correctly.[6]

In light of Blanchot, we see that only after the assurance that death has occurred can a dead body become and image. Until death is assured, we are confronted, as Kelly Oliver shows, by indexical signs, signs which imply

---

[6]   For a further elaboration of the notion the image as transparent, see Lechte (2012 and 2013).

that death – as in capital punishment – is yet to be assured even if, after this assurance, the image takes on all its disturbing ambiguity, becoming the vehicle of both life and death.

The spectacle, the king, punctual death and bare life

I pointed out above that one aspect pertaining to the moment of death is objectification where death as it happens becomes a spectacle viewed by a spectator or spectators evocative of the origin of theory in *theoria*, where a point of view is taken on the action. With regard to instant death, Oliver says that: 'Viewers want to *see* instant death, the kind that only execution could guarantee' (Oliver 2012: 84; emphasis added). Viewers thus turn death into a spectacle. In this sense, instant death governs our culture while at the same time death is disavowed: 'Does the fantasy of instant death', asks Oliver, ' – the flipping of a switch, the push of a plunger – disavow not only the process of death but also whatever relationship that death has to time and to our own finitude?' (2012: 86).

Not only is there a technical issue pertaining to the witnessing of instant death, but capital punishment goes hand in hand with the spectacle of its realization. Derrida goes further. Legal execution as a spectacle is exemplary of the dominance of the spectacle in philosophy and epistemology. To see – to witness – is thus to know, to understand. This is why, as Oliver indicates, Derrida argues that the autopic gaze generates knowledge and gives power to the one who controls this knowledge.[7] Indeed, today, 'spectral logic pervades everything' (Derrida 2004: 159) – which is to say that the logic of *theoria* and objectification pervades everything.

When in Sessions Ten and Eleven of *La bête et le souverain* (2008a) (*The Beast and the Sovereign*], Derrida refers to the dissection of the elephant witnesses by Louis XIV as an 'operation in order to know, a violence on death in order to see [voir] and to know [savoir]' (2008a: 338)[8], we should say that 'seeing' gives rise to a certain *kind* of knowing – that of the spectacle and of a viewer who takes up a position in relation to the spectacle. Here, it is noteworthy that the spectacle is death in the form of the dead animal: the elephant about to be subjected to an autopsy. No doubt this is to put the situation as it pertains

---

[7] In the case of the autopsy of an elephant at the time of Louis XIV, it is the king who demonstrates his sovereignty by orchestrating the event.

[8] The French text reads: 'une opération de savoir, une violence sur le mort pour voir et savoir' (2008a: 338).

to ordinary mortals. With regard to the king as the sovereign (Louis XIV), a different viewing is at stake. 'Sovereignty', Oliver points out, ' is the effect of death, both in the real body of the once majestic animal laying [*sic*] on the operating table in pieces and in the symbolic body that replaces the mortal body of the king' (2012: 82). We thus understand that qua absolute monarch the king transcends his mortal animal body, as Kantorwicz argues in *The King's Two Bodies* (1957), the work being cited – after Agamben – by Derrida (2008a: 382). In relation to the latter, Agamben refers to the effigy of the dead king which is 'placed in relation to the perpetuity of royal dignity which *"never dies"*' (Agamben 1998: 93; emphasis added).

The sovereign (the highest power) can also become (equivalent to) *homo sacer* in the sense that as the 'person of the king is sacred and inviolable' (cited by Agamben 1998: 102), the monarch is caught up in the so-called ambivalence of the sacred as being beyond human calculation and control. The law that applies to ordinary mortals is not applicable to monarchs as sovereign thus placing them in a never-never region of existence where violence ceases to have any relevance in law. Like *homo sacer* the sovereign is, as a result, excluded from the human community and is indeed a figure that is both human and inhuman.

What we now need to know, though, is how bare life figures in all this. For the version of *homo sacer* just announced emphasizes exclusion from humanity over mere aliveness, or over biological issues relating to life. If, as Agamben claims, 'the production of bare life is the originary act of sovereignty' (1998: 83), how does this work? Thus far, bare life has been presented as life in modernity as mere biological survival, outside any 'way of life'. In interviews and elsewhere, Agamben cautions against defining bare life as natural life. And, indeed, as there is no purely natural life in any absolute sense but only life defined as such within a biological discourse that originated in the nineteenth century, bare life is not natural life. Yet, we see that in the context of analysing the, 'biopolitical turn of modernity' (153), Agamben refers to 'the growing inclusion of man's natural life in the mechanisms and calculations of power' (119), as if there really were a domain of 'natural life'. How does this match up with the idea previously stated that bare life is a creation of sovereign power, in as far as life in the sacred sphere can be killed with impunity (cf. 83)? If the human victim in the sacred sphere is bare life (*homo sacer*), in what sense is this so? For some time, Agamben is content to play with the opposition of (all powerful) sovereignty on one side and *homo sacer* (the one completely bereft of power) on the other. Thus, for the sovereign, everyone is potentially *homo sacer*, while for the sacred man everyone is sovereign. If *homo sacer*'s only raison d'être is that he can be killed, this implies that he is nothing but a minimal biological being that is simply alive or simply dead. But this remains unclear. Instead, we are left with the impression that there could be more to bare life than minimal biological existence. Agamben is not interested in the question of what it might mean in practice for *homo sacer* actually to die.

What we do see is that there is a problem in understanding how a monarch, as absolute sovereign, might die. The point is that, much as the seventeenth-century absolute monarchs and their lackeys might have wanted it otherwise, sovereignty did not reside in their person/body but necessarily transcended their person. This is why the rituals of death become so intricate and complex in the pre-Revolutionary era, it being necessary to recognize the perpetuation of sovereign power in light of the monarch's physical death. Noticeable and relevant to the theme addressed here of the 'moment of death' is the fact that when the death of the king is at issue, there is no discrete *moment* of death. Indeed, death here is a drawn out process, as the following passage from Kantorowicz, cited by Agamben, shows:

> describing the peculiar funeral ceremonies of French kings in which the wax effigy of the sovereign, placed on a *lit d'honneur*, occupied an important position and was fully treated as the king's living person, Kantorwicz suggests that these ceremonies might well have their origin in the apotheosis of Roman emperors. Here too, after the sovereign dies, his wax *imago*, 'treated like a sick man, lies on a bed; senators and matrons are lined up on either side; physicians pretend to feel the pulse of the image and give their medical aid until, after seven days, the effigy "dies"'. (Kantorwicz 1957: 427 cited in Agamben 1998: 93)

Clearly, for the king or emperor, there is *no punctual* death, as is deemed to be the case in modernity. Even though such rituals were not applicable to the people at large, it is easy to see that for *homo sacer* (= bare life) punctual death is not the point; for this is a figure already dead – a dead person walking. To be *homo sacer* is to be absolutely powerless to prevent oneself being killed. As bare life (a life without qualities) there is no alternative to death. Prior to modernity – prior to the Revolution of 1789 – life is only very vaguely what might be called a moment or instant of death pure and simple. Only in the post-Revolutionary era does punctual death become the norm for understanding death.

In order to make solid the claim that punctual death is – qua punctual – an instance of (the practice of) bare life it is necessary to depart from Agamben's heavily political theory version of *homo sacer* as the unrecuperable underside of sovereignty.

Death, objectification and spectacle

For his part, Derrida emphasizes (as Oliver says) that the *spectacle* of necropsy affirms the monarch's sovereignty over human and animal, man and beast. Or, more precisely: sovereignty holds in check or completely (and necessarily) crushes the animal in both man and beast alike. In the human, this is done through the human sciences; with regard to animals, it is through necropsy, or more generally, through autopsy. In both cases, there is objectification and the latter is linked, says Derrida after Foucault, to power: no *savoir* without *pouvoir*: 'the order of *knowledge* [savoir] is never a stranger to that of *power* [pouvoir], and that of *power* to that of *seeing* [voir], to that of *wanting* [vouloir] and to that of *having* [avoir]' (2008a: 375; Derrida's emphasis). The one who looks and sees is sovereign, which explains the power of the human over the animal; but what about the sovereign in relation to other humans? It is in relation to power-knowledge that certain humans become the objects of knowledge. As such they also come into the category in modernity of bare life, although Derrida himself does not use this syntagm.

'It all begins', says Oliver, 'with the metaphorical death of his [the king's] animal body – and the literal death of other animal bodies, that are seen as merely bodies and nothing more – for the sake of his eternal soul and, more than that, his absolute sovereignty over all of his kingdom' (Oliver 2012: 83). The king's animal body has to be consigned to the nether regions almost as if the death of the so-called animal body were an essential element in the configuration of sovereignty. Thus, the moment of the death of the animal (and the larger the better – hence the added force of an *elephant* autopsy) prefigures the death of all animality qua physical body; or at least, as we have seen so often previously, animality must be overcome in order that the human can appear. And the purest, most imposing manifestation of the human as such becomes sovereignty as incarnate in the/a king. Thus, from the burgeoning of seventeenth-century science comes the – sometimes stronger (as in the king) sometime weaker (as in ordinary mortals) – reflection of sovereignty in the human in contrast to its complete absence in the animal. In Oliver's words: 'Within the fable of human sovereignty, the sacrifice of the elephant in the spectacle of the elephant's autopsy is a necessary part of the process of turning the animal *homo sapiens* into a man and turning a man into a king' (82).

With regard to the elephant's dissection attended by Louis the Sun King at Versailles in 1681 Derrida, as has been noted, lays great emphasis on the scene as a spectacle and as ceremonial giving rise to the 'portrait' in word and image of the diminutive King Louis XIV. A spectacle qua spectacle of course lasts only for a moment – however long – of time. Hence the call for representation to be undertaken – a representation that both captures the spectacular event for posterity and, at the same time, confirms the sovereignty of the sovereign. As such, however, representation presupposes the moment of death. Were it not for death and the dissolution of the scene the rationale for representation would be very different. The more life, or indeed the livelier and more active the animal, the closer is it to the being of 'man', so that the contrast between the human as sovereign and the animal as bare life is diminished. As such, full sovereignty presupposes the moment of death of the animal – a moment of death, as we have seen, which is the harbinger of the death of animality in the human.

*

This chapter has introduced the role of technology in human and animal relations. It thus remains in the next chapter to go into more detail on this.

8

The Human as Technics: Technicity and 'Way of Life'

In the wake of Kelly Oliver's discussion of the moment of death, this chapter addresses the question of the general relationship between technics and the human.

The three terms 'technics', 'technicity' and 'technology' evoke a field of thought, with the term 'technology' literally evoking the discourse/science of the technē. Even though technology is frequently used to refer to particular instances of technics, I will, as has become the custom, use the term 'technics' to refer to specific technical objects. 'Technicity', for its part, is reserved for activities or objects of a technical nature. A specific object might not, on the face of it, seem to have a technical aspect. But then its technicity – its quality as a technical object – comes to be revealed. An art object could be an example of this.

As this chapter is concerned with the way human being is at issue, the human's relation to the technical domain is a crucial site of debate. What we want to know is whether things technical are actually an index of human alienation and the corruption of the human or whether the human might only be fully realized in terms of its irreducible imbrication in the technical. Rousseau, as Bernard Stiegler (1998) shows, is probably the first to propose that the technical, not being part of nature, corrupts (as he saw it) the human essence, while Stiegler himself is, philosophically, the most exhaustive proponent of the second view that the human is inseparable from technicity.

Rousseau in describing the natural habitat as the original home of the first humans says that the 'body of primitive man being the only instrument he knows, is put to a variety of uses of which present-day people are incapable due to the lack of use; it is our industriousness which deprives us of the strength and agility that necessity obliges us to acquire' (Rousseau 1964: 135). No technology is therefore required; no labour is needed; for the fruits of nature are available for immediate consumption. This is the Golden Age of humanity before the techniques and tools of 'industriousness' render man separate from himself and a difference arises between the natural, authentic, totally inward-focusing self and the alienated, externalizing self that embraces every manner of artificial device as part of the development of what comes to be called civilization.

For Rousseau, the human was originally a part of nature. In light of this, we need to consider Stiegler's argument that it is more plausible to maintain that there was an original discontinuity between the human and nature, a discontinuity illustrated by the myth of Epimetheus. Because Epimetheus forgot to give humans the full gamut of qualities that would ensure their continuity with nature, the human is distinguished from other living creatures by having technics as an essential part of its being. The human thus becomes entirely incomprehensible if considered apart from the essentially constituting milieu of prostheses, or, in the broadest sense, technics. But does this not bring us back full circle to the realm of necessity? Could the driving force of technics be anything other than that of solving the problem of necessity?

Guiding the interpretation and exposition of the theme of technics is the notion of human being: Is technics inevitably concerned with solving problems of necessity in the Ancient Greek sense as, for instance, Arendt interprets it? In other words, is technics essentially tied to humanity's 'struggle for existence' in the most concrete and material sense? Would technics, then, be essentially and exclusively implicated in the articulation of human finitude and the contingent relation to time that this implies? Many writers on the history of technics give the impression that this is the case. For instance, as a leading authority on the evolution of technical objects, André Leroi-Gourhan emphasizes that 'survival', both of the group and of technical objects, is at the base of human evolution (Leroi-Gourhan 1973: 424–428). Like technical objects themselves, human groups or peoples, can evolve (= progress) at different rates in the survival stakes: 'a people is only itself through its means of survival' (425). And, 'one sees in each people chains of survival' (425). At one level, survival as such is a denial of life as a way of life. Such is encapsulated in the oft-repeated 'struggle for existence'. But, on another level, it is clear that survival as a pure struggle for existence, where necessity rules, is only thinkable within the framework of a static present. Once time is introduced, there is evolution and change that inevitably takes on a specific character. As Leroi-Gourhan recognizes, the character of a people is reflected in traditions of techniques – what can be called different programmatic activities and tools for achieving the same or similar goals. In effect, such techniques would evoke a style that, as such, is entirely non-utilitarian and thus not as such related to survival – assuming, of course that utility and survival go together, something, it has been argued, typical of the époque called modernity.

According to Arendt, labour 'never designates the finished product' and evokes, both in the past and in the present, continual toil and pain. 'Work', by contrast, can refer to both the activity and to the finished product (cf. art work) – although Arendt also says that this distinction 'was ignored in classical antiquity' (Arendt 1958: 85). This, it turns out, is another aspect of the 'necessity-freedom' dichotomy that calls to be challenged.

The zoological and the sociological according to Leroi-Gourhan

[L]et us refrain from asking whether the nature of the human is threatened by alteration or even disappearance, for one would first have to know whether humanity ever had a nature. (Stiegler 1998: 88)

Even if the French philosopher of technics, Bernard Stiegler, shows that it does not have to be the case, there is no domain where presuppositions about the nature of the human flourish more abundantly than in the field of the history of technics, a field dominated by prehistory and palaeontology, such as represented by the work of André Leroi-Gourhan.[1] The time scale addressed here concerns the period before the emergence of writing in Mesopotamia (Sumer) in 3,200 BCE.

The 'birth of graphism' introduces, as Loi-Gourhan puts it, a new relation between 'hand and tool', and 'face and language', where the 'motricity' of the hand and the face gives rise to a new modelling of thought into 'instruments of material action' and 'sound symbols' – in other words, a new relation comes to be established between speech and action, one that is evocative of humanity as such, humanity in the sense understood today, where animal and human respectively have a quite different relation to tools and vocal signs.

Without going into detail with regard to whole of Leroi-Gourhan's theses concerning the evolution of the human and technics, it is instructive to focus on the issue of the relationship between the emergence of graphic skills enacted by the hands and writing. In this regard it is proposed that depictions of animals on cave walls, such as one finds at Lascaux, have been misinterpreted when these are considered as either accurate or naive depictions of (animal) reality. The time scale Loi-Gourhan gives for Lascaux is between 11,000 and 8,000 BC, while the issue of the evolution of graphic forms concerns a much

---

[1] See, for example, Leroi-Gourhan (1964a, 1964b, 1971, 1973).

broader period – at least up to 30,000 years BC. When the latter time line is taken into account in conjunction with the development of symbolization as the precursor of phonetic writing, it makes sense to speak of the prior development of graphic abstraction over graphic mimesis (imitation of reality). Abstract forms develop, it is argued, because these are in keeping with the emergence of proto-writing that was developing over the period. It is not a matter of aesthetic or artisanal competence, as the notion of 'naive art' might imply. Graphic forms do not develop out of a desire for photographic realism but 'become organised in a period of ten thousand years in relation to signs which seem to have been initially expressed by rhythms and not by forms'. (See 1964a: 265–266.) Only after being expressed in light of rhythms of language do graphic forms appear as figures. In other words, the emergence of graphic symbols are inseparable from the evolution of language. As such, the graphic becomes the key element in the appearance of proto-writing (cf. pictographic and ideographic scripts), in which non-conventional signs and symbols refer to what is to be communicated and can only be understood if the receiver has a detailed knowledge of the context. Thus, in sum, while writing proper is a system of conventional signs, the meaning of which can be determined independently of context, proto-writing of non-conventional or 'motivated' symbols, as Saussure put it, is context specific. The more abstract graphic items become, then, the more they begin to resemble purely conventional signs and the more, taken collectively, they begin to approximate writing as a system of differences. Only through the latter can a society insure the 'permanent conservation of its individual and collective thought' (1964a: 261).

To illustrate the link between abstract graphic symbols and language as proto-writing, Loi-Gourhan refers in part to the Australian Aboriginal charinga. The latter are wood or stone tablets in the shape of shields with inscribed, rhythmical circular and linear figures. 'Two aspects of the churinga', says Leroi-Gourhan,

> appear susceptible to guide our interpretation of the [previously mentioned] Palaeolithic 'marks of the hunt': firstly, the abstract character of the representation which [...] is also present in the earliest known art; next, the fact that the charinga concretises recited incantations, which is its support, the officiant following the rhythmic figures of his declamation, with the tips of his fingers,. Thus the charinga mobilises the two sources of expression: that of rhythmic verbal motricity and that of a graphism entailed in the same dynamic process. (1964a 263)

On this basis, early art (graphism) becomes part of the gradual emergence of writing, both proto- and conventional. Already, we have mentioned the fact that a full-blown, conventional writing system is the necessary condition for the retention of evidence of the achievements of human thought and artefacts. It remains to be seen what else writing, for Leroi-Gourhan, brings about for humans, if not for animals. In the summary at the beginning of his book, the author says that the tool and language bring to an end the 'zoological' phase of human evolution (1964a: 34). This can be taken to mean that human beings pass through an animal stage prior to evolving into *homo sapiens* – the human: wise, rational user of language and inventor, in certain societies, of writing in the narrow, colloquial sense.[2]

In light of the zoological definition of man, where will the development of writing lead? The first point of Leroi-Gourhan's approach to be taken in to account is the one made at the beginning of the second volume of *Le geste et la parole* (1964b), to the effect that there is an 'essential fact' and that is that 'man belongs equally to the zoological and to the sociological worlds' (10). Leroi-Gourhan finds that there is a challenge thrown out by certain forms of scientific and philosophical thinking that aims to confound animal and human existence – a thinking that claims that there are, for instance, similarities between instinct and intelligence (think of forms of behaviourism) when it comes to providing a general definition of the human. Such thought, however, cannot account for the fact that instinctual memory typical of a species at a zoological level and memory based in language and ethnic affiliation have quite different potentials. The latter is what separates the human from the non-human: 'being external to the zoological level, ethnic memory has the important consequences of enabling the individual to transcend the established ethnic framework and the possibility of ethnic memory itself to progress' (23). In sum, 'man is free to create his own situations, even if these be only symbolic' (23). What we have here is the same idea already encountered, namely that the human becomes truly human only after becoming capable of transcending its own very real animality. Freedom is actualized in the process of this transcendence. Genetically governed species driven by instinct can never be free in the way that humans are free. How will it be with regard to the emergence of phonetic writing? And what might be the implications for societies 'without writing'? No doubt it will be a matter of determining how individuals and societies survive. In relation to this, it is important to decide whether what is being discussed is the survival of

---

[2] See Derrida (1976: 81–82), where Derrida, in discussing the positing of societies 'with' and societies 'without' writing, says that Leroi-Gourhan recognizes that to say that certain societies are without writing is, effectively, to exclude them from humanity.

individuals, or the survival only of the group or species, in which case individuals become dispensable. It is notable that an anthropologist, such as Lévi-Strauss, sees non-domesticated animals and plants as *species* that live and die, and in relation to which, we might well mourn the loss, while only humans live and die *as* individuals (see Lévi-Strauss 1974: 214).

The prospect is, according to Leroi-Gourhan, that the exteriorization of all the organs (the tool – e.g., spade – is the exteriorization of the hand) of biological humanity will continue apace making the human body (this 'osteo-muscular apparatus') entirely redundant (52) and culminating in entities (e.g., robots) that perfectly replicate the biological – or carbon – based – body inherited from the Palaeolithic era. Whether or not such a scenario will be realized is less interesting here than the proposition that complete exteriorization is necessarily preceded by the human as zoological species. While such an evolution might seem empirically self-evident, philosophically speaking, it is inscribed within a movement from the primitive to the civilized or sophisticated, from the simple to the complex, from the elemental to the complex. In other words, we perceive an echo of the movement from necessity to freedom discussed above. For, indeed, corresponding to the empirical correlates of 'primitive', 'simple', etc. are the actions necessary for material survival (cf. 58 and 61).[3] But in a section called 'Ethnic Style' (1964b: 89–94), Leroi-Gourhan describes forms or ways of life:

> the major part of culture is made of traits which belong in common to humanity or to a continent or at minimum to a region and to numerous groups which each feel distinct. This ethnic distinctiveness which transforms the banal enumeration of axes, bellows and matrimonial formulas into an expression of 'the spirit' of a people is inaccessible to verbal classification; it is a style which has its own value and which envelops the cultural totality of the group. (90)

Cultural specificity emerges in the *way* the English make cars compared to the French, or in the *way* jazz is played in New Orleans compared to Canada. Rhythms of life in relation to weather and seasons, time and space are also significant however minimal the actions involved might appear to be. Despite saying this with regard to cultural style, the latter, according to Leroi-Gourhan, is based on a biological substrate (see 87). Even so, 'form follows function' by which is implied that, for *homo sapiens*, and more minimally for certain animals, there is an aesthetic dimension to the most practical forms of activities and tools. The 'form', then, would be related to the 'personality of the group' (122).

---

[3]	As Leroi-Gourhan says, the trajectory of his research can be seen to be, 'starting with the carnivore or primate in order to arrive at the human of today' (1964b: 84).

What we are referring to here are forms of living, but, as might be anticipated, such forms of living are based on a substrate of survival: *vivre* implies *survivre* (185). And ways of living for recently evolved humanity are in urban communities. These are understood in comparison with certain animal groupings, which, like humans, also live within a 'refuge-territory' spatial formations characteristic of urban living (185). But, as opposed to animals, human integration gives rise to a rich variety of symbolizations. In short, the human as socio-cultural being is distinct from the human as zoological entity.

Let us say that very broadly conceived Leroi-Gourhan's approach involves showing how humans as zoological beings give rise to humans as societal and cultural beings, beings particularly adept at all forms of symbolization.

Bernard Stiegler's take on technics

French philosopher Bernard Stiegler has articulated one of the most interesting approaches to technics of recent times. It is an approach based on a reappraisal of the work of Heidegger, Leroi-Gourhan and Gilbert Simondon on technology. The sophistication of Stiegler's theory of technics, notwithstanding the term 'biological', that have been tracked to this point in our study and what passes for its synonyms (animality, zoological, nature, *phusis*) appears again at the beginning of the first volume of Stiegler's groundbreaking study of technics, where our author tells us:

> At bottom the issue will be to understand the dynamic of the 'technical system', to study the possibilities of a theory of technical evolution. We will see the question of a technical determinism arising in a permanent oscillation between the *physical and biological* modalities of this evolution. [… .] A central question will be that of the limits of application of the analogy between the theories of technical and biological evolution. (Stiegler 1998: 26; emphasis added)

In light of Bertrand Gille's history of technics (1978), Stiegler argues that its development 'constantly intervenes to modify everyday life' (1998: 39). This point touches upon a key feature of Stiegler's approach to technics: the latter is a universal force that comes into conflict with particular cultural systems, or with what Leroi-Gourhan calls, as we saw, 'ethnic distinctiveness', which is contextually specific. Being the opposite of all contextuality, technics is, according to Stiegler's key thesis, entirely decontextualizing. It disrupts cultures and ethnicity. It is not simply innovative, which would entail working within an existing framework, but is, as invention, essentially revolutionary, disrupting the existing state of social life across the board.

We have seen, however, that against Stiegler's claim, Leroi-Gourhan's approach – at least in *Le geste et la parole* [*Gesture and Speech*] – goes against the idea of technics as universalizing.[4] 'Ethnic style', in the context of aesthetics, individualizes what at first might appear to be the most universalizing of tendencies, such as writing and, in the modern era, industrial production. As to the latter, we mentioned that cars made in England are distinct from those made in France or Germany, even though the technology involved is identical. While Stiegler, as we shall see, wants to argue that the socio-cultural milieu has to adapt to technics, Leroi-Gourhan argues that the reverse is the case, that technics adapts to the socio-cultural. Thus, 'technique et société ne sont qu'un même objet' ['Technics and society are one and the same object'] (Leroi-Gourhan 1964a: 292–293). Moreover, at the level of art and language, it becomes near impossible to separate technics and the socio-cultural system.

While there is no doubt that Stiegler points to the zoological domain in Leroi-Gourhan's work, he at no time provides a detailed account of its essential nature. Least of all does he acknowledge that it is inseparable from nature as a whole and that it is the technical aspects of art and language, among other spheres, that separate the human from the animal or zoological domain. Stiegler, by contrast, proceeds as though the technical operates in and through the zoological – as though humans were animals endowed with a technical ability, whereas, for Leroi-Gourhan, the technical is the sign – if it is not the cause – of the human having moved beyond the zoological to the sociological realm.

On the other hand, maybe Stiegler's misreading pushes us in the right direction. For it could never be a matter here of defending Leroi-Gourhan's separation of the zoological and the socio-cultural, which ultimately leads, it has been argued, to a separation of bare life from ways of life. And indeed, Stiegler notes the issue. For, he writes that 'the human exceeds the biological, although this dimension is an essential part of the technical phenomenon itself, something like its enigma' (Stiegler 1998: 50). Then arises the paradoxical situation where as a living being the human is defined by its technical (i.e., prosthetic) ability, that is, is defined by its non-living aspect. The animal, by implication, is life that continues by means of life, although in fact this notion is problematic, given that certain primates,

---

4 Stiegler writes that Leroi-Gourhan's '*Man and Matter* [*L'homme et la matière*, 1943] proposes the hypothesis of *universal technical tendencies*, independent of the cultural localities that *ethnic* groupings compose, in which they become concrete [*se concrétisent*] as *technical facts*' (Stiegler 1998: 43; Stiegler's emphasis).

like humans, are also users of tools. According to Stiegler, Leroi-Gourhan sees technics as the primary characteristic of the human, a characteristic which more effectively than culture enables distinctions to be made between human groups (45). However, what needs to be borne in mind here is that the technical for Leroi-Gourhan includes above all, as has been shown, language and art. It is not reducible to tools and instruments, chemistry and industrialization.

No doubt Stiegler would have no problem with this; for it is through language and its derivative systems (mass media) that all internal cultural environments come under threat through globalization and the potentially massive decontextualization of living that this entails (cf. 65). But such a massive decontextualization, which is barely thinkable let alone livable, does not, even as Stiegler recognizes, result in the homogenization or uniformization of the entire world. Leroi-Gourhan's previously cited notion of a *way* of life based on small but significant differences is the counter to any thorough-going decontextualization, so that automobile technology (to recall), although necessarily derived from a single blueprint, turns out to have cultural variants. Why would it not be similar with regard to media, including the internet? Although the digital technology of the internet is identical regardless of where it is applied, how it is appropriated varies – albeit often in small, but nevertheless significant ways. Here, the 'style' of cell phone use by Kerala fishermen in India serves as an example. Through their phones the fishers have revived the tradition of cooperation (see Sreekumar 2011).[5]

Stiegler looks at the way the question of the human has been asked in philosophy and anthropology from the Greeks to Rousseau, Nietzsche and Foucault. In fact, says Stiegler, the Greeks gave up on the question and so it was only in the Enlightenment period that it was pursued with any vigour. One can

---

[5] Sreekumar points out, for example, that for the fishers in Kerala province, 'cell-phone use has actualized the collectivist logic of community sharing of information and *local knowledge*' (2011: 174; emphasis added). Moreover, the author emphasizes that 'we need to focus on the social forces the technology amplifies rather than the technology itself. In the case of Kerala fishers, the impulse toward cooperation has long been ingrained in their culture, as often happens among marginalized groups. The availability of mobile technologies has amplified this impulse and enabled new modes of cooperation' (174). This, it hardly needs saying, goes against Stiegler's thesis of technics inevitably bringing an intensification of decontextualization, the latter being exemplified by electronic communication that approaches the speed of light and where event, its 'capture' and the reading in it increasingly tend to coincide. Such communication, it is claimed, erases locality, that is, context: 'the locality tends to become everywhere identical, that is, to disappear. Decontextualization would not only be that of the utterance [énoncé], but also that of its "reception". There would then be a tendency towards a pure and simple loss of all context' (Stiegler 1996: 139). It could be argued, however, that 'reception' as used here is that of information theory, which evacuates meaning. Once meaning is understood to be indissolubly linked to interpretation context becomes it inevitable accompaniment.

point, for example, to Rousseau's question, quoted by Stiegler, in the Preface of the *Discourse on the Origin of Inequality*, to wit: 'For how shall we know the source of inequality between men, if we do not begin by knowing mankind?' (Rousseau 1982: 38, cited in Stiegler 1998: 106). Even though the aporias of Rousseau's discourse are acknowledged (a *natural* origin of man where equality ruled, but an origin that never existed, and an origin where humans are already walking using their hands and therefore are already technical, artificial – not natural), little is made of physical survival being at the origin, survival as described in the following passage quoted by Stiegler: 'I see him [natural man] satisfying his hunger at the first oak, and slaking his thirst at the first brook: finding his bed at the foot of the tree which afforded him a repast; and, with that, all his wants supplied' (1982: 47, cited in Stiegler 1998: 113). Even if a technical capacity is implied, Rousseau sees himself describing the original humans as surviving like animals:

> Self-preservation being his chief and almost his sole concern, he must exercise most those faculties which are most concerned with attack or defence, either for overcoming his prey, or for preventing him from becoming the prey of other animals. [...] Such in general is the animal condition, and such, according to the narrative of travellers, is that of most savage nations. (1982: 53)

And even though it is clear that a technical capacity is delineated, Rousseau does not see it. For what distinguishes the first humans is the development of their natural faculties in the absence of any prosthetic assistance:

> [O]ur industry deprives us of that force and agility which *necessity* [nécessité] obliges him to acquire. If he had had an axe would he have been able with his naked arm to break so large a branch from a tree? If he had a sling, would he have been able to throw a stone with so great velocity? If he had a ladder, would he have been so nimble in climbing a tree? If he had a horse, would he have been himself so swift of foot? (1982: 48; emphasis added)

'Civilized man' with his machines might be able to beat 'the savage', but without technical assistance the former would be no match for the latter. The problem Rousseau has is to distinguish natural man or humans from other animals. The best he can do is to claim that humans are cleverer than other animals even though they may not be stronger ['qu'il les surpasse plus en address, qu'ils ne le surpassent en force' (Rousseau 1964: 136)].

It is not that Stiegler does not recognize all this. It is rather a question of emphasis. For while the theorist of technics is concerned with the way that natural life – the life of survival – inevitably gives way to the emergence of prostheses and to the technical in general, the point is that survival – or, we could say, bare life – is at the origin and that were this not so the paradoxes and aporias of Rousseau's text would not exist in the way that they do. Before going into this in more detail, let us reconsider Rousseau's ideas regarding 'natural man' ('l'homme sauvage').

As is known, instead of natural existence being one of a war of all against all in the manner of Hobbes, Rousseau sees relative harmony reigning in nature, albeit unconsciously. What philosophers deem to be the woes of the state of nature are in fact those of society. Violence exists in society, but not in a state of nature. Natural man would have no reason to engage in violence, for everything is at his finger tips – this 'everything' being, for the most part, 'food, a female and sleep'. His only fears are pain and hunger and not death; for at this stage natural man is the same as the animal and does not 'know what it is to die' (Rousseau 1982: 55).

Even though he will complicate this idea, initially, humans and animals begin at the same level, one governed by instinct, so that even though, subsequently, humans raise themselves above animals (they can, very importantly, as Stiegler emphasizes, come to perceive death) they 'begin with purely animal functions: thus seeing and feeling must be his *first* condition [premier état], which would be common to him and all other animals' (1982: 55; emphasis added). Nothing indicative of society exists in the original state of nature. Thus, language is yet to be born; work does not exist as nature satisfies the needs of all living creatures; there is no need for clothing or human-made shelter; there is no economy for there is no scarcity; there are no differences between humans (in the societal sense) in the natural state, that is, at the origin: equality thus exists in nature but not in society. It is with arrival of the latter that inequalities emerge (in a nutshell, this is Rousseau's thesis).

As Stiegler recognizes, in Rousseau's text (*Discourse on the Origin of Inequality*), there is an extreme tension between the 'naturalisation of the human' and the need to distinguish humanity from animality. Ultimately, 'l'homme sauvage' is essentially animal because natural, but at the same time he is more than animal, or at least he is not entirely reducible to animality, which also means, in Leroi-Gourhan's terms, as we have seen, that the human cannot be entirely encompassed by zoology. Stiegler puts it the following way: 'There is no difference between man (in his essence) and animal, no essential difference between man and animal, unless it be an inactual possibility. When there is difference, man is no longer, and this is his denaturalization, that is, the naturalization of the animal. Man is his disappearance in the denaturalization of his essence. Appearing, he disappears' (1998: 121). Man appears through participating in his own operations, whereas animals are entirely driven by nature. Moreover, humans as a species are 'perfectible': they have 'the faculty of self-improvement'. We can also recall the adroitness of humans compared to animals. Humans, too, anticipate the future: they thus exist in time and, as mentioned, humans have a concept of death, whereas animals do not. So, in these ways 'natural man' who is essentially an animal becomes *identifiably* human.

What is the significance of Rousseau's dilemma? It is not just philosophical. It is, indeed, to do with the placing of 'Man' within the domain of bare life as the basis of human specificity, a process that begins in the post-Renaissance period and takes on apace in the nineteenth century. Even though, for Rousseau, only humans supposedly have a concept of death (Heidegger, as we have seen, will say nothing different), Rousseau also says – no doubt because the ethnology of his day confirmed it – that certain animals also show signs of mourning the loss of their fellows, that is, they also show signs of anticipation, the key to understanding the emergence of technics. For the philosopher of nature, then, humans, like animals, are *essentially* constituted in and through nature. Yet, at the same time, humans are absolutely distinct from animals, which implies, too, that they are, ultimately, absolutely distinct, qua human, from nature. Humans, indeed, are characterized by their fall from nature – a fall from whom they truly are – and into a world of appearance and noxious pretence and artificiality.[6] It is as though humans have to be nature in order to be ruled by sovereign power in society – a power that plays on the idea of the human essence as bare life, or the drive for life as biological survival.

Stiegler, by contrast, argues that it is not a matter of privileging biology, but of 'radically challenging the border between the animal and the human' (Stiegler 1998: 136). The way that this border is manipulated lays the groundwork for, to repeat, the human as essentially bare life. With regard to technics, the question is whether it comes into play uniquely to assist with biological survival, or whether it is integral to the being of beings so that technics, as we saw intimated in Leroi-Gourhan, belongs as much or even more to art and all of culture than it does to the domain of utility prostheses.

Grammē, death and the clock

In a dialogue with Derrida and the theses he presents in *Of Grammatology*, Stiegler writes: 'The *grammē* structures all levels of living and beyond, the

---

6   On this, see Lechte (1985) and (2012: 68–72).

pursuit of life by means other than life' (1998: 137). But, if certain commentators are to be believed (see, for example, Roberts (2005) and Iveson (2011)), Stiegler still fails, like Leroi-Gourhan, to go all the way and acknowledge that 'aliveness' as such is originally technical. Given this, the opposition that Stiegler invokes between epigenesis (the biological emergence of form) and epiphylogenesis (the exteriorization of life in technics) ceases to be pertinent.[7] Stiegler says, for instance, that '[e]piphylogenesis is a break with pure life' (1998: 140), thus confirming that technics is separate from something called 'pure life'. The human is also animal, Stiegler says in reading Leroi-Gourhan (170). Equally, he finds that the human frees itself from genetic constraints and that this gives rise to language and technics as exteriorization and opens the way to freedom (171), as we noted above. The problem is that there is an unilluminating circularity here: the human is also animal, but animality is what is transcended in order for the human to be fully human – that is, fully free in a way not available to animals. The human is also animal, but it is only in not being animal that the human becomes essentially human. How, in the end, does Stiegler deal with this dead-end form of thinking? He says, for a start, that social formations emerged earlier than granted by Leroi-Gourhan (173), But this hardly challenges the structure of the prehistorian's argument, only an element of its content, the point being that Stiegler accepts the form of thought which says that society began somewhere in time, that the human has not always been human, but had first of all to be prehuman before it could become human.[8] Stiegler's text is not in fact as transparent as this – as though he sensed that a real commitment to the theory of the emergence of society at some given point (however broad) would have implications to which he would not want to subscribe. Stiegler, maybe despite himself, refers to '*the moment* of the appearance of tools' (176; emphasis added) (à partir du moment où apparaît l'outillage (Fr 184)). As Michael Haworth says in an illuminating piece in referring to the break brought by epiphylogenesis: 'In Stiegler's reading, life is only an "economy of death" after the event of exteriorization, but for Derrida such an event is only possible because life is nothing other than an economy of death. Epiphylogenesis can occur only

---

[7] Roberts (2005) has suggested that this opposition merely reproduces the traditional one between nature and culture (see para 9).

[8] Surprisingly, in *La technique et temps, 2. La disorientation* (1996: 182–187), in addressing Derrida's argument against Heidegger on animals in *Of Spirit* (1991b), where the question of borders between animal and human is raised, Stiegler still does not seem to register the full consequences of what the animal/human distinction entails, particularly in relation to technics. The most that one can say is that the animal, because it is unable to relate to the world 'as such' (Heidegger), can never, other than by a reductive biologism, enter the world of technics.

because 'pure life' does not, and never did, exist' (Haworth 2016: 7). In other words, epiphylogenesis must already be 'programmed' in life in a certain sense if it is to take place, just as, for Rousseau, the 'fall' of humanity (into society and artifice) must be already a potential for 'natural man', even if Rousseau is at pains to deny this by saying that the fall is what *happens* to man from the exterior; it is not a result of man's internal makeup.[9]

To continue with the problematization of the 'break', we recall that the 'moment' has been considered in the previous chapter in relation to the moment of death. It was said there that it coalesces with bare life. Does not Stiegler's kind of 'defence' of clock time – or, indeed in defence of the clock, as a technical support of the human in his analysis of Heidegger's critique – not also enshrine the moment as the basic unit of time. The theorist wants to contest this, saying that a 'being-futural' is 'one of the clock's modalities' (221), that is, clock time is not tied to the present moment. Maybe not, but whether it is past, present or future, the moment (or time as irreversible) still dominates when it is a matter of clock time (which, obviously, is not time as duration). The difficulty for Stiegler is that the clock confirms the technical nature of time for humanity. It is prosthetic, in keeping with the human's essential technicity qua human. However, considered as a phenomenon that does not valorize bare life, clock time corresponds to a key aspect of a way of life in modernity – a way of life for which the moment is the key unit of time, but which operates as the unit of *time as such*, a notion of time that disavows life as a 'way of life'. Cinema, too, the subject of much of Stiegler's third volume of *La technique et le temps* (2001), can also be shown (as Bergson and after him, Deleuze, have made clear) to be dependent on the notion of clock time as a series of moments. In order to justify the clock as time's legitimate technical support (i.e., as an addition that in no way takes away from the notion of time as time), Stiegler cites the repetitious structure of calendars and way that time in the past has been 'measured' with sun dials, with reference to the seasons, and reference to 'day' and 'night' as countable. These, it is claimed, are the precursors of clocks, so that clocks do not, as Heidegger maintains, conceal the nature of time as time. Repetition in

---

9   Geoffrey Bennington, in his much-cited review of *Technics and Time, 1*, also takes the *moment* of the emergence of humans as being problematic: 'Stiegler wants to say that *one* moment is privileged, and that moment is the emergence of "man"' (Bennington 1996: 187; Bennington's emphasis). However, Bennington's concern is less about the politics of bare life that might be implied than it is about Stiegler's appropriation of Derrida's notion of différance in relation to 'technics'. Bennington also shows that once the question of technics becomes inseparable from the origin – or the non-origin – of the human, there is no escaping a certain positivism and determinism. This is something I failed to acknowledge in previous writing on Stiegler (see Lechte 1999).

evoking clock time continues today with the daily printing of newspapers, and we could add the examples of transport schedules, curriculum timetables, daily personal rituals (e.g., showering) media programming and so on.

Here, let us suggest that, in attempting to connect pre-modern instances of repetition in relation to time, Stiegler passes over the difference between reversible and irreversible time. For Heidegger, the modern conception of time as essentially the time of clocks does not bring into the light the nature of time as such, time *as* Dasein as 'being-towards-death'. Authentic time for Stiegler, on the other hand, is perfectly assimilable to the time of clocks, as clocks are an instance of the 'what' without which there would be no 'who', the latter being equivalent to the human qua human. As has become well known the myth of Epimetheus (Epimetheus having forgotten to give humans all the qualities needed for them to be autonomous) serves to capture Stiegler's key thesis that humans are necessarily technically constituted beings, unlike animals that are entirely self-contained and thus do not exhibit a need for prostheses (the 'what'). However, if the 'what' is crucial to the identity of the 'who', the changing nature of the 'what' will have an impact on this identity. Repetition with regard to time is thus double-edged. On the one hand, it can be made equivalent to irreversible time (today will never return). Thermodynamics and the notion of entropy in the nineteenth century becomes emblematic of essentially imperfect order and finite knowledge and the inescapability of irreversible time. In 1850s, experiments reveal that steam power, like any working system, generates friction and heat loss and that any system is destined to break down into disorder (entropy) unless energy is constantly renewed.

On the other hand, time has been understood to be reversible. For Newton and the seventeenth century, given infinite knowledge and absolute order, time is *essentially* reversible, even if such circumstances pertaining to this remain unrealized in practice. Here, there is no entropy. Repetitions are without difference, as the same recurs absolutely. Thus, with a cultural tradition based in reversible time, there is no entropy; the season is thus not another autumn (let's say) that returns (the repetition of a different autumn), but the *same* autumn recurs.

Thus, Stiegler's claim, which is that there is a 'proxying of the clock *before* all historic-natural programmatic systems (from the day and the seasons to the real-time installations of global capitalist industry)' (213; Stiegler's emphasis), is open to question when reversible time is given equal consideration with irreversible time. To see time 'before all historic-natural programmatic systems' as 'proxying the clock' is to reduce to silence the specificity of ways of life with regard to time. Consequently, Stiegler's quote from Evans-Pritchard referring to the Sudanese Nuer tribe's 'cattle clock' does not proxy the familiar clock, but is series of repeated activities so often related to cattle and their care that the anthropologist coined the term in question. The reversible time involved (repetition of the *same* daily activities) does not evoke the irreversible time that the clock presupposes. It is not indeed a matter of progress, where elementary clocks would precede the fully perfected clocks of the Industrial era.

The *polis* and 'who' and 'what' of technics

A key part of Stiegler's argument may be summarized as follows: The default of technics (the Epimetheus syndrome), qua anticipation, foresight, expectation, conjecture, presumption (1998: 196–197) and reflection, gives rise to a conception only available to humanity and not to animals: that of finitude, or mortality (Heidegger's 'being-towards-death'). This is equivalent to Dasein *as* time, as existence *in* time – as 'différance' (202). The human being defines itself in relation to the future, that is, in relation to death, something foreclosed to animals.

Supplementary to this, however, is another line of thinking dealing with the *polis* that only appears in an incidental way. It is that technics (which includes *technē*) also enables humans to accede to the *polis* as the place of citizenship. As Stiegler says quite explicitly at one point: '*technē* gives rise to the *polis*' (205). Thus, in light of the division of beings into animal and human, another consequence arises: technics enables humans to move beyond their initial animality. Or rather, we should ask again of Stiegler, as we did above in referring to epiphylogenesis: Does humanity emerge out of animality, or is there only a truly human being once there is technics, which could be neither more nor less than a conception of mortality and an expectation of death? We know already, too, that there is an original 'moment', an 'epigenetic process that is put in place from the *moment* of the appearance of tools' (176; emphasis added). And this moment is the one that, for Leroi-Gourhan, changes the human from being a purely zoological entity into one exhibiting a sociological bearing. For Leroi-Gourhan, then, humans partake of both sides of the zoological-sociological divide. Is it really similar for Stiegler as we suggested above?

Let us return to the myth of Epimetheus. In the version from Plato's *Protagoras* quoted by Stiegler, in the distribution of powers to animals, Epimetheus, lacking in foresight (= not being Pro-metheus) had forgotten about humans (Epi-metheus means hindsight) and thus ran out of powers to distribute to them. To compensate for Epimetheus's failure, Prometheus has to steal fire and the gift of skill in the arts from Hephaestus and Athena so that humans can be endowed with the means necessary for their survival (see 1998: 187–188). The question arising here concerns the nature of the beings for whom Prometheus steals fire and the gift of skill in the arts. Are we not back at the Rousseauian paradox, where the non-human human that is effectively indistinguishable from full animality is waiting to become fully human? In other words, humans *become* Pro-methean (foresight being a key index of technicity),[10] while having been Epi-methean, that is, having lacked foresight, and, most crucially, having lacked a capacity for anticipation and thus the insight into their own mortality. An Epimethean being, we can surmise, is one that, like all animals, simply perishes for lack of foresight. Humans emerge in light of the Epimethean fault. But from what? Stiegler puts it this way:

> It is by immediately deviating from the equilibrium of animals, from tranquillity […] that mortals occur. Before deviating, there is nothing. Then the accidental event happens, the fault of Epimetheus: to have forgotten humans. Humans are the forgotten ones. Humans only occur through their being forgotten. (188)

Here, Stiegler is able to complicate matters because the beings waiting to be endowed by Epimetheus with qualities do not even have the character of animals: they are in fact pre-animal, a kind of non-entity waiting to become an entity. In this sense, there is an absolute sameness between all beings prior to animals becoming animal and humans becoming human. As Stiegler no doubt rightly points out, the exploits of Prometheus and Epimetheus have their origin in the conflicts between the gods and the Titans – or between mortals and immortals. It is not, originally, a matter of differences between humans and animals. Just as lions came to be given their attributes, humans would have likewise been given their attributes, had Epimetheus not done a botched job.

Even so, distinctions have to be made and humans, potentially, were to be a variety of being or creature marked by internal equilibrium and the absence of any prosthetics leading to externalization. So, in a sense the human does pass through a purely animal stage, albeit virtually. The difficulty of course is that once technics becomes the mark of the human qua human, a pre-technical domain seems to be irrelevant. Nevertheless, the point to be reflected upon is that humans receive, acquire, create or invent technics – each of these terms implying a 'before' and an 'after' the emergence of technics. Thus: 'To make up

---

[10] As Stiegler says: 'Mortality *is prométheia*' (1998: 192; Stiegler's emphasis).

for Epimetheus's fault, Prometheus offers to man *the present* [cadeau], or *the gift*, to be outside-of-himself' (193; emphasis added; translation modified). How can 'present' and 'gift' here not be understood as being in time, so that prior to receiving the gift the humans are bereft of prostheses, whereas afterwards, they are endowed with them – to the point that they are essentially forces for externalization. Animals perish, they do not die, Stiegler, following Heidegger, has affirmed. But humans, had Epimetheus been successful, would also have been beings destined to perish and not to die. We can even read that: '[t]he qualities of animals make up *a sort of nature*' (193; emphasis added). Everything suggests humans being something other prior to the 'deviation' of externalization in tools and all forms of prosthesis. Everything, indeed, has the appearance of being framed with the horizon of a trajectory that moves, à la Descartes, from the simple to the complex: from a simple animal existence to a complex human existence founded in technics. Stiegler seems to sense that this is a problem and so he says very explicitly that '[b]efore the deviation there is nothing' (188). Our reading has suggested that the idea of nothing of the human existing prior to the gift of a technical capacity is implausible. Even if one says with Stiegler that humans are the forgotten ones and that they 'only appear in disappearing' (188), we are still dealing with the category of humans. Humans have to exist in a certain way, *as* human, prior to existing as mortals, as beings where the 'who' (subject) and the 'what' (technical object) coalesce indistinguishably. Even if Stiegler calls upon Vernant's reading of Hesiod in order to confirm that there is no origin – no 'golden age' (190) – prior to the birth of the human, his discourse seems riven by metaphysics in the sense that even to pose the question of origin is in keeping with the idea of a human before technics in contrast to a human after technics.

After the birth of technics, as Leroi-Gourhan has shown, particularly with regard to phonetic writing, sociality comes into existence. The equivalent for Stiegler is the birth of the political – of the *polis* and citizenship; indeed, politics, as we have already noted, is fundamentally technics: 'Politics is an art, a technics imprinted in every mortal [chacun] as the originary feeling of the divine coup of technicity itself' (201). As with Heidegger, an animal could never enter the *polis*, for it can never be endowed with technics. Thus, if there is a 'default' of origin in the case of the human, it is, first, specifically humans (and not animals or other living beings) that are in default and, secondly, to specify the human as emerging through the 'coup of technicity', or through the birth of technicity, contradicts the claim of a default of origin. If one wanted to speak truly and rigorously of a default of origin, it would be necessary to suppress all ideas in relation to technicity that evoke: coup, birth, deviation, rupture, arrival, emergence, invention (of the human), instantiation, etc. The reason Stiegler does not do this, no doubt, is because he wants to explore the specificity of the human as the 'who/what' conjunction – the human and nothing but the human, the human circumscribed and ultimately identified and open to analysis, an object of reflection in a philosophy driven by différance in the sense that analysis and reflection as the way to possibility and anticipation are also part of *technē* and so also constitutive of the human qua human. To be sure, in terms of différance, the human is that being whose origin is to be in default of origin. Is this not a reasonable way of putting things? It allows, after all, for the presence/absence of origin and thereby enables a reflection on the 'who' subject as being nothing without the 'what' technical object. In response to this, I say that it is the very notion of origin – its existence as much as its non-existence – that is at issue. It is a term that, if Stiegler wanted to achieve his end, should at least be placed under erasure. But it also can be dealt with by exploring the possibility that there is no rupture or discontinuity between human and animal, so that technics would exist in that domain that has hitherto been called 'nature'.[11]

If, regarding the 'origin' of technics, the structuralist path regarding language is followed, we would say that, like language, technics must have 'arisen all at once. With language, things cannot have begun to signify gradually' (Lévi-Strauss 1997: 61). Language, because it is a system, either exists or does not exist; there can be no evolution. If we can for a moment curb our tendency to be dazzled by progress in the history of technics, we can say, equally, that technics, *as the essential marker of humanness*, either exists or does not exist. The evolution from primitive simplicity to civilized complexity is thus misleading.[12] The complexity of technical evolution must be present *in potentia* from the start, something which only confirms its orientation towards the future.

---

[11] It is precisely with regard to nature being implicated in technics that Bennington draws attention to the insightfulness of Kant, the philosopher neglected by Stiegler in the first volume of *Technics and Time*: 'The thought of a technic of nature is intrinsic to what Kant calls *teleological* judgement: we attribute a technical capacity to nature by analogy with human technical activity' (Benningtion 1996: 185; Bennington's emphasis). Thus, Kant brings 'technic' and 'nature' together, whereas Stiegler's approach makes them the basis of an essential separation.

[12] In an essay on Stiegler's interpretation of Leroi-Gourhan, Christopher Johnson cites Derrida in *Of Grammatology* as apparently being critical of Lévi-Strauss's 'all at once' theory of language (Johnson 2013: 51n.8). Rather, however, Derrida is critical of the radical separation of speech from writing which accompanies Lévi-Strauss's theory. Cf. 'We might well find numerous questions to raise about this paragraph, which ties sense to signification in the *spoken* language' (Derrida 1976: 120; Derrida's emphasis). To be sure, Lévi-Strauss is no doubt remiss in limiting language to its purely symbolic aspect, to the detriment of its semiotic (Kristeva) aspect. Nonetheless, this is far from accepting that there can be a 'concrete' language based on signs that are wholly natural or 'motivated' (Saussure), that is, not arbitrary.

Tracy Colony has recognized (but not with reference to Heidegger) that: 'Following the narrative of the ancient myth, Stiegler rethinks the specifically human attribute of mortality as deriving from technical materiality. However, in doing so, he can be seen to preserve a traditional opposition between human temporality as mortal and nonhuman temporality as merely a naturalistic duration' (2011: 81). Colony claims that Stiegler's approach in separating human from non-human life is anthropocentric (75). The question, as Colony recognizes, is not whether non-human life untouched by technics is 'un-ruptured or pure' (78), but whether, as Stiegler claims, there is such a life.

In his essay already cited, Haworth shows, not only that the invocation of epiphylogenesis creates a problem of the 'moment' that commits Stiegler to the double origin to which he says Rousseau and Leroi-Gourhan are forced to resort, but that the whole idea of the separation of genetic memory – or the memory that every member of a succeeding generation of a species inherits – from individual epigenetic memory, which can only ever be passed on 'by means other than life' (i.e., by epiphylogenesis) is now being questioned. Indeed, it is now being asked whether an experience an individual has could be passed on to the next generation via 'transgenerational memory', thus putting in doubt Stiegler's thesis of the necessity of tertiary memory of technics to provide access to a past that one has not lived. As Stiegler puts in the second volume of *La technique et le temps* (*Technics and Time*), 'Technics does *not aid* memory: it *is* memory as "retentional finitude", originally *assisted*' (1996: 83; Stiegler's emphasis). Haworth acknowledges that it is still early days in this neuroscientific research and thus too early to say that tertiary memory is superfluous to requirements, as it were. It would also seem that knowledge of 'transgenerational memory', were it to be a validated, becomes another empirical stage in the evolution of humanity and thus, ultimately, does not escape the problem of the origin of humanity being founded in bare life. Indeed, rather than this being a new development, it would seem necessary to concede that transgenerational memory – even more than technics – was there *in potentia* from the start and is thus part of the constitution of the human. Like technics the content of trangenerational memory would be open-ended because based in individual experiences that are essentially contingent – or 'improbable', as Stiegler says in referring to the 'who', or to Dasein in Heidegger's terminology (1998: 215). It turns out, of course, that the improbable is the probable as the 'delay' (Derrida) of certainty in uncertainty and the delay of immediacy in mediacy. Were human life totally programmable, totally predictable, say, in the manner of seventeenth-century reversible time, everything would be calculable leaving no room for difference in identity. Death would cease to be a general horizon in the manner of 'being-towards-death' and become a 'natural' empirical certainty, like day and night. By contrast, anticipation and possibility enable the future to be a sphere of change and creativity accompanied by an awareness that one will never experience death even though it is ultimately certain.

Nature as interiority, as we saw in Rousseau, entails that beings and the world are entirely coterminous. A similar view pertains in the contemporary view of animals as being continuous with their environment. Heidegger, influenced by von Uexküll, holds to this view. Research in the 1950s on 'the frog's eye view' (Lettvin et al. 1959) was geared to show how the frog (like other animals) is totally integrated into its environment. To be totally integrated into the environment is to be bereft of any hint of the exteriorization made so explicit in the prostheses of technics. The interiority of nature contrasting with the exteriorization of technics as wielded by humans does nothing if not confirm the opposition between nature and technics/culture in the life of 'man'.

As with Heidegger, the clear marker of the separation of technics from nature is, for Stiegler, the *polis*, within which 'speech', in Hannah Arendt's words, 'is what makes man a political being' (Arendt 1958: 3 quoted by Stiegler 2011: 120). Even though humanity comes into being through epiphylogenesis as a separation from nature, once this separation has taken place, there is, Stiegler says to his credit, no human life as subsistence life:

> within the *polis* the banality and everydayness [*ordinaire*] of existence, is the very thing that means there *is* an everydayness of existence itself, one which forgets that *bodily reserve* is as such extra-ordinary – and thus this is an *ordinariness* that is *irreducible to subsistence behavior*. (Stiegler 2011: 117; emphasis added to the last four words; previous emphasis is Stiegler's)

From this passage we could conclude that 'within the *polis*' there is no essentially banal activity geared exclusively towards the satisfaction of the needs of the body in order that it might survive at a subsistence level. Like Arendt's valorization of speech in the *polis*, Stiegler privileges, 'grammatization', in relation to which, he says, Arendt 'remained completely blind' (2011: 123). Grammatization is that sphere of technics which concerns writing, and all processes of media, especially those concerned with memory (mnemo-technics) and the dialectic of retention and protention. Only through grammatization and the evolution of writing (or the 'letter') can there be law and thus the 'possibility of citizenship as a singularity posed *in law*' (2011: 142; Stiegler's emphasis). Does it need to be said that beings other than human cannot figure in the *polis*, even though

Stiegler quotes again in epigraph, the following passage from *Of Grammatology*: 'Instead of having recourse to the concepts that habitually serve to distinguish man from other living beings (instinct and intelligence, absence or presence of speech, of society, of economy, etc. etc.), the notion of *program* is invoked' (Derrida 1976: 84; Derrida's emphasis)? Here, Derrida implicitly problematizes the discontinuity between nature and culture, human and animal, necessity and freedom, interiority and exteriority. It remains now to establish what path Gilbert Simondon's theory of technics and individuation follows.

Simondon: Humans and technics

Technical objects

In Gilbert Simondon's theory, technical objects cannot be defined by their use, only by their genesis: 'The genesis of the technical object makes up part of its being. The technical object is that which is not anterior to its becoming, but is present at each stage of this becoming; the technical object is a unity of becoming' (Simondon 2012: 22–23). Significantly, Simondon argues that it is insufficient to understand technicity by taking the already-constituted technical object as the starting point (226). The same, we will note in passing, is said of individuation, where the latter cannot be validly understood if the (hypothetical) already-constituted individual is taken as the point of departure. Technicity, then, is not reducible to the totality of technical objects (226). Rather, it is a matter of studying the phases of the genesis of technical objects.

Simondon seems, nevertheless, to define the animal as 'le vivant élémentaire' [elemental life] (2012: 198). He also refers to Ancient Greek society, where technical objects were excluded from the City because associated with the work of slaves (124). Moreover, he discusses the relation of the human (l'homme) to the world, implying that there is a unity called the human. Indeed, living beings are essentially distinguishable from technical beings in terms of reproduction: 'living beings engender beings similar to themselves', whereas 'a technical being does not possess this capacity' (226). The technical object is the mediator between humanity and the world (227).

The world of magic is an important aspect of Simondon's understanding of technical objects and their genesis. It is a world where there is no distinction between subject and object – where, in an echo of Rousseau, there is no distinction between the human and the world, only continuity. Thus, we read:

'The unity of primitive magic is the relation of a vital liaison between man and the world, defining a universe at the same time both subjective and objective, anterior to any distinction between subject and object' (2012: 227). Simondon goes on to speak of a 'primitive union, before any splitting into subjectivity and objectivity' (228), a world in fact prior to the world of magic, where a 'figure and ground' kind of division appears, which Simondon calls 'the first structuration' (228). There is interaction, or exchanges between humans and the world, such that humans have an impact on the world and vice versa.

Simondon reveals his traditionalist streak when he refers to work as 'the mediation between the human species and nature' (328). Again, in his definition of 'social group', Simondon is hardly innovative. As with animals, the social is constituted, 'according to an adaptation to the conditions of the milieu' (332). The technical object, we recall, is not essentially defined by utility. Being detachable it can serve in many varied contexts (334).

Having established that there is a sphere of nature in his theory of technical objects, what is the case with regard to Simondon's intricate theory of individuation?

Individuation

Living beings, Simondon says right at the beginning of his treatise on individuation, exhibit a 'perpetual' and 'permanent activity of individuation', and it is not the result, like the case of crystal, of a single individuation (1989: 16). Instead of identity – which is homeostatic – being the key to understanding the individual, the latter 'maintains metastablity' as 'the condition of life' (17). Metastability means being open to change, not being permanently fixed.[13] The living individual, unlike the purely physical individual, has an interiority and is a system of individuations (17–18). The foundation of individuation in its various levels is transduction (28). Transduction is both a form of thinking and a process. As a form of thinking it may be compared with deduction and induction and is evocative of analogy as the movement between different dimensions or contexts, a movement constitutive of an openness that is absent in identity. Invention, says

---

[13] Something similar can be seen in Julia Kristeva's notion of the 'subject in process/on trial' as part of her theory of the semiotic (Kristeva 1984), and in her appropriation of the theory of the open system as a way of describing Freud's theory of the 'death drive' as 'the greater complexity of the individual' (1987: 14) and of the transference as equivalent to 'self-organization' (14). Here, it is interesting that the term 'individual' (individu') is used instead of Kristeva's usual one of the 'subject'. Needless to say, Kristeva does not have a theory of preindividuality.

Simondon, is neither deductive nor inductive but *trans*ductive (1989: 26). As a process it is without a 'blueprint'; it is an individuation in progress (25) where emergent stages build on one another.

However, the starting point for Simondon's notion of individuation is the preindividual, or the indefinite, *apeiron* – the pre-Socratic Greek term for 'nature' (1989: 196). What, precisely, is the significance of the preindividual sphere? In an introductory remark, Simondon implies that preindividual reality more than overlaps any given individuation and becomes the source of future metastable states giving rise to new individuations (18). It is the 'existence of potential' for individuations (27). Can such a notion avoid the opposition, human/nature that we have discussed so far? The short answer given by Simondon is: 'Nature is not the contrary of Man, but the first phase of being, the second being the opposition of individual and milieu' (196). And Simondon adds: 'According to the hypothesis presented here, some ἄπερον [*apeiron*] would remain in the individual' (196). But then, like some sort of ethnic memory, there is a residual nature, distinct from the individual's individuality, which recalls what Simondon refers to as 'the primitive and original phase' which has an echo in the second phase of the individuation of the individual (197).

Equally, Simondon formulates the concept of the 'transindividual' that is exterior to the individual, 'is not structured' (195), nor is it 'in a topological relation' (195) with the individual, but which, being unstructured, traverses the latter. Moreover, transcendence and immanence only have relevance in relation to the individuated reality, not to the transindividual. As with the preindividual, there is 'an anteriority of the transindividual in relation to the individual', which, Simondon says, is what prevents it being defined in terms of transcendence and immanence. Once again, it is the indefinite, non-conceptual nature of transindividuality that allows it to be a phase of the individuated individual. It is present without being present; it is present and absent simultaneously.

To speak approximately, while the preindividual as Nature reverberating is the individuated individual understood diachronically, transindividuality, which would tap into the individual's group or social being, is the individual understood synchronically. The point is that Simondon adds to the diachronic dimension the descriptors of 'primitive', 'original' and 'Nature', as though, not only would there be a move from the simple to the complex, but that unstructured or indefinite reality (the Greek *apeiron*?) were something to be overcome, not to say transcended. A similar point can be made with regard to transindividuality in that the latter is overcome in the structuration of the social reality of community. In Simondon's words:

the transindividual and the individual are not the same phase of being: the two phases coexist like amorphous water in a crystal. This is why the group can appear as a milieu: the personality of the group is constituted on a foundation of preindividual reality, which bears, *after structuration*, an individual aspect complementary to the individual. (195; emphasis added)

Be this as it may, structuration is an ongoing process as is individuation. Thus: 'By this ἄπερον [*apeiron*] that is borne within, each human being is not only an individuated being but is also the couple: individuated being and nature; it is by this reverberating nature that humans communicate with the world and with other individuated beings' (197). In other words, rather than being transcended, which, as we have seen, is often the way it has been understood, Nature, as preindividual reality, remains the driver of both individual and collective being.

However, in more schematic formulations, Simondon says that the 'subject being' can be conceived as a 'more or less perfectly coherent system of three *successive* phases: the pre-individual, the individuated, the transindividual, corresponding partially but not completely to what is designated by the concepts of nature, individual, spirituality' (205; emphasis added). Here, the 'successive' would seem to imply one phase is overtaken by the next.

Whatever might be the case, the fact is that nature as a reality and concept plays a key role in what has been seen as Simondon's highly innovative and original thinking. Some, such as Chabot, see this nature as a 'pre-Socratic' 'reservoir of becoming' (Chabot 2013: 86), or, as with Deleuze referring to the individual, as a 'reservoir of its singularities' (Deleuze 1994: 246), rather than as a primitive stage of objectivity. More specifically, we have noted the indeterminate or indefinite character of pre-Socratic nature which would reverberate in the process of individuation. An ambivalence in Simondon's approach can also be observed, when he refers to this nature as 'primitive' and that it is the first of three 'successive' phases of human being. When referring to how emotion should be understood, Simondon again evokes Nature in that emotion 'manifests in the individuated being the reverberation [rémanence] of the preindividuel' (211). Here the preindividual is the '*naturally* indeterminate' (211; emphasis added).

In his conclusion to *L'individuation psychique et collective* (1989), Simondon asks the following revealing question: 'Of what use is it to cast into the unknowable state of the preindividual being the forces destined to account for ontogenesis if this state is only known by way of the subsequent state?' (231) This is to say that the state of preindividuality is *deduced* from the state of individuality. Is the form of this logic any different from Freud's when he says that the primary process is only knowable indirectly via the secondary process of consciousness and is 'to that extent a theoretical fiction' (Freud 1976: 763). Or, is it really very different from seventeenth- and eighteenth-century political philosophers (including Rousseau) deducing the state of nature from the present state of society without knowing whether or not such a state ever really existed? Just as Freud 'needed' the existence of the primary process in order to explain enigmatic features of the secondary system and political philosophers 'needed' the state of nature in order to explain society, so Simondon apparently 'needs' the state of preindividuality to explain indivdiuation. Parenthetically, let it be noted that the existence of bare life is based on the same form of hypothetical deduction. Simondon in fact rejects this line of argument (cf. 232) while at the same time recognizing (at least in part) the problem raised by the hypothetical deduction of the state of preindividuality and asks whether this is analogous to hypothesizing a 'creator being' to account for instances of creation. Simondon calls this a 'creationist hypothesis' (232). His response is that it is not analogous because such a creator determines the nature of the created, whereas this is not the case in the relation: preindividual–individual. While this is quite true, especially given the indefinite character of *apeiron*, and while there is no radical opposition between the human and nature, nevertheless preindividuality does not appear *as such*.

In a further move, Simondon would seem to counter the latter point by emphasizing that the 'hypothesis of a preindividual state is not totally gratuitous', that there is more to it than how it relates the existence of individuals and that 'it is derived from a certain number of schemas of scientific thought' (232). To illustrate, Simondon claims that although physics does 'not show the existence of a preindividual reality' (232),[14] it does 'show that geneses of individual realities do exist in light of the conditions of a state' (232). Simondon then gives the examples of the photon and the electron as illustrative of 'individuals' being, in first case, an individual and a 'quantity [*sic*] of energy' and in the second, 'an interaction with fields' (232). Physics, Simondon claims, allows us to think an individual as a state of exchanges against 'the structural modification of a system, thus against a certain defined state of a system' (232–233). Or again: 'the individual is not an absolute starting point' and one 'can study its genesis in light of a certain number of conditions both energetic and structural' (233).

---

[14] Despite this statement, a little later, Simondon will conclude that 'There is in physics a predindividual and a postindividual being; a photon disappears and becomes a change in the structure of an atomic edifice' (1989: 233).

Few non-physicists (including the author of this book) would have the competence to evaluate Simondon's claims. What can be said, however, is that photons pertain to the whole field of quantum mechanics and its theory of the behaviour of particles in the atom. In this regard, photons are individual quanta (not quantities?) or discrete bundles of energy related to the behaviour of electrons as the latter move in different orbits in relation to the nucleus of an atom, a lower orbit giving rise to the energy loss called photons. A photon is also defined as an elementary particle, which means that its substructure (if it has one) is unknown, a fact that would seem to tell against the relevance of Simondon's notion of genesis. Moreover, the movement of electrons between orbits leaves no trace these occurring by way of a *quantum* leap, something that, once again, renders problematic the notion of genesis. If, as Simondon also says, 'ontogenesis is inscribed in the becoming of systems; the appearance of an individual corresponds to a certain state of a system' (233), does it make any sense to speak of the becoming of the atom as a system? Or again: If the individual in physics 'is relative and not substantial', how does this gel with the notion of the photon as an 'elementary particle'?

None of this should be interpreted to mean that Simondon's characterizations of the individual in physics being explicable in terms of genesis might not indeed be valid.[15] What is more certain, however, is that it is difficult to see how the resort to physics actually enhances the justification of the state of preindividuality with its connotation of origin, nature and amorphousness, giving rise to the specific modes of individuation.

At the end of his chapter in the published version of his whole thesis dealing with individuation in physics, Simondon provides the following revealing observation: 'Living beings, in order to live, *need* physico-chemical individuals; animals *need* vegetable life which, for them, is Nature, in the proper sense of the term' (Simondon 2013: 153. Simondon's capitalization; emphasis added). With the emphasis on 'need', here the echo of bare life would seem to be inescapable despite all the subtlety of Simondon's discussion of individuation

---

[15] A mark of Simondon's competence in physics is the fact that, as reported by Chabot (2013: 1), Simondon often substituted for the physics teacher during his tenure (1948–1955) at the Lycée Descartes in Tours. Simondon goes on to talk about electron waves in Undulatory Mechanics (233), which, for obvious reasons, I cannot comment on. Moreover, the definitive edition of Simondon's thesis on individuation (defended in 1958) includes a chapter, 'Form and Substance' on individuation in quantum mechanics and in the history of physics (see Simondon 2013: 99–153). This chapter was not included in the first published part of the thesis in 1964 (PUF), although it is to be found in the later Millon (1995) edition (see also Chabot 2013: 83n9). This text is further evidence of Simondon's competence in the field and shows him to be a specialist in his own right.

Perhaps the point to be made is that it is not a matter of the physics but of what one does with it in relation to the social milieu.

in physics. Moreover, if the latter field reveals a form of preindividuality in non-living matter, this is, to all appearances, a preindividuality that is prior to, and contemporary with, the individual that emerges from individuation. That is, in the now frequently talked about example of crystal formation the individual crystal emerges from an unstable (amorphous) *pre*-crystalline, meta-stable state, a state which, when subjected to some kind of event or 'structural germ' (a shock to the system) initiates the process of crystal formation (2013: 151). This preindividual – precrystalline – state Simondon calls, 'singularity capital' (151) (cf. cultural capital), which, unlike living matter, inert matter cannot augment. We have seen that it is precisely at this point that there is, at the very least, an ambiguity in Simondon's discussion of the preindividuality of living beings such that it is unclear as whether the preindividual state is prior to – as a remnant of 'nature' – or is contemporaneous with individuations and the emergence of the individual.

Individuation and technics

In discussing the human–machine relation in a complementary note at the end of, *L'Individuation psychique et collective*, the second published part of his doctorat d'état, Simondon opposes the view that the machine is nothing but a human plaything with the characteristic of the slave of former times, as well as the reverse idea: namely, that man is enslaved by the machine or by technics more generally. The view presented is that machines cannot be understood in isolation from one another and only have meaning within a network of 'coordinated technical beings' and 'this coordination can only be thought by man and constructed by him, for it is not given in nature' (1989: 279).

Not only, then, is there an implicit opposition at work between human and nature, but, unlike Stiegler's theory, the human, instead of being formed by technics, is quite distinct from the technical object. Here, perhaps it would be more accurate to say that two worlds face each other: the world of humans and that of technical objects. While these two worlds relate to each other they are separate and distinct worlds, so that the human world is already given as a world before confronting the world of technics. This, of course, is precisely the opposite of Simondon's theory of individuation, where the individual cannot be assumed to be prior to the process of individuation. By contrast, the human world *can* be assumed to be prior to the world of technics and not to be formed (in part or in whole) by the latter world, as is the case for Stiegler. Thus, to confirm the point, for Simondon, '*man confers on the machine* its integration into the constructed world where it assumes its functional definition in relation to other machines' (279; emphasis added). From the natural world, Simondon says, the machine takes its condition of materiality and all the spatiotemporal coordinates that this implies. So that this relation between man and the machine can exist, there must be a technical culture 'made from intuitive and discursive, inductive and deductive knowledge of the mechanisms constitutive of the machine and implying a consciousness of the schemas and technical qualities which are materialised in it' (279).[16] In short: technical culture requires scientific knowledge (279).[17] Here, once again, is the human confronting the machine, objectifying it so that it becomes part of science. Technical knowledge becomes a form of mediation 'between man and the natural world' (280). There are then, three worlds: the human, the technical and the natural. Even though these worlds interpenetrate, they are three distinct worlds.

In an interesting and significant aside, Simondon says that a technical taste must be acquired and that many people act towards machines in a 'crude' and 'primitive' way, treating machines in a 'frenzy of possession' simply as utilitarian objects there to serve humans' needs: 'Machines', adds Simondon, 'are treated like consumption goods by a crude and ignorant humanity' (280). In short, within the commercialized world of consumer society the ignorant have no respect for machines treating them like slaves. In a final gesture, Simondon says that it is ultimately via the machine that humans have a relation 'beyond the reality of the community in order to institute a relation with Nature' (290; Simondon's capitalization).

The 'natural world'

In the first part of his thesis on individuation dealing with physical individuation, Simondon refers to '*le monde naturel*' (2013: 52; Simondon's emphasis), when discussing the permanence in thought of the 'hylomorphic schema'. The natural world is where supposedly brute matter is to be found before it takes any form. But, in fact, Simondon argues, matter is already – in its natural state, we might say – possessed of certain qualities that will facilitate its taking of form as a result of human intervention. In effect, brute matter already has a kind of form

---

[16] In fact, Simondon says that there must be a double condition 'in man' and 'in the machine' (1989: 279). However, the condition on the side of the machine is seemingly only given by implication. It is that the machine must not simply be a tool or a consumer object.

[17] Simondon later goes further saying that there should be a 'technical taste' in much the same way as there is taste in aesthetics (see 1989: 280).

before taking form: 'The taking of technical form uses the natural taking of form anterior to it' (52). Thus, the specificity of nature is proposed: a quantity of wood from a given tree or trees is always of a particular type; it is not a totally amorphous and abstract brute matter supposedly lacking any kind of shape or not having any attributes. It in fact exhibits *eccéité*, translated as haecceity – 'thisness', in the language of Duns Scotus, that evokes having discrete qualities. There may indeed be discrete qualities in nature; the point however is that there is a sphere of nature and it is *anterior* to human intervention, which means anterior to technics. Thus: 'a technical operation reveals and utilizes *natural*, already existing forms' (2013: 56). Technical operations use the already-existing, implicit forms in nature rather imposing totally new forms. All of this is no doubt valid – but there is still an autonomous sphere of *pre-existing* nature. Rather than concluding that there is a continuous way of life, where the opposition nature–culture becomes redundant, Simondon argues for a discontinuity between nature and human activity, even if nature is the irreplaceable source of this activity.

9

Levinas, the Absolute Other, and Humanness

Thus far in this study, it has been found that, in key texts in philosophy and cultural theory, the human is fundamentally related to a prehuman state from which the fully human arises: animality, nature, epigenesis (the biological emergence of form) or the preindividual *apeiron*, as we saw in Simondon's theory. The question in filigree in this chapter on the philosophy of the Other of Levinas is: To what extent does Levinas's thought on responsibility and the Other confirm or undermine the notion of a prehuman humanity?

More specifically, to what extent does Levinas's philosophy of the absolute other do justice to the transcendence of the human? For Levinas, the human, as originally other, is also originally transcendent. Human history is a 'permanent state of war' and it is here that politics in the current, conventional sense takes place. We need to examine Levinas's approach to conventional politics and his philosophy of the face of the Other (Autrui) in relation to war and peace. As we have seen, freedom will be essentially political freedom raising the prospect that its price would be equivalent to the sacrifice of the other.

Ultimately, it is a matter of working out how political position-taking might affect an ethical stance (the 'Thou shalt not kill') and of assessing how politics as practised in the twenty-first century could possibly give rise to transcendence and thus to a reinvigorated appreciation of the human. The 'answer' to be explored is that it is a question of what philosophy can achieve today, given the hyper-pragmatic inflection of the practice of politics. While the effects of thinking cannot be spelt out in a blueprint, it is not a matter either of effects brought about entirely arbitrarily. Rather, it is a matter of (re)establishing faith in the practical achievements of thought.

Even though Levinas says that life is the love of life – thereby defying the reduction of life to bare life – nevertheless, he also says that we 'live from our work [*travail*] which ensures our subsistence' (1969: 112; translation modified). It remains to establish how firmly 'subsistence' sits with Levinas's philosophy as an ethics of otherness with emphasis on the actually existing other person, or persons (autrui).

It is Levinas who has substantially problematized existing philosophical language that, deriving its inspiration from Ancient Greece, has attempted to 'capture' the otherness of the other. Such a philosophy, he argues, has failed in its mission, and, instead of enabling the Other to appear, has become, as we noted in Chapter 1, an 'egology' (1969: 44)[1] – a philosophy of self, or of the order of the Same. The way that Levinas has gone about this task and the insights into ethics that have come to the fore have been the subject of wide-ranging debates, a notable early contribution being by Jacques Derrida, who concluded his meditation by posing the question of whether ultimately Levinas's thought is in good part driven by Judaism as an 'experience of the infinitely other' and the need, despite the intention to the contrary, to invoke the language of philosophy inspired by Ancient Greece (Derrida 1967: 226), given that this is the language through which the very problem of 'egology' becomes manifest.

Be this as it may, let us put existing interpretations of Levinas to one side for the moment, and look, with regard to the Other, at the relation it might have with the notions of subsistence and bare life. As Levinas's thought evolved out of an interpretation of Husserlian phenomenology, it is worthwhile considering aspects of the *epochē*, defined as the bracketing, disconnection or abstention in relation to the natural world, and this particularly in relation to phenomenological description as Husserl intended it.

Husserl and the 'natural attitude'

With reference to technics, the previous chapter discussed the relationship between interiority and exteriority. Rousseau's depiction of 'natural man', we saw was a classic illustration of the human as interiority because as Man was coterminous with Nature or the environment which sustained him. Stiegler, inspired by Leroi-Gourhan, proposed that technics as exteriority appears even before the first concrete tools, in as far as anticipation in general and a recognition of death in particular, come to constitute a mode of exteriorization. The issue was, however, that there was still a nascent nature in Stiegler's account, a nature most explicit in the theory of epiphylogenesis – or the exteriorization

---

[1] In fact, prior to its appearance in *Totality and Infinity*, Levinas had attributed the neologism, 'egology', to Husserl (see Levinas 1994: 168).

of life in technics, also described as 'the pursuit of life by means other than life'. Epiphylogenesis wrenches the human from its putatively natural biological rhythm evoked by the process of the stages of epigenetic development. The epiphylogentic wrench opens the way to the appearance of a residual 'nature' and all that this implies for understanding the human as having a natural origin as pure interiority.

Levinas, like Stiegler, but with a different orientation, is an avid reader of Husserl – the Husserl of intentionality and all that this implies, while Stiegler focuses on the Husserl of temporal objects as exposed in *On the Phenomenology of the Internal Consciousness of Time* (1991: 19, 21–71), a text which brings to a head the critical status of consciousness as pivoting on the opposition between interiority and exteriority.

The natural and cultural worlds, summarized under the rubric of the 'natural attitude', plays a crucial role in the development of Husserl's outline of 'pure phenomenology', where being and consciousness as absolute are one. Here, Husserl begins from being in the world and nature, from the everyday world, or the natural standpoint 'as it confronts us, from consciousness as it offers itself in psychological experience' (1982: XIX). Psychologically, individuals are *in* the world, which Husserl sometimes divides into the real and natural worlds. Humans as natural beings share the natural world with animals even if the latter might be excluded from language and culture. In other words, to begin, Husserl posits the human – including the thinker philosopher qua human being – as being *interior* to the world not external to it. This world as reality which includes nature is a contingent world: it could have been other than it is. It has no *essential* (designated by Husserl as 'eidetic') aspect, the aspect that a pure phenomenology will seek to disclose after effecting the *epochē*, or phenomenological reduction which puts the natural attitude out of play in order to give consciousness complete ascendency. 'The existence of a Nature', says Husserl, '*cannot* be the condition for the existence of consciousness, since Nature itself turns out to be a correlate of consciousness: Nature *is* only as being constituted in regular concatenations of consciousness' (1982: 116; Husserl's emphasis). Nothing external to consciousness is necessary to it. It is 'a *self-contained complex of being*, as complex of *absolute being*, into which nothing can penetrate and from which nothing can slip' (112; Husserl's emphasis). The 'whole *spatiotemporal world*' (112; Husserl's emphasis) to which humans and animals belong is thus subordinate, or secondary to consciousness. Being now equates with the being of consciousness, not with the contingent world as that which constitutes being. Could we say that consciousness, nevertheless, is *exterior* to the contingent world? – in as far as the *epochē* implies a disconnection of some sort even though Nature is a 'correlate of consciousness'. Does this imply, despite Husserl, perhaps, that consciousness is autonomous and not dependent on human being? Does this mean, further, that no 'who' is necessary for the being of consciousness so that consciousness would think the 'who' – think the human as 'who', as the incarnation of consciousness – rather than the reverse? In answer to these questions, it has to be said that it would be naive in the extreme to think that, in the end, Husserl does not make the 'who' the privileged vehicle of consciousness. The who-human may be part of the natural contingent world, but it is also destined to make itself external to this world as the one in pursuit of a pure phenomenology. Indeed, the whole point of phenomenology is that it can be established *by* a 'who' as thinker, which is the human as thinker – a point confirmed by the following passage:

> instead of *effecting* the acts pertaining to our Nature – constituting consciousness with their positings of something transcendent, and letting ourselves be induced, by motives implicit in them, to effect ever new positings of something transcendent – instead of that, *we* set all these theses 'out of action', *we* do not 'participate in them'; *we* direct our seizing and theoretically inquiring regard to *pure consciousness in its own absolute being.* (113; emphasis added to 'we')

A 'who'-*we* is thus 'carrying out' these acts, so that even if consciousness cannot be qualified as 'human', it is the human who has privileged access to this consciousness. No other living being can have such access. Instead of living *in* the natural world as 'positings' of one kind or another, 'we effect acts of *reflection* directed to them; and we seize upon them themselves as the *absolute* being which they are' (114; Husserl's emphasis). Thus, the who-human, we can maintain, is uniquely the one destined to reflect and apprehend 'absolute being'.[2]

We have then a situation where the essential nature of pure phenomenology and absolute consciousness as being can be accessed by the act of pure consciousness, even though such consciousness is incarnate in a human being as a being that is part of the real world. In other words, the *epochē* is effected in a natural body that, qua natural entity, does not impinge upon the purity of

---

[2] Paragraphs 53 to 55 of *Ideas* go some way in clarifying Husserl's meaning with regard to absolute consciousness. To summarize what is at stake, it could be said that reflection of the purest kind can reveal that consciousness is necessarily incarnate in a personal ego. The key to the latter statement is that it is universalizable – that is, it could be validated by any personal ego whatsoever. Moreover, in paragraph 64, Husserl even acknowledges the presence of 'we' in his text. However, he simply concludes that, like any thinker of eidetic truths, such as the mathematician, the phenomenologist excludes himself from the eidetic content. This, though, is evocative of an issue of method rather than an answer as to how a thinker can marshal consciousness to bring about the *moment* of the *epochē*.

consciousness; for such consciousness can apprehend the body for what it is: that is, an entirely contingent entity. Of course, if it is in pure phenomenology as eidetic science that philosophical thinking also emerges, it is clear that an opposition between philosophy and non-philosophy is also constituted. Those who remain in the 'natural attitude' – the attitude, Husserl says, of everyday life – would remain also in the quintessentially non-philosophical attitude.

The problem introduced here is that of the conditions of possibility for the taking place of the *epochē*. How does the philosopher, as part of the natural world, arrive at the *moment* where the *epochē* is effected and the philosophical naïveté of the natural attitude transcended? Do we not have here, yet again, the assertion of the possibility, if not the necessity, to break free of nature so that a fully human status can be realized? Levinas, who as early as 1930 was also troubled by the status of consciousness in Husserl, puts it this way: 'How does man in the naïve attitude, immersed in the world suddenly become aware of his naïveté? Is there an act of freedom which is metaphysically important for the essence of our life?' (Levinas 1998c: 157). Being immersed in the world – or in Nature – entails, as we have proposed, the human as interior to the world and nature. The point (and Husserl is not different here to most philosophers of the modern era) is to initiate a process of exteriorization, a process understood in modernity as the initiation of language, thought and technics. Just as for Rousseau humanity was originally ensconced in Nature from whence it suffered its 'fall' into society, so, for Husserl, the naïve, natural attitude is the necessary precursor of the *epochē* as performed by a philosophy of absolute consciousness: a pure phenomenology.

What is of further note here is that for Husserl actual sciences both natural and human (with the possible exception of all fields of mathematics) can only study contingent realities and to this extent they are continuous with, or interior to, these realities. Psychology is Husserl's most quoted example of this.

Levinas on the infinite and phenomenology

With his writing just prior to the publication of *Totality and Infinity*, Levinas's focus turns to the infinite, which is the Other (Autrui) as 'absolutely exterior' (Levinas 1994: 172). The infinite is that which cannot be contained in the idea of it. It exceeds its idea. It therefore cannot also be contained within the order of the Same, which, as an object, includes social and cultural life. The infinite, Levinas says in short, 'is the radically, the absolutely other (autre)' (172). The infinite is thus one avenue (perhaps the most important) taken by Levinas in going against the prevailing philosophy which reduces the Other to a version of the Same.

Significantly, in the context of Simondon's appropriation of the pre-Socratic notion of *apeiron* as indeterminate preindividuality and the basis of individuation, Levinas refers to the same term as the precursor of the infinite in thought, 'the source of all things, enveloping and directing them all' (Levinas 1999: 60). But while Levinas argues that the infinite challenges, if not destabilizes, the order of the same not permitting individuation as a mode of identity, Simondon, as we saw, makes *apeiron* the basis of ever-new individuations. In other words, while for Simondon *apeiron* is a principle of infinite transformation open to being thought, for Levinas, qua infinite, it can never be transformed or transposed, for to do so is to render it part of the order of the Same, whereas the infinite cannot be assimilated in this way.

But even Heidegger's notions of being and Dasein, Levinas says, ultimately reduce the Other to the Same (1994: 169). Although Being is the being of beings (of Dasein), Being itself is not a being. Being includes the disclosure of the ways that Dasein is in the world. Dasein, or existence, thus comes within the purview of a philosophical revealing that is also an objectification. Certainly Dasein is never described by Heidegger as an infinity, for disclosure as aletheia – as a bringing into the light – is the basis of the most profound meaning of being. Dasein's finitude – its mortality – only serves to confirm Dasein's being in the order of the Same. Being, in other words, is fundamentally identical with itself, something that infinity does not support. Thus: 'Heideggerian philosophy marks precisely the apogee of a mode of thought where finitude does not refer to infinity' (170). Heideggerian philosophy thus marks the confidence in philosophy as thinking in the deepest sense to do justice to otherness. As Being is absolute, or a totality, there is nothing – no entity – which cannot potentially come into the light – that is, into philosophy. Levinas refers to the latter in Heidegger's thought as the Neutral because Being cannot be an entity, an individual Dasein, *a* being, or *a* point of view. 'Heideggerian ontology', says Levinas, 'subordinates the relation with the Other [l'Autre] to the relation with the Neutral, which is Being' (170). Again, he says: 'Being excludes all alterity' (1994: 213). The infinite, by contrast, is 'unassimilable alterity' and thus bypasses Being.

With regard to the ethical, as we shall see, everything turns around a certain notion of Desire: not a desire for material things, but the desire for the infinite that puts finitude in question: 'the Desirable of Desire is infinite' (215). But what is the nature of finitude in relation to Desire if not that which can be conceptualized? It is a breaking free from identity.

True experience transports us beyond Nature (1994: 165). Does this imply that, were there no Nature as such, there would be no 'beyond'? It is not possible to give a clear-cut answer to this question, mainly because the subtlety and complexity of Levinas's thought entails that there is no clear-cut Nature,[3] as in Husserl, but rather a qualified nature that is inseparable from culture – or, better, from a way of life. Moreover, if morality is the foundation, it is the foundation of culture (Levinas 2006: 38), not of Nature. While it is difficult to find evidence of a pure nature in Levinas, there, are nevertheless hints that humans must work in order to live, even if life is also, and essentially, a love of life.

No one could say that Levinasian philosophy has any direct relation to a notion of the human understood in purely biological terms. Levinas was only too well aware that biology was the basis of the National Socialist programme, which stated that only those of 'German blood' could be compatriots and that Jews could not be compatriots (see Rolland 2003: 32). In *On Escape*, first published in 1935, it is said, in effect, that need as privation cannot be the defining quality of humans, in as far as it would not affect the 'existence of the existent' (Levinas 2003: 57) or, by extension, all living creatures, although Levinas does not go so far as to say this. Thus, to interpolate, neither biology nor psychology – nor economy, for that matter – can define beings. Nor, in any case, can satisfaction eliminate a need – such as the need for food. Levinas is thus against the efficacy of need as privation in defining beings (existents): 'What gives the human condition all its importance is precisely the inadequacy of satisfaction to need' (60). Even though need here is not yet the transition to desire that evokes the infinite, it is not a matter, as Jacques Rolland says in one of his annotations to *On Escape*, of the '*quid* [what] of being but its *quomodo* [in what way]' (Rolland 2003: 86). Such would evoke, it now goes without saying, the notion of a way of life (of being) that has been the concern of this investigation.

The section in *Totality and Infinity* entitled 'Interiority and Economy' is worth revisiting. We have noted that Levinas does draw a link (briefly) between labour and subsistence, that is, labour serves to ensure *subsistence* and this is an indicator of how tenacious this notion is in European thought, given that its presence in Levinas tends to oppose the thesis that Levinas is presenting, namely that in his terms life, fundamentally, 'is *love of life*' (1969: 112; Levinas's emphasis). Or, more specifically, the subsistence view of labour quickly reverts to one where labour 'delights' or 'saddens'. Subsistence there is as evocative of

---

[3] This is where my analysis would diverge from that of Dieham, who sees nature in Levinas as the exact equivalent to a Darwinian 'struggle for life' (2000: 51).

bare life – or bare existence, in Levinas's terms – but it quickly loses its persuasive power. Instead, the human incarnates the equivalent of Bataille's general economy: 'To enjoy without utility, in pure loss, gratuitously, without referring to anything else, in pure expenditure – this is the human' (133). The essential human as proposed here, therefore, links up not only with Bataille's notion, but also with Agamben's vision of humanity as essentially 'Sabbatical' without a project in the Hegelian sense, and where the political sphere would one of 'inoperativity', an inoperativity mirroring that of God. (Agamben 2011b: 248, 250–251). Needs are what make it possible to love life; they are not what must be satisfied in order to continue to live. This is the key nuance that Levinas brings to this notion. Needs become part of the general economy of life rather than giving rise to the dominance of utility, which is what has been so often assumed. And yet, there is still animal life quite separate and distinct from human life. To all appearances, in this perspective no animal *loves* life. From this it can be concluded, too, that there is Nature, that humanity is always already separated – if it does not separate itself – from Nature and thus from animals as Nature. Animals, seemingly, do not have a face, and they do not constitute a theme in Levinas's work, as Derrida noted (Derrida 2008b: 105–118). This has led to a re-evaluation of Levinasian thought with a view to determine whether, despite all, it might give rise to animals as Other.

In this regard, Peter Atterton has argued that if Levinas's idea of the radically Other is applied to an animal, it entails that one is responsible for it (2011: 635) – responsibility being the key element of Levinas's ethics. And there is no reason as to why *an* animal cannot be radically other because, says Atterton:

> The Other is *radically* individual and not merely a specimen of a species like humanity subsumable under a common genus (*Homo*). This is why I am not able to explain the Other, for all explanations require appeal to general or common features, whereas the Other qua Other cannot be analyzed into general terms. (636; Atterton's emphasis)

For this to work, however, the question of what can be designated as the radically Other cannot be avoided, thus:

> if as Levinasians we assume that ethical responsibility is a direct response to suffering in the sufferer, then I can be responsible only *to* a being that is capable of suffering. Since, then, the capacity for suffering and enjoyment is a prerequisite for my being responsible *to* and *for* that being, only beings capable of suffering can be said to be capable of provoking a response (and responsibility) that is Levinasian. (641; Atterton's emphasis)

Atterton goes on to conclude that as there are undoubtedly animals that can express suffering there are undoubtedly animals that must be included within the ethical domain.

Be this as it may, it is clear that Levinasian thought has difficulty avoiding relying on the division between the so-called natural beings (animals) and human beings, just as it is clearly dependent on the broad division between nature and culture. This is reinforced by Atterton's quoting from an interview Levinas gave in 1986, where he was asked about whether an animal face is set apart from a human face. Levinas says: 'We understand the animal, the face of an animal, in accordance with *Dasein*. The phenomenon of the face is not in its purest form in the dog. In the dog, in the animal, there are other phenomena. For example, the force of nature is pure vitality. It is more this which characterizes the dog. But it also has a face' (1988: 169, cited in Atterton 2011: 643). 'The force of nature as pure vitality' suggests that the dog (and no doubt animals in general) are entirely circumscribed by their environment where, as we saw earlier, there is no exteriorization, only complete immanence. On this basis, it becomes difficult to conceive of an animal as being able to respond – as having any capacity for communication in the form of language.[4] Nonetheless, the issue becomes more complex when children and language are brought into the picture. Thus, in the interview already cited, Levinas remarks: 'Children are often loved for their animality. The child is not suspicious of anything. He jumps, he walks, he runs, he bites. It's delightful'. (1988: 172). Suggested here is view that children and animality are one, that children are yet to engage fully in language and other forms of exteriorization, that, furthermore, as children, all humans go through a period of being 'pure nature', of being entirely innocent, just as the lion that kills to feed itself cannot be held responsible because it is following the precepts of nature: it is thus innocent.

To be sure, what Levinas says in an interview is not necessarily the same as what appears in his published work. Indeed, one reference to the child in *Totality and Infinity* occurs in the context of paternity. There, Levinas says, evoking Isaiah 49, that the son is a stranger who 'is not only mine, for he *is* me. He is me a stranger to myself'[5] (1969: 267; Levinas's emphasis). There is ambiguity here, for what does it mean to be a stranger to oneself? Nevertheless,

---

4   Atterton, nevertheless, takes up the idea of expression as the means through which animals can communicate through the face. As a result, the gap between human and animal face is significantly narrowed.

5   This phrase, 'stranger to myself', recalls that of Julia Kristeva, who, in a more psychoanalytical mode, argues that we are all 'strangers to ourselves' ('*étrangers à nous-mêmes*') (Kristeva 1988).

it seems safe to say that 'being' the son does not here entail innocent animality; for, I, the adult, am an adult – am a father – to the extent that I have transcended all animality. As if things were not already complicated enough, Levinas says that, in the context of erotic relations, animality as play emerges: 'The face fades, and in its impersonal and expressive neutrality is prolonged, in ambiguity, into animality. The relations with the Other [autrui] are enacted in play; one plays with the Other [autrui] as with a young animal' (1969: 263). Playing with the Other is thus evocative of youthful animality, an animality that recalls that of children as referred to by Levinas in the interview. Presupposed here is the notion that one can speak about the Other as the other person (autrui) in the same terms that one uses to speak of Nature and animality. Does this not mean that the Other in eroticism *can* be captured by the discourse of the Same? Or at least it raises the question as to where exactly animality figures in Levinas's philosophy of Other (autrui).

In a text on the infinite, first published in 1957, Levinas describes Nature as that which surrounds us (la Nature qui nous entoure) (1994: 165). True experience must go beyond Nature, including human nature, even though humans feel at home and comfortable in Nature. Nature is thus there to be transcended – to be transcended in order to attain truth and the 'Absolute other' (165). Is the Nature referred to here not a radical intimacy that nullifies any form of outside – one not so different from the Nature of Rousseau? Be this as it may, an individual's 'nature' is his or her identity, easily appropriated by philosophy as the order of Same (166). Clearly, there is a close proximity between Nature, identity and the Same – the order that the radical Other (autrui) must transcend – will transcend – as infinity. We should mention here, too, the phenomenon of freedom as autonomy, for the latter is essentially implicated in the Same, where freedom is the freedom of identity. The whole of Western philosophy (la philosophie occidentale) has privileged freedom, the Same and identity – has, as we have seen, reduced the Other to the Same (166). Freedom as autonomy is also self-justifying; being like Narcissus it requires no external reference, no founding philosophical explanation other than the constitution of identity. Freedom, in short, like nature is a pure interiority. External challenges to the autonomy of the ego – anything truly Other that arises must be integrated into the order of the Same. Harking back to Descartes, the 'I think' 'will triumph when the monologue of the soul [l'âme] becomes universal, having encompassed the totality of being' (167).

As concerns the theme of animality, the face as the infinite exteriority of the Other [autrui] 'differs from the animal face', which is always localized in the

Same. While the face of the Other (autrui) expresses my responsibility for him, animality is the seat of irresponsibility – the beloved is opposed to the lover as 'an irresponsible animality which does not speak true words' (1969: 263). Moreover – and this is important in light of Levinas's characterization of the child in the interview – 'the beloved, returned to the stage of *infancy without responsibility* [...] has quit her status as a person' (263; emphasis added). It is within erotic relations that one play with the Other, as we saw, 'as with a *young animal*'. In the erotic, too, identity and identification are enacted, to the point, indeed, of there being a 'trans-substantiation' (266). In other words, a number of the elements said to be characteristic of identity and the order of the Same appear in eroticism, only to give rise to transcendence. The explanation given by Levinas for this is that as the 'simultaneity of need and desire', the erotic 'is *the equivocal* par excellence' (1969: 255; Levinas's emphasis)[6]. Moreover, although later refusing transubstantiation and fusion,[7] Levinas claims that voluptuosity, 'is simultaneously fusion and distinction' (270).

It goes without saying that innocence as pure interiority is, as we have seen in the discussion of technics, applied by Rousseau to the origin of Man and that, synchronically, the 'childhood' of Man (e.g., in the Pacific) as proposed by eighteenth-century voyagers and philosophers is life as essentially interiority (interior to Nature and the environment). By travelling in space and 'discovering' other societies, it was thought to be possible to go back in time to the origin of humanity because this origin was Nature itself. The question is: Does Nature remain the bedrock for Levinas as, in a sense, it is for the Heidegger of Parmenides' seminars, where no animal can attain to the status of pure Being – Being as aletheia? To put the question in another way: Is my responsibility to the Other to be fulfilled against a *natural* tendency to place myself first? In responding we can point to Levinas's idea that life is not purely utilitarian, but is essentially a 'love of life', as *Totality and Infinity* contends. On this basis, it is not a natural tendency towards physical self-preservation which guides existence, but rather life as a joyous engagement with the world. The philosophy of Same, a philosophy that entails a certain system of conceptualization, one that cannot accept the infinite, is the obstacle to responsibility. Moreover, we know that this philosophy cannot accept exteriorization, which transcends totality; nor can it accept the Other as

---

[6] Also, the heading for the section in *Totality and Infinity* is 'The Ambiguity of Love' (1969: 254). It is thus a matter of both 'the equivocal' and 'ambiguity' with regard to the erotic and love.

[7] Here is the passage from *Otherwise than Being* that refers to transubstantiation: 'As a substitution of one for another, as me, a man, I am not a transubstantiation, a changing from one substance into another, I do not shut myself up in another identity, I do not rest in a new avatar. A signification, proximity, saying, separation, I do not fuse with anything' (Levinas 1998a: 14).

transcendence or the subject as born 'in the beginninglessness of an anarchy', as it is said in *Otherwise than Being* (1998a: 140). It is almost as though the birth Levinas is concerned with is anything but a natural birth as defined by biology. Indeed, in *Entre Nous*, Levinas declares, 'Thought cannot be *deduced* from biological consciousness' (1998b: 16; Levinas's emphasis). Just as 'essence' (which is also finitude) is put out of play, thus preventing the reduction of entities to an origin, is Nature also put out of play? Or, is Nature an inevitable component of the philosophy of the Same from which one must always endeavour to escape – which one must surmount? Thus, we read: 'Man has overcome the elements only by surmounting this interiority' (1969: 131). Again: humanity 'gets a foothold in the elemental by a side already appropriated: a field cultivated by me, the sea in which I fish and moor my boats; the forest in which I cut wood; and these acts, all this labor, refer to the domicile. Man plunges into the elemental from the domicile, the primary appropriation' (131). Nature here is thus mediated by the domicile; but it is nonetheless Nature.

Nature, at minimum, is part of the interiority constituting the philosophy of the Same. Instead of focusing exclusively on Nature, then, it makes sense to consider the Same in more detail, specifically with regard to whether the Same must be surmounted, overcome, transcended. After all, in a world where statelessness and migration have become the norm, reducing others to the Same – homogenizing them – has become a regular occurrence.

The domicile, although favoured by Levinas, is to all appearances, interiority par excellence. Thus, the human 'is *within* [*intérieur* à] what he possesses, such that we shall be able to say that the domicile, condition for all property, renders the inner life [la vie intérieur] possible. The I is thus at home with itself' (132; Levinas's emphasis). Crucially, '[t]he interiority of immersion is not convertible into exteriority' (132). Finally: 'The element separates us from the infinite' (132). But the element also gives rise to the 'general economy', as we saw earlier. Enjoyment, then, is still an ego-state, without reference to the Other (autrui) and as if the Other were still to be encountered, as if interiority precedes exteriority, or precedes a thought 'making its way towards the outside' [une pensée qui se dirige vers le dehors] (135; translation modified). Enjoyment is sensibility is contentment and is prior to the 'finite-infinite' distinction. But, we are brought up sharply to learn that what is delineated through enjoyment and sensibility does not refer to actual individuals – individuals in the here and now. For the latter already exist in society and thus do have an idea of the infinite (139). How are we to interpret this? Does it mean, nevertheless, that actual human beings will have always *already* followed the trajectory outlined in order to 'arrive' at the social situation? Or, on the contrary, is it to be understood that a pure state of enjoyment must always be a retrospective projection, not unlike the State of Nature for the Enlightenment? In short, does the human engage in an odyssey of renouncing and overcoming interiority so as to encounter exteriority, infinity and the face of the Other (autrui)? – or is the encounter with exteriority, etc., always already possible, given that the analytical starting point must always be the social situation? If we were to take the actual sequence of Levinas's exposition as a guide, then, assuredly, it is a renouncing and an overcoming of interiority that is at stake. However, if one gives precedence to the actual argument, the human has always already arrived at the point where encountering the infinite is possible. The least that can be said is that the issue of Nature and enjoyment as a going beyond utility is central to Levinas's discussion as it is for much of modern Western philosophy. Thus, not only will an origin of sorts be smuggled in to the debate, but this origin is more likely than not to be about a natural origin that must be overcome if the human qua human is to emerge as a truly distinct form of being.

Even though the *apeiron* is said to be, in its indetermination, 'refractory to identification' (1969: 141), it is not equivalent to the infinite. It escapes things and still remains elemental.

Eventually, contentment, enjoyment and sensibility give way to something else – something that opens onto the infinite. Initially, this 'something' is a kind of shock that prompts a descent towards the interior of interiority:

> in this descent a shock must be produced which, without inverting the movement of interiorization, without breaking the thread of the interior substance, would furnish the *occasion* for a resumption of relations with exteriority. Interiority must be at the same time closed and open. The possibility of arising from the *animal condition* is assuredly thus described. (149; emphasis added to 'animal condition')

Despite strong intimations that domestic life is a *way* of life, animality, as that domain from which the human must extricate itself, is nevertheless evoked. This is to be explained, we could propose, by the fact that Nature and the animality integral to it has become so deeply embedded in Western thinking in modernity that even a thinker as subtle as Levinas succumbs to the idea of Nature as the foundation of human materiality. We find Levinas saying, a short time after referring to 'the animal condition', that, for the human, 'the happiness of enjoyment is stronger than every disquietude' and that this reveals the 'gap [décalage] between the animal and the human' (149). It is, moreover, characteristic of Levinas's phenomenological description and analysis to posit the hypothetical individual as the centre of attention, an individual that has material needs to be satisfied and happiness to be enjoyed and life to be lived over and above all animality – as if ontogenesis, rather than a way of life, were driving the analysis. Thus, just as for every human childhood, as an interiority so evocative of animality, precedes adulthood, so does every human necessarily extricate him- or herself from the 'animal condition'. But Levinas can also write: 'in reality no human need exists in the univocal state of an animal need. All needs are culturally interpreted. Only needs approached on the level of underdeveloped humanity can give this false impression of univocality' (2006: 22). Although the separation between animal and human persists, the notion of 'all human needs as culturally interpreted' clearly evokes life as a way of life. However, what is also implied by the phrase 'underdeveloped humanity'– and this is the worrying part – is that humans can be reduced to animality as a form of bare life, despite the fact that the idea of culture implies that one is never poor in the sense of being reduced to bare life, that one is never thrown back into pure Nature. Consequently, there is no avoiding it: for Levinas there *can be* an underdeveloped and thus subsistence humanity and this, even in light of our being enjoined to define 'man' 'as capable of living for the Other [autrui] and of *being* on the basis of the Other [autrui] who is exterior to him' (149; Levinas's emphasis).

Although, no doubt, the real starting point of Levinas's study on totality and infinity is infinity and exteriority (he has already expressed this in earlier writings), there is a clear attempt to move from human life as a concrete materiality – in which interiority dominates – to the human being as being for the Other (autrui) – the Other as transcendence, exteriority and infinity filtered through the face. And so even though we have an analysis of the 'dwelling' in all its tangible everydayness, it also ushers in 'intimacy' and 'gentleness' (the feminine) that opens up the separation leading to the shock revelation of the Other. It is in the context that the issue of labour is discussed. Characteristically, labour in the dwelling, incarnate in the body, initially does not evoke the infinite; it begins as an activity of pure interiority. The familiarity of the home leads to a sense of being unable to 'quit the space in which I am steeped', so powerful is the hold of interiority. So how can the Other (autrui) be revealed? That the Other needs to be revealed implies that there must be an event of the Other. It begins (does it begin – or has it always already begun?) with 'the negative moment of this *dwelling*' which tears me from my immersion in it. And so, this event 'is the relation with the Other [autrui] who welcomes me in the Home, the discreet presence of the Feminine' (170). So follows the full emergence of the absolutely

Other (autrui) as the 'epiphany of the face' as language (171). Teaching signifies the Other as exteriority and infinity because the first teaching is the teaching of ethics – not an ethics that is formulated first, then taught; but an ethics that *is* itself teaching.

The Other (autrui) is then an epiphany – a manifesting of himself or herself as Other in the midst of interiority. To manifest oneself as a face is 'to *impose oneself* above and beyond the manifested and purely phenomenal form' (200; Levinas's emphasis). Everything points towards a breaking out of interiority – the Same as interiority – even if this event has always already begun.

In *Otherwise than Being*, ambiguity remains about whether, in each individual case, an epiphany of the face and transcendence is an actual event or whether, after all, transcendence has always already taken place, that the human as the infinity of the fact of the Other (autrui) is always already 'otherwise than being'. Or, more pointedly still: What is the precise status of the Same – thus of essence, being, totality and finitude? Are they a condition of possibility of transcendence and infinity? Levinas assuredly wants to say 'no'. Finitude is not the way to the infinite, essence and totality are not necessary for transcendence. Substitution, where 'I exist through the other for the other', where I am always already responsible for others[8] – am 'hostage' to others – 'is not an act; it is a passivity inconvertible into an act' (1998a: 117). In discussing passivity, Levinas seems to be aware that something might be amiss with the idea of responsibility. For, he ponders whether ontological language might have crept into his exposition (113), so that the fulfilment or failure of responsibility would be a mode of being in the world – a mode where irresponsibility becomes the necessary hither side of responsibility. It is in this light that we read: 'Responsibility for another is not an accident that happens to a subject, but precedes essence in it, has not awaited freedom, in which a commitment to another would have been made' (114). Indeed, the very use of 'I' 'means *here I am*, answering everything for everyone' (114; Levinas's emphasis). There is thus no doubt that the intention is to avoid falling into the trap of oppositions, where each component is, symmetrically, necessary to the other, and, in this regard, we can recall that, most of all, the Other and the Same are not symmetrical, if only because the Other is Absolute.

We are left, then, to ponder the following question: Are we to think that in the very midst of the Same – in the midst of Being, in the midst of interiority – there is something which is more primordial than Being and interiority and that as such,

---

[8] This is why Levinas is so attracted to Dostoyevsky's statement in the *Brothers Karamazov* (1982), to wit: 'Each of us is guilty before everyone and for everyone, and I more than the others' (Levinas 1998a: 146). Responsibility, clearly, is the inseparable accompaniment of guilt.

responsibility, the infinity of the Other's face, exteriority and the Other in me, etc., are not to be attained but are what is interior to the human – or better: Are what always already exist in existents? If a response in the affirmative is correct, I can say that I am also in the world as described by phenomenology and that this is always my first port of call because knowledge and consciousness – including self-consciousness – are constitutive of my existence, an existence entrenched in interiority. Thus, the phenomenal world – as the world of Being and the order of the Same – *seems* to be what is fundamental because knowledge, logic and thought (including the history of thought) are the basis of consciousness and subjectivity. We might even call this the ineluctable seduction of the Being and the Same. The world thus evoked is perfectly viable: it has an origin, death is pragmatic and material, the opposition, animal–human, is perfectly appropriate to it, as is the notion of the animality of the human and the natural environment, in other words, the notion of Nature. This, then, is a world from which I would never think of exiting from or of being exterior to; for thought is the firm ally of interiority. Or, more than this: I can indeed think of existing from, or being exterior to the world, but this exiting or this exteriorization in thought still confirms interiority; for absolute exteriority, like the Absolute other cannot be thematized, that is, cannot be thought philosophically. Or again, to play on the words of the title of Levinas's book: it is not a matter of thinking otherwise, but of otherwise than thinking. But if, finally, what has been said is valid and that it is within the phenomenal world – within interiority – that transcendence (the 'beyond essence' as 'being-in-the-world' (1998a: 152)) would occur, are we to assume that the infinity of the face of the Other, etc., is *immanent* to the world of interiority? This is a crucial question, but a detailed response is beyond the scope of this chapter.

The analysis undertaken, has, however, suggested a different status for what we have broadly termed the 'phenomenological world', the world as uncovered in good part by Heidegger. In this case, the order of Same is to be, as it were, brought to account for 'absorbing' the Other (autrui) as the other person into the Same and of reducing the Other to the Same. How can one not interpret this as an event that has happened? Thus, in his essay on the infinite, Levinas writes: 'philosophy would be concerned with reducing to the Same what would oppose it as *other*' (1994: 166; Levnas's emphasis). The 'reduction of the Other to the Same' in Western philosophy (including Heidegger's) is, from the late 1950s onward, almost a mantra for Levinasian thought. Indeed, Levinas is on a mission to turn things round – to do justice to the Other (autrui) that has been hitherto deprived of justice. Of Heidegger's philosophy – the most important of the twentieth century – it is written that 'this supremacy of the Same over the Other seems to us to be integrally maintained by Heidegger's philosophy' (169). Such a supremacy of the Same is also equivalent to the stifling closure resulting from interiority and totality, an interiority and totality that becomes the central point of departure for the essay on *exteriority* that is *Totality and Infinity*.

To all appearances, therefore, a tension in Levinas's thought exists between the phenomenal world as made available by phenomenological description and the sphere evoked by all the terms that Levinas has made famous: the Other (autrui), infinity, exteriority, responsibility, the face, substitution, transcendence, etc. Our aim here, however, has not been to give a new interpretation of the *oeuvres* of phenomenology, including that of Levinas, but to show how a certain view of Nature and biological existence giving rise to bare life is firmly encrusted in the work of undeniably innovative thinkers whether this be in terms of a Nature that must be overcome, or whether it is only via phenomenological description and analysis that something entirely different is destined to arise, just as the trace would arise in a description of the everyday, where, as we noted in Chapter 1, in gestures and acting one leaves traces, whether in the putative everyday or in other contexts, one leaves traces:

> The comedy begins with our simplest gestures. They all entail an inevitable awkwardness. Reaching out my hand to pull a chair toward me, I have folded the arm of my jacket, scratched the floor, and dropped my cigarette ash. In doing what I willed to do, I did a thousand and one things I hadn't willed to do. The act was not pure; I left traces. Wiping away these traces, I left others. (Levinas 1998b: 3)

Wiping away the traces thus results in making traces.

It is worthwhile having repeated this Levinasian notion about traces because, clearly, it can be interpreted on (at least) two levels. The first is as a meta-philosophical statement about acting in the world: traces producing traces, which as traces have effects because they are irrevocable. There will always be something rather than nothing. The second level, however, would refer to the way that Levinas himself *has* left traces in wiping away traces. A rich vein of research is foreshadowed here that, for one thing, would touch on aspects of Levinas's biography – on his life. For instance, the notebooks containing poems Levinas wrote in the 1920s also show erasures of words, and despite Levinas's best efforts these words have been reconstituted in the *Oeuvres d'Emmanuel Levinas*.[9]

---

[9] The poems in question can be consulted in Levinas (2013: 296–367).

Although Levinas may only have intended his description as an example, it is clear that to take the example seriously leads to engaging with the tension between the utterance as what is uttered (énoncé or the 'said') and the utterance as an act of stating or a performative (énonciation or the 'saying'). In the latter case, Levinas's own actions leaving traces become part of the philosophical terrain. And indeed Levinas brought the everyday and philosophy together in his argument in an influential article on the trace, an article referred to by Jacques Derrida in his discussion of the trace in relation to writing in *Of Grammatology* (1976: 70).

Transcendence, then, surely, takes off from the everyday, and must in some sense overcome it, otherwise there is nothing but immanence. Levinas's writing had already tended in this direction in *Le Temps et l'autre* (1989) (*Time and the Other*), where it is said that 'our existence in the world constitutes a fundamental effort by the subject to *overcome* [surmonter] the weight it is to itself, to *overcome* its materiality, that is, to untie the knot between the self and the ego' (44; emphasis added). It is within the everyday that human animality is also extant. This is reinforced in the text just cited by the idea that the world is not, as Heidegger said, a collection of tools, but a collection of nourishments (45). Food comes before tools, in other words – food, which is necessary in order to exist. Crucially – perhaps we could even say, definitively – it is said that 'our everyday life is already a way of becoming liberated from the initial materiality through which the subject is realised' (46). Such would be the basis of a transcendence prompted by 'the eternal futurity of death' (59). Death comes; it is never assumed (61). Death *comes* – is an event – precisely because we are 'always immersed in the empirical world' (62).

Levinas goes on to say that like death, the erotic relation, too, cannot be assumed; the future comes, it is not assumed. But most of all, the face-to-face with the Other is the event which cannot be assumed. Thus, it is undoubtedly in existence assumed – equivalent to being submerged in the empirical world – that the event comes. To conclude, then, it is only because I am in the world in my animal being as a being of needs that an event can come to me, an event that would shatter my life of tranquil immanence.

The *polis* and politics

In his preface to the 1961 edition of *Totalité et infini* (*Totality and Infinity*), Levinas claims with admirable succinctness that '[p]olitics is opposed to morality, as philosophy to naïveté' (1969: 21). If we focus on politics for a moment, this can be understood in a colloquial sense to mean that, in the political sphere, unscrupulous behaviour, if it is not encouraged, is inevitable. In addition, it is only via the political sphere that war and its violence take place.

But Levinas also understands politics to be opposed to morality in a much more profound sense. This is the sense in politics participates in the order of the Same with its finite freedom is the freedom of the ego-self, a freedom reinforced by the political institutions of the State that is a denial of justice; for the latter can only be enacted in my responsibility for the Other (autrui) as a negation of my finite freedom. Politics as practised is thus anything but transcendent – which of course means, in Levinas's terms, anything but morality. Politics, too, as Levinas conceives it, privileges the universal, which is quintessentially of the order of the Same – hence the philosopher's scepticism towards 'universal' human rights. The project, also a quintessential attribute of political existence, is foreign to ethics. Most importantly, while the ethical is welcoming of the Other (autrui) as the stranger and is, on that account, a principle of hospitality, the political attitude valorizes the exclusion of strangers who are, qua strangers, essentially stateless persons. It thus becomes impossible to deal with statelessness politically – or at least it is not possible to ameliorate statelessness only through political means. Ethical responsibility must also be allowed to play a part.

Above all, though, politics, in Levinasian terms, becomes a stifling interiority where violence can potentially rule the day and egos pit themselves mercilessly against one another. And here we could ask whether politics is not the play of a human animality that calls to be transcended. Although not treating of politics directly, the closing pages of *Otherwise than Being* refer to breathing, first in its biological sense 'answering a fundamental need for energy' (1998a: 181) and then in a transcendental sense, where breathing becomes an 'opening to the other [autre] and [a] signifying to the other [autrui] its very signifyingness [signifance]', as it becomes 'transcendence in the form of an opening up' (181). The biological – the natural, interiority – is posed only to be transcended. Such seems to be the way Levinas proceeds in all his thinking. As if to confirm this interpretation, the same text pointedly asks: 'Is not the diachrony of the inspiration and expiration separated by the instant that belongs to an *animality*? Would *animality* be the openness upon the beyond essence? But perhaps *animality* is only the soul's still being short of breath' (181; emphasis added). Then human breathing 'in its everyday equality' is invoked, an invocation that opens onto references to the growth and flowing of Nature, which, says Levains, Heidegger was able to speak of as 'parousia' (182).

The *polis*, to refer to it, as the disclosedness of the being of beings in Heidegger's sense, or as the sphere of glorious words and deeds achieved by equals in Arendt's sense, are both anathema to Levinas. For it, too, reinforces the order, as we have said, of the Same as universality, the order of interiority as opposed to the exteriority of transcendence. As others have noted (see Caygill 2002 and Bernasconi 1999), Levinas does not turn his thought extensively towards analysing the nature of politics. The latter has to be gleaned – to the extent that it can be – from various indirect comments – such as the reference to Heraclitus to the effect that 'being reveals itself as war' (1969: 21). War occurs within the order of the Same – within totality. It destroys identity (21).

It could be argued that the picture evoked by assimilating war and politics is the Hobbesian one where the state of war among individuals in nature becomes in organized politics a state of war between states, which is to say the war beyond the State of Nature is institutionalized. Political society then ceases to be – as the received idea would have it – the overcoming of war as such and is instead a state of war institutionalized in a state apparatus. What this thesis implies, speculative as it might seem, is that the overcoming of (a State of) Nature as war gives rise to politics as inherently institutionalized violence, which in turn gives rise to the transcendence of political totality and the welcoming the Other (autrui) in hospitality, in ethics. Whether or not this is plausible, the presence of nature, of animality, of need in a biological sense is undeniable in Levinas's thinking.

10

Ways of Life – Not Bare Life: Being as Acting

We return now to the key idea that there is no human life that is not a *way* of life and that, consequently, living is always acting or doing in a specific way. Inspired by Giorgio Agamben's, *The Highest Poverty* (2013a) dealing with monastic rules as the institution of a form of life, and *Opus Dei* (2013b) dealing with duty as acting. In light of the means–ends rationality and abstraction, Australian Indigenous art will be considered as practices that show that abstraction always has a content and as art it is embedded in the everyday activities of the social group. It is the mechanism that makes ordinary objects and actions extraordinary. In short, here, what has often been interpreted in utilitarian terms turns out to be possessed of a certain transcendence.

Our discussion of way (or ways) of life will initially engage with Marcel Mauss's 'Techniques of the Body' (Mauss 2009) and his unfinished thesis on prayer (Mauss 2008). In the former text, Mauss begins an ethnography of the body in everyday life showing that there is no bare life. In the latter text, Mauss's focus is on Aboriginal living and acting in the context of religion and the sacred.

In relation to rule, or a model for action, it will be seen that there is no set of rules that is not also part of a way of life, just as there is no way of life that does not have a pattern or set of regularities, which may be made extant by the description of a set of rules.

When we reflect upon the idea of modernity as incarnate in secular society, a society considered to be the incarnation of Weber's means–ends rationality (zweckrationalität), the question of formalization arises. For Weber, modern bureaucratic institutions are based on formal rather than substantive criteria. However, when, for the example the origins of 'office' (= bureau) are considered in light of Agamben's genealogy of office in *Opus Dei*, it becomes clear that in the religious context, office as *officium* is what brings about a life as form, as order, a life inseparable from office as duty, and this has been taken over from the religious sphere.

The conclusion reached is that a way of life has to be understood as 'ways' of life and that what means to act in a given socio-cultural context needs to be reflected upon and analysed.

Mauss on the body and prayer

Marcel Mauss in the field of anthropology is seen by many as a pioneer in the approach to life as a way of life – the theme to be elaborated in this chapter. Thus, in 'Techniques of the Body' (2009), walking, running, marching, sleeping, eating, childbirth, sexual intercourse, climbing, coughing and spitting, swimming, washing and many more actions are all part of the great field of techniques of the body, techniques, qua techniques, that are learned – or are ways of doing – despite often being termed 'natural'.

Techniques of the body vary according to context. Notoriously, in Japan, and also in China, women's feet were bound and the resultant manner of walking referred an 'alluring gate'. With regard to walking, Mauss offers a personal 'revelation' which came to him while after he had been in hospital in New York. American nurses imitated the gait of women in the cinema. Mauss says: 'Returning to France, I noticed how common this gait was, especially in Paris' (Mauss 2009: 80). This prompts Mauss to observe that various ways of life show different styles of walking. A girl raised in a convent will walk differently to someone born into a middle-class family (cf., 80).

Again, with regard to ways of sitting, Mauss, while in the army during the First World War, noticed that Australia soldiers could rest by squatting in their haunches, whereas he, as a Frenchman, could not (84). Consequently, Mauss argues, that there is no *natural* way of walking, sitting, running, marching or of whatever 'technique' of the body we are talking about.

In the following discussion, this point will be taken as proven so that the main focus will be on the way that the natural as bare life in fact continues to have a determining effect in understanding the human–animal relation.

Thus, if Mauss has the natural implicitly in his sights in analysing techniques of the body, this is far less clear in his increasingly well-known study – derived from his unfinished doctoral thesis – *On Prayer* (2008). In attempting to study prayer in its broadest sense, Mauss says that his approach is to examine the 'elementary' and primitive instances of prayer before coming to analyse contemporary forms. Indeed, the simile Mauss uses to illustrate his method is biological: studying elementary forms of prayer is like studying single-cell organisms before moving on to the study of those that are multicelled. A clearer example of the move from simple to complex would be difficult to find. Thus, despite his methodological precautions with regard to the definition of prayer and of avoiding defining it through the prism of the researcher's own cultural lens, Mauss still adopts what amounts to a Cartesian method founded on the move from simple to complex. This has ramifications. Indeed, the focus on Australian religious practices in *On Prayer* can be explained by the method outlined: Australian practices exemplify elementary forms of prayer in elementary societies. Thus, Mauss says of Australian societies that 'we know of none that presents to the same degree incontestable signs of a primitive and elementary organization. Small, poor, sparse, technologically backward, stagnant from a moral and intellectual viewpoint with the most archaic social structures imaginable, they even help us to form a schematic view of the first human societies from which all others developed' (2008: 64). Such societies could, on this assessment, be described as close to a pure interiority (cf. 'technologically backward'), where the difference between nature and the human is minimal. Indeed, we have here a clear evocation of bare life.[1]

In primitive forms of social organization, religious rituals are of a collective type and 'linked to the totemic system' (67). Prayer, too, is thus linked to the totemic system, that is, according to Mauss, linked 'to the most archaic religious system hitherto discovered by history and ethnography' (67). Broadly, prayer is defined as 'a religions rite which bears directly on the sacred' (2008: 57) and is not 'mere incantation' (74). In the Australian context, prayer is an action or practice that involves demanding action of the god or totemic power, while, in its most highly developed form, prayer is essentially an oral rite performed by an individual. Thus, higher forms of prayer are more than a demand for the god to do something. Instead, they are, as Howard Morphy says, 'more supplicatory and increasingly form part of an abstract individual dialogue with God' (Morphy 2008: 146), although it should also be noted that for Mauss the origin of individual prayer is, as already noted, fundamentally social (see Mauss 2008: 36). Indeed, we may confirm that whatever else it is, prayer is a 'social institution' (37). Notably, in terms of Mauss's genetic method, higher types of prayer are derived from lower types (cf. 46), even if it is also recognized that flexibility of approach is important.

---

[1] In fact, Mauss seemingly rehearses the already noted eighteenth-century view that certain societies are the incarnation of the childhood of humanity, that travelling forward in space on voyages of discovery to encounter hitherto unknown societies often enables one to travel backward in time to the origin of humanity.

Agamben on the oath, ethics and acclamation

Giorgio Agamben, in *The Kingdom and the Glory* (2011b), cites Mauss's unfinished thesis with the aim of showing that it reinforces his claim that prayer, like various rituals of acclamation in relation to the sacred, not only acts on the deity so that benefits might be obtained, but the deity itself *needs* to be praised, worshipped and glorified. As a result, prayer, as a key religious rite, comes to be seen as part of a two-way process where the people who pray need the deity but the deity also needs the people, that is, it needs acclamation, praise and humility in order to exist.

Agamben's broader aim is to view the form of this religious practice as having reverberations in the domain of power and government, so that in place of the deity people call upon power for benefits, while power and the governmental machine call for – or even need – glory and acclamation in order to be what they are. Thus: 'profane acclamations are not an ornament of political power but found and justify it' (2011b: 230). Prayer can thus be convoked as illustrative of the structure of praise and acclamation in the political domain.

While Agamben is interested in appropriating Mauss's view on prayer solely for gaining an insight into the Western political structure centred on power and glory, Mauss is essentially concerned in his thesis on prayer in revealing the nature of prayer as understood in its cross-cultural evolution. In this regard, what Agamben fails to notice – or at least fails to make explicit – is that a certain conception of primitivism and thus of bare life ultimately underpins Mauss's account.

Then comes the oath as a sacrament of language in which blasphemy and the oath are symmetrical (2011a: 40). Perjury, too, is part of a symmetrical relation: 'The name of God, isolated and pronounced "in vain" corresponds symmetrically to perjury, which separates words from things' (see Agamben 2011a: 41). Agamben proposes that the oath is not only a key element in the political system of the West to the extent that it participates in the foundation of the law, but that 'the term *oath* can only be made intelligible if it is situated within a perspective in which it calls into question the very nature of man as a speaking being and a political animal' (2011a: 11). How, precisely Agamben sees the oath as integral to 'man as a speaking being' will be addressed in a moment. Now, we need to clarify how exactly bare life figures in Agamben's thesis concerning the oath.

Bare life does so in relation to the nexus that Agamben claims holds between the oath and the curse. Ultimately, the task of the oath is to ensure the relationship between words and things – and in particular, when these things are actions.

To break the oath, therefore, is to break the word–thing nexus and to open up language to profanities, or, in the case of the name of God to open the way for the deity's name to be taken in vain. The curse functions, Agamben says, 'as a genuine "sacrament of power"' (37). Bare life, as *homo sacer*, thus becomes the part excluded from the community through the sacrament of power. *Sacramentum*, as Agamben quotes Benveniste as saying, 'implies the notion of making "*sacer*"' (Benveniste 1971: 498 in Agamben 2011a: 30). Through some malediction (which, in the end, is a breaking of the oath of language) the *homo sacer* is subject to the curse, or, as Agamben puts it, to the *sacratio*[2] 'which has struck him' (38). The *sacratio* is the form of the curse which has the power to *make* '*sacer*'. The one so 'cursed' has no power to resist, in particular because, in participating in the oath – that is, in participating in language, in the space language allocates for the speaking being – one also participates in the curse, that is, agrees to be punished if one breaks the oath. As Agamben observes, '[s]cholars in fact tend to consider the curse as the very essence of the oath and therefore define the oath as a conditional curse' (30). Here, then, is bare life in one of the incarnations Agamben gives to it, an incarnation which repeats the notion that bare life is the symmetrical other of power, with the sacred man being excluded from all human intercourse. '*Sacertas*', as the production of bare life, is, indeed, to be interpreted as 'an orginary performance of power' (66). This symmetricality is also characteristic of the relation between two of Agamben's books: 'From the perspective of Agamben's oeuvre, then, we must consider *Homo Sacer* and *The Sacrament of Language* as symmetrical studies: they chart the construction of bare life from political and linguistic origins respectively' (Tell 2012: 457).

Need it be said that this notion is not identical with the biologically inspired notion of bare life operating throughout this book? As I have suggested at the outset, the asymmetry within which life *becomes homo sacer* as the asymmetrical other of power is possibly *too* perfect, the opposition just *too* neat. Be this as it may, the biologically inspired version of bare life is referred to intermittently in the *Sacrament of Language*. For the emergence of the oath as the sacralization of language is also the 'becoming human of man', or anthropogenesis where human becoming arises through its separation from animality. And if one can still talk of animal language, it then becomes the difference between human and animal

---

[2]   Of the *sacratio* Agamben writes: 'Another institution with which the oath is closely connected is the *sacratio*. The ancient sources and the majority of scholars, in fact, agree in seeing in the oath a form of *sacratio* (or *devotion*, another institution with which consecration tends to be confused). In both cases a man was rendered *sacer*, that is, consecrated to the gods and excluded from the world of men' (2011a: 29).

language, as linguists have sought to define it (cf. 2011a: 68). More specifically: 'In order for something like an oath to be able to take place, it is necessary, in fact, to be able above all to distinguish, and to articulate together in some way, life and language, actions and words – and this is precisely what the animal, for which language is still a part of its vital practice, cannot do' (69). Thus, in an interesting variation on the animal–human relation, it is not that the animal is bereft of language, as many thinkers have hitherto argued, but *how* the animal is in language. In short, the animal cannot experience language as an oath – that is, in a way in which account is taken of how actions do, or do not, correspond in language. Agamben, at the end of *The Sacrament of Language*, goes further. He refers again to the human as a 'speaking animal', which has history distinct from nature, even if this history is also 'intertwined' with it. For the human being, language is a blessing if it conforms, as we have seen to action, and is a curse if it does not. Language thus gives rise to an experience for its user of ethical proportions. Indeed, language is the condition of possibility of human ethics; it is something that cannot exist, it is implied, in the animal domain. Each time propositions such as these are proclaimed, the more the human, qua speaking being, is separated from animality, the more, as a result, the human has a specific identity attributed to it. In addition, the invocation of anthropogenesis only serves to instil even further the animal–human difference and the consequent consolidation of a certain humanism. Thus, only the human being 'must put himself at stake in his speech' (71).

In today's Western society, the oath has fallen into desuetude. The result, as Agamben sees it, is a collapse of human language into 'vain' speech, speech that testifies to the breakdown of the bond between words and things, words and actions. In a somewhat enigmatic gesture, Agamben also seems to revive the biological interpretation of bare life, which, truth be told, had never entirely disappeared from his discourse after the initial foray into *zōē* and *bios* at the beginning of *Homo Sacer* (1998). Agamben thus writes of the 'moment when all European languages seem condemned to swear in vain and when politics can only assume the form of an *oikonomia*, that is, of a governance of empty speech over *bare life*' (2011a: 72; emphasis added).

On another level, however, bare life is given short shrift in *The Kingdom and the Glory* to the extent that inoperativity liberates 'the living man from his biological or social destiny' (2011b: 251). Inoperativity is politics qua politics. It is about acting for the sake of acting, the glory of power as the truth of politics.[3]

---

[3] In Arendt's approach to politics glory, as we have mentioned, is also a key factor.

Moreover, *zōē* and *bios* 'coincide without remainder' (251). While there is no *bios* without *zōē*, there is equally and, more importantly, no *zōē* without *bios*.

Everyday life and utility

If the foregoing equations mean that there is no bare life in the biological and subsistence sense, how does it happen that the sphere of politics is also a zone of exclusion? This is the question that will subsequently be addressed. For now, however, it is important to return to where we began and reconsider the domain of everyday life that is integral to Mauss's approach to techniques of the body and other aspects of living deemed to be unique to the human.

As we have seen, what Mauss does in making the most intimate, everyday actions of the body part of education and imitation is to inscribe such actions in a way of life. Mauss is of course not alone in this. In Heidegger's philosophy of 'being-in-the-world', phenomenological descriptions are offered of everyday life – or rather, of 'everydayness'. The latter is the object of fundamental ontology: 'This decisive mode of the Being of Dasein – seen solely from the standpoint of Fundamental Ontology – we call everydayness' (Heidegger 1990: 160). To invoke fundamental ontology implies that descriptions of everydayness are not done for their own sake – as frequently happens in anthropology and psychology – but as a way of accessing the Being of beings. Thus, descriptions of everydayness in Heidegger do not simply illuminate *what* beings do, but draw out the transcendence of the doing as 'Being-in-the-world' (1990: 160). It is not a matter of simply describing 'how we use a knife and fork' (160).

In their own way, as we have already seen, Leroi-Gourhan and Levinas give descriptions that open up life as a way of life.[4] Such descriptions, even in being intentionally limited to describing actions and phenomena for their own sake, are able to break through the 'taken-for-grantedness' – or, as Heidegger describes it, the closeness that, as such is furthest, ontologically speaking – accompanying what is supposedly uniquely utilitarian. Mauss's 'Techniques of the Body' is thus an instance of how what is taken to be the utility of the everyday becomes transcendent. The minimalist existence of bare life (of life as subsistence) is also transcended. We do, however, need to go further than this. Although it is necessary, it is not enough to note the transcendence of everydayness – or, to put it another way, to note the extraordinariness of the ordinary. It is not enough

---

[4] See, for example, Chapter 8 for Leroi-Gourhan and Chapter 9 for Levinas.

either to offer more (ethnographic) descriptions of the everyday, even in cross-cultural contexts, such as that of Australian Aboriginal art, where art and life can be seen to be in a symbiotic relationship.[5] Certainly, we have here a beginning, but it is possible to go further.

Let us start with a reconsideration of 'a way of life', often taken to be equivalent to culture. What would *a* way of life in the singular be? Does it not imply that a given group, or a people, exhibits a single pattern in their activities, so that they can be identified by this way of life? Is this not a totalizing notion? Indeed, anthropological characterizations of human cultures present them as so many totalizing identities. There is a quest to find the pattern of identity when randomness or chance – for one thing – is also an indelible part of lived existence. Do we not have here a classic instance of the dominance of the Same in the characterization of human cultures?[6] Is it not clear that in order to attribute *a* way of life to a collectivity otherness must, by definition, be excluded? Not only this, but referring to *a* way of life can imply that a culture or society is not open to change because this would mean the destruction of the collective identity, there being only a single way of life that defines this identity and nothing more. Lévi-Strauss's conception of 'cold societies' evokes this idea of destruction, as such societies can only change from without (colonialism, natural and chance events), not from within, external change being equivalent to the collapse of the cultural identity of the 'cold' society. This is a society, too, based in reversible time. The 'hot' society (industrial society), by contrast, is one of irreversible time – a thermodynamic society where the loss of energy from a given system must be replenished, even if the total energy neither increases nor

[5]   Here, I could point to my own experience in September 2015 of being introduced to the Aboriginal rock art of the 'Rainbow Serpent' found just outside Cook Town in Northern Queensland. At one level, it might be thought that this rock art consists solely of designs on the walls of caves and shelters in the rock, designs that seem to be removed from actual social activity and that, for this reason could be compared to the relative separation from everyday life of Western art objects. However, in fact all significant social actions pass via the many incarnations of the Rainbow Serpent, including birth, marriage, death and ancestral communication. For example, the cave of the rock art where a child birth image is present 'legitimates' the cave as the place for childbirth.

[6]   Here, let it be noted, too, that without due precautions, what is called the 'religion' of peoples can be entirely misunderstood. The problem is to know how a secular, profane science or philosophy can do justice to religious, sacred phenomena without making a prior judgement about the scientific basis of religion or without making a prior judgement about the validity of a 'science of religions' (cf. Mauss 2008:46)? We have seen that even as sensitive an analyst as Mauss, when it comes to prayer, cannot avoid linking the form of the practice of prayer in Australian Aboriginal culture to the perceived 'primitiveness' of the material conditions. Indeed, for Mauss, the primitiveness of prayer practices – or their 'elementary' forms – correspond to the primitiveness of the material society or culture within which they are inscribed, the point being that 'higher' forms of prayer are always rooted 'in the lower type immediately preceding it' (Mauss 2008: 46). What Mauss actually refers to are elementary forms of social life from which, as he sees it, elementary forms of prayer arise (cf. 2008: 64), not elementary forms of prayer as such.

decreases (see Charbonnier 1973: 32–42). These characterizations are clearly homogenizing.

We need, therefore, to work towards a more subtle conception of 'way of life'. The concept of a way of life needs to evoke ways of acting and doing. A way of life is perhaps not unlike a *habitus* in Pierre Bourdieu's sense, or style in Agamben's sense, where neither of these concepts function as a predictor of the actions that might occur within their auspices. Moreover, actions might well exceed an existing *habitus* or style giving rise to a totally new framework. Indeed, just as a truly unique work of art cannot, qua unique, be integrated easily, if at all, into the framework of 'art in general', such might equally be the case with regard to society as a whole as concerns terms such as *habitus* and 'style'. The latter are at best approximations.[7]

Furthermore, the issues of hospitality, of responsibility and relations with others move the centre of gravity towards a more dynamic form of existence for a given collectivity. Resistance – hostility – to the external world itself can initiate change. Unless a group were isolated in an exceptional sense, a total absence of an impetus for change is impossible. Chance alone would seem to entail that things could rarely remain the same. But total isolation can only ever be hypothetical; a totally traditional society, a society that was a pure interiority, can, as Rousseau's discourse showed, only ever be hypothetical. For as soon as a people is known about, empirically, its isolation is at an end. Moreover, it is well nigh impossible that a circumscribed community would not have an 'other' – an 'outside' – against which it constituted itself. Indeed, a sense of tradition, of communal identity, or of totality, entails that there *is* an outside. Identity entails difference; sameness entails otherness; interiority entails exteriority.

From what has been said, it follows that 'way' of life should be understood as 'ways' of life, that there is no simple way of life, that ways of life are complex, that within a so-called way of life, there will be ways of life. Such complexity is evoked by the French term, 'hôte', which is effectively untranslatable as it means 'host' *and* 'guest', so that, as Derrida points out, 'the inviting and welcoming host [hôte] becomes the guest [l'invité] of his guest [de son invité]' (Derrida 1999: 118). As Derrida's suggests, this is indicative of the fact that there is never a pure interiority (of the host) perfectly turned in on itself. Language, which is the precondition of being a host, is exteriorizing. My language is also always the 'other's' language. In this sense, the notion of a 'maternal' language is misleading.

---

7 Evoked here, too, is Levinas's claim that the order of the Same – the order of generality – has reduced the Other to a version of itself.

What is more, the other always 'has' language. This is a key point in relation to stateless people reduced to bare life. There is never bare life, if only for the fact that there is language and all that it makes possible: symbolic and imaginary realms, including religious symbols, words and iconography.

As Matthew Abbott says, in referring to Agamben's essay, 'Form-of-Life' (Agamben 2000: 3–12), which echoes the syntagm, 'ways-of-life' developed here:

> Form-of-life is unrepresentable (for it disrupts predicative logic) and yet intelligible (for we can get to know it, recognise it, and fall in love with it); it is a figure of pure equality (for it is impossible to judge or place in any hierarchy) that does not sublate difference (for it is singular, absolutely unrepeatable). (2012: 29)[8]

This reiterates the point that 'ways-of-life' are effectively emergent. They are not the result of conformity to a pre-existing plan or model, the latter also being typical of the hylomorphism against which Simondon pitches his thinking. We are then always dealing in ethnography with acts, often made up of actions, of doing.

Agamben himself has attempted to instantiate his idea of 'form-of-life' in texts that analyse monastic life and the liturgy in the history of Christianity – life as, in his words, a 'form-of-life' (see Agamben: 2013a and 2013b). Thus, in *The Highest Poverty* (2013a), Agamben writes that 'the "sacred habit" is something more than "the holy clothes", because it expresses the way of life of which they are the symbol' (2013a: 15). Moreover, a link can be made between the monk's habit and a *habitus* as a way of life: 'To inhabit together thus meant for the monks to share not simply a place or style of dress, but first of all a *habitus*. The monk is in this sense a man who lives in the mode of "inhabiting" according to a rule and a form of life' (2013a: 16). 'Rule' and 'form of life' become interchangeable, so that whether life is formed by system of rules or rules are the result of a form of life becomes indeterminate.

The liturgy, which is also addressed in *The Highest Poverty*, is treated in more detail in *Opus Dei* (2013b). Liturgy is found to be inseparable from office as duty.

---

[8] Although the tenor of Abbott's essay evokes the key idea – that there is no bare life – developed in this study, there is a difference. Thus, he says: 'Bare life, like pure being, can never exist (has never existed). But this is not to say that it plays no role in ontic politics' (Abbott 2012: 27). The difference from what I am doing is that Abbott endeavours to show that Agamben is working within a political ontology paradigm indebted to Heidegger. And this may well be true. However, in approaching bare life ontologically, rather than revealing the secret of Agamben's thought, one runs the risk of forgetting some of the consequences of Heideggerian ontology as brought out by Levinas as well as Heidegger's very definite equating of the *polis* uniquely with the unconcealedness of beings in their being, which, as we have seen (cf. Chapter 6), results in animality (or what is defined as such) being excluded from the *polis*. In short, the human becomes the equivalent of the exclusion of animality.

In particular, the following principle is made explicit in Agamben's archaeology of office: I am what/how I do/act and I do/act according to what I am. Thus: 'The priest must carry out his office insofar as he is a priest and he is a priest insofar as he carries out his office' (87). Note, too, the *opus operatum*, the work effected regardless of who administers is characteristic of the liturgy. But then the impact of the liturgy cannot fail to have consequences for the one administering it. Gradually, in the period of early Christianity to the time of Aquinas (thirteenth century) and beyond, the distinction between *opus operatum* (action in its effectiveness) and *opus operans* (the one who acts – the priest) is diminished insofar as the latter is determined by the office, which comes to be understood as the *duty* of office. Hence, the point previously noted where priest and office coincide.

Consequently, if rules evoke a form or way of life, it is not in the sense that they function as a blueprint or model to be followed. Or in Agamben's words: 'The form is not a norm imposed on life, but a living [in the case of monastic life] that in following the life of Christ gives itself a form' (2013a: 105). Thus, to reiterate, no distinction can be made between life and way of life, which also means that there cannot be a life that is bare existence, a life without any form, a life distinct from a way of life.

It is, however, within a strictly religious context that Agamben has confirmed most decisively the principle of 'form-of-life' enunciated some time before the present studies.[9] How appropriate is it, one might ask, to draw analogies with the putatively secular world of modernity? In this regard, the whole idea of 'office' and the notion of 'duties of office' have undeniably filtered through into modern industrial society. Max Weber's theory of bureaucracy as 'rule by office' confirms that 'office' has been taken over from its more explicitly religious precursor (see Weber 1970: 196–204). Regarding the 'official', Weber says, inter alia: 'Office holding is a "vocation" [...] Furthermore, the position of the official is in the nature of a *duty*' (198–199; emphasis added). If there is a sense of duty, there is also a sense of loyalty – not to any person or persons, but to 'impersonal and functional purposes' (199). From this we could conclude that despite the fact that officials are appointed on the basis of formal qualifications and for a salary, there is nevertheless an ethics of office conduct that can be made explicit by deontology. In other words, strictly formal, functional actions of an office can only be instituted up to a certain point, especially at the higher levels of bureaucracy. Rules cannot be mechanically enforced in any absolute sense,

---

[9] This text, 'Form-of-Life', was first written in the early 1990s and is dated '1993'.

which is to say that ethical conduct must be part of every official's character if bureaucracy is to operate efficiently and justly. Scandal occurs when ethical conduct breaks down.

Moreover, Weber, as we have seen uses the term 'vocation' (Beruf) to describe the job of the official with all the elements of the Christian heritage of 'calling' – that is, being called to the service of God – that this evokes. Thus, vocation refers to the inner voice that calls one to service regardless of the material arrangements that might pertain. Consequently, what Weber sees as *the* distinguishing feature of modern capitalist societies – the office and its official acting out of a sense of duty – clearly has a religious genealogy.

Of course, the distinction between a public and private self characteristic of modern secular existence suggests that the official's status contrasts radically with priest's in the liturgy. Indeed, in the latter case there appears to be a complete fluidity between the public and private self that does not pertain in the case of the official. For the official, it is in part a matter of keeping his or her private beliefs and concerns out of view in the performance of the duties of office. Such is the basis of the deontology of bureaucracy. In this sense, the academic teacher is – or should be, Weber contends – like a bureaucrat. Thus, in 'Science as a Vocation', Weber says, the duty of an academic teacher is to respect the distinction between 'fact' and 'value' and not 'imprint' upon his students 'his personal political views' (1970: 146). Equally, it would be wrong in Weber's eyes for religious views to be imprinted on students.[10]

In the religious context of monastic life and its rules or in the case of *Opus Dei* and the liturgy, life and way of life become one. In the secular society that succeeds the religiously based social arrangements of the pre-modern era, bare life comes strongly to the fore and rules, or the law determines life; necessity becomes the precursor to freedom and a way of life. Subsistence must be overcome before culture can truly arise. On this basis, bureaucracy becomes a fundamentally utilitarian set up, governed by the instrumentalism of means–ends rationality (zweckrationalität). Furthermore, just as modern bureaucracy is unthinkable without a highly developed money economy, so there is a division of labour in bureaucracy, just as there is in the broader economy, the implication being that one works above all else to earn money. This to be sure is an old story.

---

[10] It is worth mentioning in passing that the fact–value distinction has come in for much criticism (e.g., see Latour 2004: 95–102). Let it be said here, as Weber also admits, that adhering to the distinction is, at least in good part, based on value, so that, at this level, fact and value flow into each other. Or, as Latour says, 'respect for matters of fact appears essential to the *deontology* of scientists' (96; emphasis added).

However, three things render this thesis problematic. The first is that the deontological aspect of official's holding office blurs the distinction between private morality and public performance, for the demonstrated ability to keep one's private views private or to resist exploiting the vulnerable when in a position of power can be seen to be ethically admirable in itself. Referring to the academic, Weber says: 'one cannot demonstrate scientifically what the duty of an academic teacher is. One can only demand that the teacher have the intellectual integrity to see that it is one thing to state facts […] while it is another thing to answer questions of the *value* of culture' (Weber 1970: 146; Weber's emphasis) and to tell people, Weber goes on, how they should act culturally or politically. Could one find a clearer case of where the 'duty of office' forms the academic teacher as much as the same academic is suitable for the office? In short, an academic teacher is so to the extent that he performs the duties of the office of being an academic teacher. And he will perform the duties of office to the extent that he is an academic teacher. In a religious context, this has been called, as we have seen, the blurring of the distinction between life and way of life. In the professions (medical, legal, pedagogical, etc.) where a deontological dimension is made quite explicit, but also in other work areas where hierarchy governs relations between workers, or where veridical integrity is crucial, such as is the case of journalism,[11] life and way of life become indistinct. This is not to say that a denial of this indistinction is not also part of the social reality characteristic of modern, capitalist societies.

It is significant to note that the bureaucratic form of administration, although perfected to a high degree in modern societies based on a capitalist market economy, is not exclusive to the latter. As Weber points out, historical precedents are to be found in Ancient Egypt, in Roman and Byzantine political and religious structures, in the Catholic Church at the end of the thirteenth century and in China. In particular, Weber points to the fact that bureaucratic administration is necessary to meet the needs of empire and a standing army (Weber 1970: 204). As this historical, comparative view makes clear, modern bureaucracy, despite its ostensibly formal and calculative basis, is nonetheless culturally specific. Indeed, only by beginning completely afresh in the construction of bureaucratic institutions – as in the most thoroughgoing of revolutions, which to date remain entirely hypothetical – could there be

---

[11] On 16 December 1991, in France a faked interview with Fidel Castro by the journalist Oliver Poivre-d'Avor went to air. The fraud was exposed by *Télérama* journalist Pierre Carle. The point here is that integrity with regard to truth is a key element of journalists' deontology, given, in particular, that opportunities for fraud are frequent in this profession.

anything like a bureaucratic formation that was culturally neutral without any character of its own. Because Weber and other thinkers have argued that there is clearly an element of cultural and for that matter political neutrality in modern bureaucratic forms, it is often taken as read that this is the case across the board, while in fact it is not at all the case. The development and refinement of the writing of history, which includes philosophy as the history of philosophy, only serve to reinforce the distinctiveness of modern culture as a reworking of the past. Even though it might seem that pure labour power and the division of labour that this presupposes are bereft of culture as a way of life, the context in which it is realized (the coal mine, the Northern-England factory, the steam transport system) is not neutral. To evoke Bernard Stiegler's notion of 'de-contextualisation', it can be argued that the latter only ever takes place up to a certain point and that numerous cultural indices always remain, thus confirming life as a way – or as ways – of life.

Weber refers to the market as being, like bureaucracy, based on formal, rational principles of calculability and 'impersonality', principles both enacted and symbolized by the refinement of money in the economy and accompanied by contractual freedom (Weber 1970: 192). Because the focus in the market is, according to Weber's influential view, on the commodity to the exclusion of all else, 'there are', he says, 'no obligations of brotherliness or reverence, and none of those spontaneous human relations that grow out of intimate personal community' (192). But what Weber tends not to thematize in any extended way are the implications of the notions, also specific to the market, of scarcity, efficiency and utility in relation to necessity or subsistence, notions already analysed above in Chapter 2 in the context of modern consumer society. Instead, Weber resists making any judgement with regard to the foundation of economically oriented social action. It is nevertheless possible to conclude, on the basis of statements made in relation to his definition of certain concepts related to social action, that Weber accepts the basic assumptions of economic theory, namely, that scarcity entails that, with regard to the distribution of resources, a choice must be made;[12] that the 'technical question' is fundamentally about efficiency (= minimum input for maximum output[13]) and that subsistence, referring to the minimum

---

[12] Thus, in Weber (1964) we read: 'If anything, the most essential aspect of economic action for practical purposes is the prudent choice between alternative ends. The choice is, however, oriented to the *scarcity* of the means which are available' (160; emphasis added). Again: it is a question 'of asking what would be the effect on the satisfaction of other wants if this particular means were not used for the satisfaction of one given want' (162).

[13] See Weber (1964: 161).

of resources necessary to sustain bare life, can apply to certain economic units.[14] Thus, Weber's formalism, as discussions in the scholarly literature show, is only successful up to a point.

Formalism and abstraction

Taken to its purest point, formalism implies a complete decontextualization of practices, which, as a consequence can be enacted without regard to time, place or purpose whether this be religious or otherwise. Formalism in the artistic sphere would go hand in hand with abstraction qua pure form. In Weber's terms, formalism overcomes substantive rationality (wertrationalität), as exemplified by religious practice. It also privileges quantification over the qualitative as related to value. It is thus in harmony with a biological definition of life – of life, ultimately, as bare life. Formally understood, life here is not 'ways of life'. A kind of substantive rationality as a rationality of ends, not of means, and of content rather than form is to be found in ways of life; for there can never be a *purely* formal, instrumental rationality that excludes the quasi-substantivism of ways of life.

We know, though, that according to Weber and the received idea, modern industrial society exemplifies the separation of formal and substantive rationality to the nth degree. Formal rationality, decontextualization and the transformation of art into an art object that, qua object, can be made available in the art market, seem to characterize the domain of art in the modern era. However, there are also artworks which problematize this.

Looked at externally, certain forms of contemporary Indigenous Australian art (e.g., the dot and line paintings of Papunya Tula artists of the Western Desert)[15] appear to be highly abstract, to be appreciated more for their form rather than for their content. And, indeed, many works are produced in a slightly modified, secular form for the market. But such works, in their original version, have a substantive, religious aspect and evoke the Dreaming. Their quasi-geometrical nature is no impediment to the evocation of a narrative and the precedence of

---

[14] Cf.: 'in cases of relative impoverishment in *means of subsistence,* as determined by a given standard of living and of the distribution of economic advantages, there have been wide variations' (1964: 167; emphasis added). Although it seems here that Weber attributes a relative meaning to subsistence existence, this goes against the commonly accepted meaning. Also, Weber refers to 'The chronic scarcity of the means of subsistence in the Arabian desert' (167).

[15] For examples of this art, see Perkins and Fink (2001).

content over form. Or rather, we could say – in order to avoid a hylomorphic interpretation where form is supposedly prior to content (where content 'fills' form) – that there is no impediment to the indistinguishability of form and content. The 'pattern' often being reproduced in a variety of contexts – on bodies or in the sand – is another important aspect of this art, one that renders many renditions transitory and susceptible of erasure. In short, the work ceases to have a strictly 'object' status and thus becomes a partial instantiation of a way of life.

Again, it is often thought, following Weber, that art is removed from the mainstream of living and that it is now part of a sphere of (high) culture, a sphere that people only enter occasionally. Abstract or non-figurative art would be exemplary of the way all art, but particularly abstract art, is removed from the ordinariness of everyday life in relation to which artworks would be extraordinary. Once one expands the notion of art to include craft activity and have it defined as the realm of aesthetics then all of living can be incorporated into art, recalling with Deleuze that the instantiation of artworks, including abstract artworks, are the harbingers of sensation.[16] However, even though the notions of sensation and affect in relation to art are insightful, they tend to be so from a subjective, if not a subjectivist, point of view. Also, abstract art – as, say, exemplified by abstract expressionism – is never *simply* formal – never simply an abstract form, if by this is meant that the form is significant to the exclusion of content. What is called abstract always in fact includes a content – be it colour, shapes, pattern. Even the idea that abstraction is non-figurative is open to question because it is assumed that figurative means the representation of a complete human or natural figure. Yves Klein's International Klein Blue would thus be non-figurative in this sense. But absolute abstraction – a purely formal entity without content – would also be without incarnation. In short, it could not appear. Such is not at all the case with International Klein Blue, which has always had an incarnation, most notably on the bodies of models, then on paper, in the 'Anthropométrie de l'époque bleue' (Klein 1960). But anything from sponges to plaster casts and dinner plates as well as canvases could serve this purpose. International Klein Blue – to subvert the usual cliché – is the *figure* of blue.

Design, architectural structures of all kinds, fashion, cuisine and even sexual conduct can be incorporated into the domain of art, a point that has already been made.[17] Even Weber acknowledges that instrumental rationality is characteristic

---

[16] See Deleuze (2003). Recall here that the origin of 'aesthetic' is found in the Greek, 'aisthesis', meaning sensation.

[17] See, for example, Featherstone (2000 and 2007).

of *Western* culture and differentiates the latter from other cultures. Moreover, he points out that decimal numbers were invented in India even if the implications of decimals for arithmetic were not pursued (see Weber 2001: xl). Speaking rigorously, therefore, we are forced to conclude that there are no *purely* formal or *purely* abstract phenomena.

Formalism and contradiction

If, albeit from a non-specialist's point of view, we consider for a moment the treatment of formalism in the philosophy of mathematics, it seems clear that a key issue has been about contradiction. A strictly formal system would be one where there is no contradiction. In his very accessible paper on three famous approaches to establishing a valid foundation for mathematics – namely, Logicism, with the work of Russell and Whitehead; Intuitionism, with the work of Brouver; and Formalism proper, with Hilbert's theory – Ernst Snapper (1979) shows that none of these approaches in philosophy dealing with the foundations of Mathematics has been able to eliminate contradiction. Hilbert had realized quite rightly that 'formalization is the proper technique to tackle foundational questions' (1979: 214). However, spectacularly, Kurt Gödel, in 1931, showed 'that formalization cannot be considered as a mathematical technique by means of which one can prove that mathematics is free of contradiction' (214–215).

As is now known, contradiction is an instance of the excluded middle (or the excluded third) characterized by 'either/or': thus, to avoid contradiction, either p or not p (p¬p) (disjunction) must be the case, not both p and not p (p ∧¬p) (both/and (conjunction)). This in fact has been the focus of much of Jacques Derrida's philosophy,[18] which has raised the question of the problematic notion of purity at every turn, as well as that of Michel Serres, who has pointed out that 'the middle', or third place is essentially that of education, of communication (Hermes) as mediation, of scientific objectification; but it also the place of exclusion (see Serres 1991: 78–79, 81). However, the *place* of science itself does not figure in science, or mathematics. Were it to do so, the objectivity of science would be put in question. So, science excludes the third absolutely even though it is the condition of its possibility.

---

[18] Focusing on the notion of undecidability, David Bates (2005) places Derrida's philosophy within the broader historical context (especially that of the interwar era) of mathematicians, biologists and historians of science (c.f. Canguilhem) that showed the inherent instability of all instantiated, formal systems. Systems theory, for example, would emerge out of this context.

No formalization is therefore possible without leaving traces related to the exclusion to the third element.[19] On this basis, formalization, based in the law of contradiction, is not just a mode of organization or ordering, but is also a practice with political implications, albeit often indirect. The stateless person, as a person without a formal civil identity – as an 'anomaly' – is neither 'friend' nor 'enemy', to use Carl Schmitt's terms. This is why Hannah Arendt could write:

> Since he was the anomaly for whom the general law did not provide, it was better for him to become an anomaly for which it did provide, that of the criminal.
>
> The best criterion by which to decide whether someone has been forced outside the pale of the law is to ask if he would benefit by committing a crime. If a small burglary is likely to improve his legal position, at least temporarily, one may be sure that he has been deprived of human rights. (Arendt 1968: 166)

Once deprived of civil identity, that is, once deprived of what often were thought to be the formal accoutrements of humanness, no evocation of a way of life, such as language, kin relations, symbolic practices, would suffice to prevent the fall into a perception of animality. Or, as in the oft-quoted line from Arendt: 'Only the loss of a polity itself expels [the human] from humanity' (1968: 177). This is because, to be included in the *polity* entails having a formal status – most often, that of citizen – something stateless people lack, as do the members groups supposedly reduced to subsistence life – life as bare life.

The citizen – the person with formal rights and duties – is a public figure, as are bureaucracy, parties and the institutions of government. 'Citizen' is thus an element of the public part of the public–private opposition. Weber's theory of means–ends rationality is essentially a public phenomenon. However, the idea of ways of life is neither entirely public nor private. Ways of life are just not reducible to one or other pole of this opposition. Indeed, in relation to the latter, ways of life are the excluded third element that rarely appears as such despite being the basis of the living – a living not reducible to formalization. It is living as action, much as liturgy is action:

> Action as liturgy, and the latter as a circular relation between being and praxis, between being and having-to-be: this is the disquieting inheritance that modernity, from the moment it put duty and office at the center of its ethics and its politics, has more or less consciously accepted without the benefit of an inventory. (Agamben 2013b: 88)

---

[19] Serres suggests that the exclusion of the Third also takes on incarnations in, for example, the idea of the Third World, or the 'third person' in a conversation, or as the other as enemy third party excluded from the community (see Serres 1991: 82–85).

More broadly, liturgy also opens onto the notion that styles of action and the gestures of living, as Agamben might say, are what render ways of life perceptible if one has the eyes to see. Such seeing would confirm the fallaciousness of the idea of bare life.

Conclusion

In liturgy, Agamben says, 'being and acting enter into a threshold of undecidedability' (2013b: 63). Another way of putting this is to say that being and acting cannot be formalized precisely because they are the equivalent of the excluded middle – the fact of conjunction, of 'both/and'. This is also evocative of the 'logic' of carnival as Kristeva theorized it (see Lechte 1990: 108–109), which is not a logic of true or false (0–1, p or not p), but a conjunctive logic of both/and: there is no excluded middle. The living of life as a way of life is living 'in the middle' – in the milieu. Through the trajectory of this chapter, we have arrived at the point where the externalization of life is absolute. Or rather there is no interiority – no secret enclave – that is not eminently susceptible to externalization. A way of life is indeed inseparable from externalisation.

Mauss has contributed to the rich ethnographies that provide material showing that the so-called everyday life is in fact life, in its gesture, style, design, praxis and ceremony (going to the toilet can indeed be ceremonial – or the opposite (see V.S. Naipaul!), life as extraordinary. But the chapter has endeavoured to go further than this in order to show, in light of Agamben's insight, that a way of life is not a life that follows an already-formulated rule, but one in which rule and action, or praxis as a given orientation in the world, become indistinguishable: life follows rules, but rules are the outcome of acting.

While, on the one hand, ethnographies (c.f. those of Mauss and Lévi-Strauss) have been able to reveal ways of life, this, on the other hand, has often been achieved on the basis of a theory of the evolution of societies, an evolution that entails an explicit or implied trajectory that moves from primitiveness (animality, subsistence existence) to civilization (European society), or, in the case of Lévi-Strauss, from 'cold' societies that resist change to 'hot' societies, where change is structural and essential.

Even if secularization or disenchantment, to use Weber's term, is deemed to point to the essential nature of modern society based in 'means–ends' rationality (zweckrationalität), an investigation inspired by Agamben's work shows that acclamation, deriving from the supposedly uniquely utilitarian sphere of the *oikos*, and now incarnate in the mass media is the necessary complement to power. In addition, abstract, non-figurative art, whether exemplified within a Euro-American or Australian Aboriginal frame, is never separable from content. It is never, in other words, a pure form, as a strictly formalist analysis would have it.

But perhaps even more importantly, a study of the nature of formalization in, for example, the philosophy of mathematics shows that the principle of the excluded middle upon which formalization is based is inapplicable when it is a matter of ways of life. The conjunctive nature of carnival logic, based on 'both/ and' rather than on 'either/or', is the logic applicable to ways of life. And, indeed, in the so-called society of disenchantment, it is still essentially a matter of *ways of life* not, ultimately – as so often implied – a matter of bare life.

What of the Arendtian distinctions between *oikos* and *polis*, necessity and freedom, private and public, human and citizen? Here, a binary logic evokes, in the first instance, 'a dark background of mere givenness, the background', says Arendt, 'formed by our unchangeable and unique nature' (Arendt 1968: 181). This, we could say, indicates Arendt's assumption that pure nature underpins the *polis* and society, and that nature, as akin to the striving to overcome necessity, is the condition of possibility of the *polis*. Societies can therefore be assessed on the basis of the extent to which they have solved the problem of necessity and created as a result a political community, or *polis* characterized by word (artifice) and deed and the quest for glory. What this binary logic conceals is that there is no 'givenness' or necessity – there is no nature that is not essentially a way of life. A particular way – or ways – of life create the *polis*. Or at least it would do if it made sense to speak of politics as delineated in a *polis*. This approach to politics is, as we have said, founded on inclusion and exclusion, implying that the political is not a description – is not a political sociology – of the conflictual nature of the human condition that could be resolved or managed through politics, but is an achievement of certain societies. 'Savage' societies, because they are frequently deemed to be subsistence societies, can be defined on this basis as those lacking a *polis* (see Arendt 1968: 180–182).[20]

Historically, subsistence, as a struggle for survival, and primitiveness, described by Mauss in relation to religion as elementary – that is, religion, if not at its origin, 'at least in its earliest infant cries' (Mauss 2008: 25) – these two features became the focus for external intervention by missionaries,

---

[20] In short, Arendt, like many political theorists, accepts the presuppositions of 'classical' economic anthropology (referred to in the Introduction to this work), where subsistence means: incessantly working to prevent starvation and to ensure survival.

administrators and, at its height, by European colonial powers. 'Savage' societies did not have religion properly speaking, so they had to be given one; they had no genuine economy that would give rise to a surplus, so they had to be changed to allow this to happen; they had no politics, no state apparatus, no real art, so conditions had to be created where a local version of the European state and culture could emerge. In other words, once defined negatively as bare life, genuine life (= economy, religion, culture) – a genuine way of life – had to be brought in from the outside.[21] Such intervention would of course also and in particular be necessary if the 'right to have rights' – the key Arendtian principle – were to be realized in 'savage' societies. All of which serves to demonstrate how a negative view of the society of the 'other' is concomitant with making such societies the object of external intervention, one indistinguishable from paternalism.

As has been said on many occasions throughout this book, the relationship between humanity and animality is fundamental when thinking the human. As a reminder of a European vision on the primitive as animal, Pierre Clastres evokes the point made in Lévi-Strauss's *Race and History*, where, in relation to the Spanish intervention in Mexico, the indigenous peoples asked whether the Spaniards were gods or men, while the Europeans asked whether the natives were human or animal (Clastres 1980: 49). We know that to ask whether a people is human or animal is, by implication, to ask whether they have evolved beyond subsistence existence and whether they have religion and political community – that is, whether they have evolved beyond their essence in bare life. What this book has been able to show is that animality has haunted, and doubtless still haunts, a view of the human in philosophy, theories of technology, political theory and anthropology, to the point where animality as bare life is the explicit or implicit origin of humanity. Even though it is true that the range of thinkers canvassed here is far from exhaustive, those whose texts are analysed are strategically important for showing the origins of humanity in animality. Such texts (recall of those of Hegel and Schelling, for instance) do not think for one moment that it is a matter of thinking the animal as in any way participating in transcendence, that is, in being able to communicate, think or respond (c.f. Derrida 2008b).

What is the connection – if there is one – between bare life and people as stateless? Agamben has argued that it is the stateless person that, today, is the incarnation of bare life. One aspect of Agamben's argument here is that bare life

---

[21] The intervention into Australian Indigenous culture, first by the British colonial administration and subsequently by Australian governments, is exemplary here.

concerns the asymmetry of power relations. As bare life, the stateless are the equivalent of *homo sacer* – the being totally bereft of power, who, as the complete counterpoint to the absolute power of the sovereign, may be killed (or allowed to die?) without this being a crime.

The question that this raises is whether such an asymmetry is entirely plausible. Stateless people are, after all those still possessed – and essentially so today – of language and cultural memories and practices. And, in any case, can there be an absolute sovereignty today? Certainly, if one is referring to nation states, it seems more appropriate to speak of 'sovereignties'. But of course with the pluralizing and thus divisibility of sovereignty comes a diminution of power. The only context in which Agamben's theory would be plausible is if there were an absolute sovereign as the basis of international law.

A more convincing way to proceed in relation to stateless people is to challenge the assumption that lack of citizenship or any of the formal accoutrements of social and political life, means those concerned are the equivalent of bare life – as though, indeed, they lacked language and a cultural heritage, as though they lacked any signs of or did not in any manifest a way of life.

Consequently, we need to break through the hold that bare life has on defining the human. For in so doing, beings (humans and animals) might experience a taste of genuine freedom.

References

Abbott, Mathew (2012) 'No Life Is Bare, the Ordinary Is Exceptional: Giorgio Agamben and the Question of Political Ontology', *Parrhesia*, 14: 23–36.

Agamben, Giorgio (1998) *Homo Sacer: Sovereign Power and Bare Life*, trans. Daniel-Heller-Roazen, Stanford: Stanford University Press.

Agamben, Giorgio (1999) *Potentialities: Collected Essays in Philosophy*, trans. Daniel Helle-Roazen, Stanford: Stanford University Press.

Agamben, Giorgio (2000) *Means Without End: Notes on Politics*, trans. Vincenzo Binetti and Cesare Casarino, Minneapolis and London: University of Minnesota Press.

Agamben, Giorgio (2004) *The Open: Man and Animal*, trans. K. Attel, Stanford: Stanford University Press.

Agamben, Giorgio (2011a) *The Sacrament of Language: An Archaeology of the Oath*, trans. Adam Kotsko, Stanford: Stanford University Press.

Agamben, Giorgio (2011b) *The Kingdom and the Glory. For a Theological Genealogy of Economy and Government* (Homo Sacer *II, 2*), trans. L. Chiesa, Stanford: Stanford University Press.

Agamben, Giorgio (2013a) *The Highest Poverty: Monastic Rules and Form-of-Life*, trans. A. Kotsko, Stanford: Stanford University Press.

Agamben, Giorgio (2013b) Opus Dei: *An Archaeology of Duty*, trans. Adam Kotsko, Stanford: Stanford University Press.

Arendt, Hannah (1958) *The Human Condition*, Chicago, London: The University of Chicago Press.

Arendt, Hannah (1960) 'Freedom and Politics: A Lecture', *Chicago Review*, 14(1): 28–46.

Arendt, Hannah (1968 [1951]) *The Origins of Totalitarianism. Part Two*, San Diego, New York, London: Harvest/HBJ.

Arendt, Hannah (1970 [1969]) *On Violence*, San Diego, New York, London: Harvest/HBJ.

Arendt, Hannah (1982) *Lectures on Kant's Political Philosophy*, Brighton: The Harvester Press.

Arendt, Hannah (1990) 'Philosophy and Politics', *Social Research*, 57(1): 73–103.

Aristotle (1995) 'Politics' in Jonathan Barnes (ed.), *The Complete Works of Aristotle. The Revised Oxford Translation*, Volume Two, Princeton: Princeton University Press.

Arnould-Bloomfield, Elisabeth (2012) De « L'Aspect » au Sacrifice: L'Animal dans les Premiers Textes de Georges Bataille, *Contemporary French and Francophone Studies*, 16(4): 497–505.

Atterton, Peter (2011) 'Levinas and Our Moral Responsibility Toward Other Animals', *Inquiry*, 54(6): 633–649.

Balibar, Étienne (2004) 'Is a Philosophy of Human Civic Rights Possible? New Reflections on Equaliberty', *The South Atlantic Quarterly*, 103(2/3): 311–322.

Balibar, Étienne (2013) 'On the Politics of Human Rights', *Constellations*, 20(1): 18–26.

Balibar, Étienne (2014) *Equaliberty: Political Essays*, trans. James Ingram, Durham and London: Duke University Press.

Bataille, Georges (1957), *Éroticisme*, Paris: Minuit.

Bataille, Georges (1970a) *Oeuvres complètes I: Premiers écrits, 1922–1940*, Paris: Gallimard.

Bataille, Georges (1970b) *Oeuvres complètes II: Écrits posthumes, 1922–1940*, Paris: Gallimard.

Bataille, Georges (1976) *Oeuvres completes VIII*, Paris: Gallimard.

Bataille, Georges (1986) *Visions of Excess: Selected Writings, 1927–1939*, trans. Allan Stoekl with Carl R. Lovitt and Donald M. Leslie, Jr, Minneapolis: University of Minnesota Press.

Bataille, Georges (1988a) *Inner Experience*, trans. Leslie Anne Boldt, Albany, New York: The State University of New York.

Bataille, Georges (1988b [1944]) *Guilty*, trans. Bruce Boone, Venice, CA: The Lapsis Press.

Bataille, Georges (1990a) 'Hegel, Death and Sacrifice', trans. Jonathon Strauss, *Yale French Studies*, 78: 9–28.

Bataille, Georges (1990b) *The Tears of Eros*, trans. Peter Connor, San Francisco: City Lights Books.

Bataille, Georges (1994) *Theory of Religion*, trans. Robert Hurley, reprinted, New York: Zone Books.

Bataille, Georges (1992) *On Nietzsche*, trans. Bruce Boone, New York: Paragon Press.

Bataille Georges (1997) *The Bataille Reader*, Fred Botting and Scott Wilson (eds), Oxford: Basil Blackwell.

Bates, David (2005) 'Crisis Between the Wars: Derrida and the Origins of Undecidability', *Representations*, 90: 1–27.

Bateson, Gregory (1972) 'A Theory of Play and Fantasy' in Gregory Bateson (ed.), *Steps to an Ecology of the Mind. Collected Essays in Anthropology, Psychiatry, Evolution and Epistemology*, Chicago: Chicago University Press.

Baudrillard, Jean (1981[1972]) *For a Political Economy of the Sign*, trans. Charles Levin, New York: Telos Press.

Baudrillard, Jean (1993) *Symbolic Exchange and Death*, trans. Iain Hamilton, London, Thousand Oaks, CA, New Delhi, Singapore: Sage Publications.

Baudrillard, Jean (1998 [1970]) *The Consumer Society: Myths and Structures*, trans. C. Turner, London: Sage.

Belting, Hans. (1996) *Likeness and Presence: A History of the Image Before the Era of Art*, trans. Edmund Jephcott. Chicago: University of Chicago Press.

Beltrán, Cristina (2009) 'Going Public: Hannah Arendt, Immigrant Action, and the Space of Appearance', *Political Theory*, 37(5): 595–622.

Benjamin, Andrew (2011) *Of Jews and Animals*, Edinburgh: Edinburgh University Press.

Benjamin, Walter (1986) *Reflections: Essays, Aphorism, Autobiographical Writings*, trans. Edmund Jephcott, New York: Schocken Books.

Benjamin, Walter (2004) 'Capitalism as Religion' [fragment] in Eduardo Mendieta (ed.), *The Frankfurt School on Religion. Key Writings by the Major Thinkers*, 259–262, New York and London: Routledge.

Bennington, Geoffrey (1996) 'Emergencies', *Oxford Literary Review*, 18: 175–216.

Benveniste, Émile (1971) *Problems in General Linguistics*, trans. Mary Elizabeth Meek, Coral Gables, FL: University of Miami Press.

Benveniste, Émile (1973) *Indo-European Language and Society*, trans. Elizabeth Palmer, London: Faber and Faber.

Bergson, Henri (1993) *Matière et mémoire*, Paris: Presses Universitaires de France.

Bernasconi, Robert (1999) 'The Third Party. Levinas on the Intersection of the Ethical and the Political', *Journal for the British Society of Phenomenology*, 30(1): 76–87.

Blanchot, Maurice (1955) *L'Espace littéraire*, Paris: Gallimard, Folio.

Bourdieu, Pierre (1986) *Distinction: A Social Critique of the Judgement of Taste*, trans. Richard Nice, London and New York: Routledge and Kegan Paul.

Braidwood, Robert (1957) *Prehistoric Men*, Chicago: Chicago Natural History Museum, Popular Series Anthropology, Number 37.

Buchanan, Brett (2007) 'The Time of the Animal', *PhaenEx*, 2(2): 61–80.

Calarco, Matthew (2004) 'Deconstruction Is Not Vegetarianism: Humanism, Subjectivity, and Animal Ethics', *Continental Philosophy Review*, 37: 175–201.

Calarco, Matthew (2007) 'Jamming the Anthropological Machine' in Matthew Calarco and Steven, DeCaroli (eds), *Giorgio Agamben: Sovereignty and Life*, 163–179, Stanford: Stanford University Press.

Calarco, Matthew (2010) 'Faced by Animals' in Peter Atterton and Matthew Calarco (eds), *Radicalizing Levinas*, 113–133, Albany, New York: State University of New York Press.

Calarco, Matthew (2011) 'Identity, Difference, Indistinction', *The Centennial Review*, 11(2): 41–60.

Calarco, Matthew (2014) 'Being Toward Meat: Anthropocentrism, Indistinction and Veganism', *Dialectical Anthropology*, 38: 415–429.

Calarco, Matthew (2015) *Thinking Through Animals: Identity, Difference, Indistinction*, 'Stanford Briefs', Stanford: Stanford University Press.

Caygill, Howard (2002) *Levinas and the Political*, London and New York: Routledge.

Charbonnier, Georges (1973 [1969]) *Conversations with Claude Lévi-Strauss*, London: Jonathan Cape, 32–42.

Chabot, Pascal (2013) *The Philosophy of Simondon: Between Technology and Individuation*, trans. Aliza Krefetz with the participation of Graeme Kirkpatrick, London and New York: Bloomsbury.

Clastres, Pierre (1980) *Recherches d'anthropologie politique*, Paris: Seuil.

Colony, Tracy (2011) 'Epimetheus Bound: Stiegler on Derrida, Life, and the Technological Condition', *Research in Phenomenology*, 41: 72–89.

Cottegnies, Line (2002) 'Codifying the Passions in the Classical Age: A Few Reflections on Charles Le Brun's Scheme and Its Influence in France and in England', *Etudes Epistémè*, 1: 141–158.

Critchley, Simon (2004) 'Five Problems in Levinas's View of Politics and a Sketch of a Solution to Them', *Political Theory*, 32(2): 172–185.

Dallmayr, Fred R (1984) 'Ontology of Freedom: Heidegger and Political Philosophy', *Political Theory*, 12(2): 204–234.

Darwin, Charles (1981 [1859]) *On the Origin of Species*, A Facsimile of the First Edition, 6th printing, Cambridge, MA and London: Harvard University Press.

Debreuil, Laurent (2006) 'Leaving Politics: *Bios, Zōē*, Life', *Diacritics,* 36(2): 83–96.

Dieham, Christian (2000) 'Facing Nature: Levinas Beyond the Human', *Philosophy Today*, 44(1): 51–59.

Deleuze, Gilles (1988) '"A Philosophical Concept …"', *Topoi*, 7: 111–112.

Deleuze, Gilles (1989) *Cinema 2: The Movement-Image*, trans. Hugh Tomlinson and Barbara Habberjam, Minneapolis: University of Minnesota Press.

Deleuze, Gilles (1994) *Difference and Repetition*, trans. Paul Patton, New York: Columbia University Press.

Deleuze, Gilles (2001) *Pure Immanence: Essays on A Life*, trans. Anne Boyman, New York: Zone Books.

Deleuze, Gilles (2003) *Francis Bacon: Logic of Sensation*, trans. Daniel W. Smith, London and New York: Continuum.

Deleuze, Gilles and Guattari, Félix (1991) 'Le plan d'immanence' *Qu'est-ce que la philosophie ?*, Paris: Minuit.

Derrida, Jacques (1967) 'Violence et métaphysique: Essai sur la pensée d'Emmanuel Levinas' *L'Écriture et la différance*, 117–228, Paris: Seuil.

Derrida, Jacques (1976) *Of Grammatology*, trans. Gayatri Chakravorty Spivak, Baltimore and London: The Johns Hopkins University Press.

Derrida, Jacques (1978) 'From Restricted to General Economy: A Hegelianism Without Reserve' *Writing and Difference*, trans. Alan Bass, 257–277, Chicago: The University of Chicago Press.

Derrida, Jacques (1987) 'Geschlecht II: Heidegger's Hand', trans. J.P. Leavey, Jr in John Sallis (ed.), *Deconstruction and Philosophy: The Texts of Jacques Derrida*, trans. J.P. Leavey Jr, 161–196, Chicago and London: University of Chicago Press.

Derrida, Jacques (1991a) '"Eating Well", or the Calculation of the Subject: An Interview with Jacques Derrida', trans. Peter Connor and Avital Ronell in Eduardo Cadava, Peter Connor and Jean-Luc Nancy (eds), *Who Comes After the Subject?*, 96–119, New York and London: Routledge.

Derrida, Jacques (1991b) *Of Spirit*, trans. Geoffrey Bennington and Rachel Bowlby, Chicago: Chicago University Press.

Derrida, Jacques (1993) *Spectres de Marx: L'État de la dette, le travail du deuil et la nouvelle International*, Paris: Galilée.

Derrida, Jacques (1995) *The Gift of Death*, trans. David Wills, Chicago and London: The University of Chicago Press.

Derrida, Jacques (1997) *Politics of Friendship*, trans. George Collins, London and New York: Verso.

Derrida, Jacques (1999) 'Responsibilité et hospitalité' in Mohammed Seffahi (ed.), *Manifeste pour l'hospitalité: Autour de Jacques Derrida*, 111–124, Grigny, France: Editions Paroles D'Aube.

Derrida, Jacques and Roudinesco, Elisabeth (2004), *For What Tomorrow … A Dialogue*, trans. Jeff Fort, Stanford: Stanford University Press.

Derrida, Jacques (2008a) *Séminaire: La bête et le souverain, Volume I (2001–2002)*, Paris: Galilée.

Derrida, Jacques (2008b) *The Animal That Therefore I Am*, trans. Wills D., New York: Fordham University Press.

Derrida, Jacques (2012) *Séminaire: La peine de mort, Volume I, 1999–2000*, Paris: Galilée.

Descartes, René (2010) *Oeuvres philosophiques: Tome III – 1643–1650*, Paris: Editions classiques Garnier.

Dietz, Mary G. (1995) 'Feminist Receptions of Hannah Arendt' in Bonnie Honig (ed.), *Feminist Interpretations of Hannah Arendt*, University Park, PA: Penn State University Press.

Dostoyevsky, Fyodor (1982 [1880]) *The Brothers Karamazov*, trans. David Magarshack, Hamondsworth, Middlesex: Penguin.

Elden, Stuart (2005) 'Reading Logos as Speech: Heidegger, Aristotle and Rhetorical Politics', *Philosophy and Rhetoric*, 38 (4): 281–301.

Esposito, Roberto (2012) *Third Person*, trans. Zakiya Hanafi, Cambridge, UK and Malden, MA: Polity Press.

Esposito, Roberto (2014) *Third Person. Politics of Life and Philosophy of the Impersonal*, trans. Zakiya Hanafi. Cambridge, Reprinted, UK; Muldon, MA: Polity Press.

Faucher, Kane X (2005) 'The Transcendental Empiricism of Georges Bataille: The Incommensurable Object', *Culture, Theory and Critique*, 46(2): 163–176.

Featherston, Mike (2000) 'Life Style and Consumer Culture' in Martyn Lee (ed.), *The Consumer Culture Reader*, 92–105, Oxford: Blackwell.

Featherstone, Mike (2007) 'The Aestheticisation of Everyday Life' *Consumer Culture and Postmodernism*, 2nd edition, 64–80, London: Sage.

Fei, Cao (2006) *Whose Utopia?* (film). Available at: https://vimeo.com/76026916

Finlayson, James Gordon (2010) '"Bare Life" and Politics in Agamben's Reading of Aristotle', *The Review of Politics*, 72: 97–126.

Foucault, Michel (1974) *The Archaeology of Knowledge*, trans. A.M. Sheridan Smith, London: Tavistock.

Foucault, Michel (1982 [1966]) *The Order of Things: An Archaeology of the Human Sciences*, trans. from the French, London: Tavistock.

Foucault, Michel (1984a) *L'Usage des plaisirs: Histoire de la sexualité 2*, Paris: Gallimard.

Foucault, Michel (1984b) *Le Souci de soi: Histoire de la sexualité 3*, Paris: Gallimard.

Foucault, Michel (1987) 'The Ethic of Care for the Self as a Practice of Freedom: An Interview with Michel Foucault on January 20, 1984', conducted by Raúl Fornet-Betancourt, Hemet Becker, Afredo Gomez-Müller, trans. J.D. Gauthier, *Philosophy and Social Criticism*, 12(2/3): 112–131.

Foucault, Michel (2011) *The Courage of Truth: The Government of the Self and Others, II. Lectures at the Collège de France, 1983–1984*, trans. Graham Burchell, New York: Picador.

Franco, Paul (1999) *Hegel's Philosophy of Freedom*, New Haven and London: Yale University Press.

Freud, Sigmund (1976 [1900]) *The Interpretation of Dreams*, The Pelican Freud Library Volume 4, trans. James Strachey, London: Penguin Books.

Gaughan, Judy (2010) *Murder was Not a Crime: Homicide and Power in the Roman Republic*, Austin, Texas: University of Texas Press.

Gehrke, Pat J. (2006) 'The Ethical Importance of Being Human: God and Humanism in Levinas's Philosophy', *Philosophy Today*, 50(4): 428–436.

Gille, Bertrand (ed.) (1978) *Histoire des techniques*, Paris: Gallimard, Encyclopédie de la Pléiade.

Glaskin, Katie (2006) 'Death and the Person: Reflections on Mortuary Rituals, Transformation and Ontology in an Aboriginal Society', *Paideuma: Mitteilungen zur Kulturkunde*, 52: 107–126.

Glinister, Fay (2007) 'Constructing the Past' [on Festus], *Bulletin for the Institute of Classical Studies*, 50(S93): 11–32.

Grosz, Elizabeth (2004) *In the Nick of Time: Politics, Evolution, and the Untimely*, Durham and London: Duke University Press.

Grosz, Elizabeth (2008) *Chaos, Territory, Art: Deleuze and the Framing of the Earth*, New York: Columbia University Press.

Guerlac, Suzanne (2012), 'Derrida and His Cat: The Most Important Question', *Contemporary French and Francophone Studies*, 16(5): 695–702.

Haraway, Donna (2003) *The Companion Species Manifesto: Dogs, People, and Significant Otherness*, Chicago: Prikly Paradigm Press.

Haraway, Donna (2008) *When Species Meet*, Minneapolis: Minnesota University Press.

Harrison, Peter (1991) 'Do Animals Feel Pain?', *Philosophy*, 66(255): 25–40.

Haworth, Michael (2016) 'Bernard Stiegler on Transgenerational Memory and the Dual Origin of the Human', *Theory, Culture & Society*, 33(3): 151–173.

Hegarty, Paul (2000) 'Bataille Conceiving Death', *Paragraph*, 23(2): 173–190.

Hegel, Georg Wilhelm Friedrich (1956) *The Philosophy of History*, trans. J. Sibree, New York: Dover Publications.

Hegel, Georg Wilhelm Friedrich (1966 [1812–1816]) *Hegel's Science of Logic, Volume Two*, trans. W.H. Johnston and L.G. Struthers, fourth impression, London and New York: George Allen and Unwin.

Hegel, Georg Wilhelm Friedrich (1975 [1821]) *Hegel's Philosophy of Right*, trans. T.M. Knox, reprinted, London, Oxford, New York: Oxford University Press.

Hegel, Georg Wilhelm Friedrich (1979 [1807]) *Phenomenology of Spirit*, trans A.V. Miller, Oxford, New York, Toronto, Melbourne: Oxford University Press.

Hegel, Georg Wilhelm Friedrich (1993 [1820]) *Lectures on the Philosophy of World History: Introduction*, trans. H.B. Nisbet, Cambridge: Cambridge University Press, reprinted, Oxford: Oxford University Press.

Hegel, Georg Wilhelm Friedrich (2010) *Hegel's Aesthetics. Lectures on Fine Art, Volume I*, trans T.M. Knox, reprinted, Oxford: Oxford University Press.

Heidegger, Martin (1971) *Schellings Abhandlung Uber das Wesen der menschlichen Freiheit (1809)*, ed. Hildegard Feick, Tubingen: Niemeyer.

Heidegger, Martin (1975) *Gesamtausgabe* (GA), Frankfurt am Main: Vittorio Klostermann.

Heidegger, Martin (1978) *Being and Time*, trans. John Macquarie and Edward Robinson, Oxford: Basil Blackwell.

Heidegger, Martin (1985) *Schelling's Treatise on the Essence of Human Freedom*, trans. Joan Stanbaugh, Athens, Ohio, London: Ohio University Press.

Heidegger, Martin (1990) *Kant and the Problem of Metaphysics*, trans. Richard Taft, Bloomington and Indianapolis: Indiana University Press.

Heidegger, Martin (1992) *Parmenides*, trans. A. Schuwer, and R. Rojcewicz, Bloomington and Indianapolis: Indiana University Press.

Heidegger, Martin (1993a) 'The Origin of the Work of Art', trans. A. Hofstadter in David Farrell Krell (ed.), *Martin Heidegger, Basic Writings*, revised and expanded edition, 143–203, London: Routledge.

Heidegger, Martin (1993b) *Basic Concepts*, trans. Gary E. Aylsworth, Bloomington and Indianapolis: Indiana University Press.

Heidegger, Martin (1995) *The Fundamental Concepts of Metaphysics: World, Finitude, Solitude*, trans. W. McNeill and N. Walker, Bloomington and Indianapolis: Indiana University Press.

Heidegger, Martin (1996) *Hölderlin's Hymn 'The Ister'*, trans. W. McNeill and J. Davis, Bloomington and Indiana: Indiana University Press.

Heidegger, Martin (2002a) *Grundbegriffe der aristotelischen Philosophie* (GA18).

Heidegger, Martin (2002b) *The Essence of Human Freedom: An Introduction to Philosophy*, trans Ted Sadler, London and New York: Continuum.

Heidegger Martin (2009) *Basic Concepts of Aristotelian Philosophy*, trans. R.D. Metcalf and M.B. Tanzer, Bloomington and Indianapolis: Indiana University Press.

Hollier, Denis (1989) *Against Architecture: The Writings of Georges Bataille*, Cambridge, MA: The MIT Press.

House Ian (1991) 'Harrison on Animal Pain', *Philosophy*, 66(257): 376–379.

Husain, Nasser and Ptacek, Melissa (2000) 'Thresholds of Sovereignty and the Sacred', *Law and Society Review*, 34(2): 495–515.

Husserl, Edmund (1982 [1913]*Ideas Pertaining to a Pure Phenomenology and to a Phenomenological Philosophy. First Book: General Introduction to a Pure Phenomenology*, trans. F. Kersten, Dordrecht, Boston, London: Kluwer Academic Publishers.

Husserl, Edmund (1991 [1966]) *On the Phenomenology of Internal Consciousness of Time*, trans. John Barnett Brough, Dordrecht, Boston, London: Kluwer Academic Publishers.

Iveson, Richard (2011) 'Misreading Derrida: Stiegler, originary technicity, and the différance of différance'. Available at: https://zoogenesis.wordpress.com/2011/10/03/misreading-derrida-stiegler-originary-technicity-and-the-differance-of-differance/ (Accessed 6 July 2016).

Johnson, Christopher (2013) 'The Prehistory of Technology: On the Contribution of Leroi-Gourhan' in Christina Howells and Gerald Moore (eds), *Stiegler and Technics*, Edinburgh: Edinburgh University Press.

Kant, Immanuel (1970 [1781]) *Immanuel Kant's Critique of Pure Reason*, trans Norman Kemp Smith, London and Basingstoke: Macmillan.

Kant, Immanuel (1997 [1788]) *Critique of Practical Reason*, trans. Mary Gregor, Cambridge: Cambridge University Press.

Kant, Immanuel (1998 [1797]) *The Metaphysics of Morals*, trans. Mary Gregor, Cambridge: Cambridge University Press.

Kantorwicz, Ernst Hartwig (1957) *The King's Two Bodies: A Study in Mediaeval Political Theology*, Princeton, NJ: Princeton University Press.

Klagge, James C. (1986) 'Marx's Realms of "Freedom" and "Necessity"', *The Canadian Journal of Philosophy*, 16(4): 769–778.

Klein, Yves (1960) *Athropométrie de l'époque bleue*. Available at: http://www.yveskleinarchives.org/works/large/ant82.jpg and http://a136.idata.over-blog.com/0/02/40/16/images-tasons/Anthropom-trie1.jpg (Accessed on 8 August 2016).

Kovecses, Zoltan (2002) *Metaphor: A Practical Introduction*, Oxford: Oxford University Press.

Kristeva, Julia (1984) *Revolution in Poetic Language*, trans. Margaret Waller, New York: Columbia University Press.

Kristeva, Julia (1988) *Étrangers à nous-mêmes*, Paris: Fayard.

Kristeva, Julia (1987) *Tales of Love*, trans. Leon S. Roudiez, New York: Columbia University Press.

Kristeva, Julia (1999) *Le Génie féminin, Tome premier: Hannah Arendt*, Paris: Fayard.

Latour, Bruno (2004) *Politics of Nature: How to Bring the Sciences into Democracy*, trans. Catherine Porter, Cambridge, MA and London: Harvard University Press.

Leach, Edmund R. (1964) 'Anthropological Aspects of Language: Animal Categories and Verbal Abuse' in E.H. Lenneberg (ed.), *New Directions in the Study of Language*, 23–63, Cambridge: MIT Press.

Lechte, John (1985) 'Woman and the Veil – or Rousseau's Fictive Body', *French Studies*, 39 (4): 423–441.

Lechte, John (1988) 'Ethnocentrism, Racism, Genocide …' in Marie De Lepervanche and Gill Bottomley (eds), *The Cultural Construction of Race*, 32–45, Sydney: Sydney Association for Studies in Society and Culture.

Lechte, John (1990) *Julia Kristeva*, London and New York: Routledge.

Lechte, John (1999) 'The *Who* and the *What* of Writing in the Electronic Age', *Oxford Literary Review*, 21: 135–160.

Lechte, John (2003) *Key Contemporary Concepts: From Abjection to Zeno's Paradox*, London, Thousand Oaks, New Delhi: Sage.

Lechte, John (2013) 'Beyond the Ontology of the Image?', Bradford, UK: National Media Museum. Available at: http://eitherand.org/photographys-new-materiality/beyond-ontology-image/

Lechte, John and Newman, Saul (2012) 'Agamben, Arendt and Human Rights: Bearing Witness to the Human', *European Journal of Social Theory*, 15 (4): 505–521.

Lechte, John and Newman, Saul (2013) *Agamben and the Politics of Human Rights: Statelessness, Images, Violence*, Edinburgh: Edinburgh University Press.

Lemke, Thomas (2005) '"A Zone of Indistinction" – A Critique of Agamben's Concept of Biopolitics', *Outlines*, 1: 3–13.

Leroi-Gourhan, André (1964a) *Le geste et la parole I: Technique et langage*, Paris: Albin Michel.

Leroi-Gourhan, André (1964b) *Le geste et la parole II: La mémoire et les rythms*, Paris: Albin Michel.

Leroi-Gourhan, André (1971) *L'homme et la matière*, Paris: Albin Michel.

Leroi-Gourhan, André (1973) *Milieu et technique*, Paris: Albin Michel.

Lettvin, J.Y., Maturana, H.R., Mcculloch, W.S., and Pitts, H.R. (1959) 'What the Frog's Eye Tells the Frog's Brain', *Proceedings of the IRE*, 47 (11): 1940–1951.

Levinas E. (1963) 'La Trace de l'autre'. *Tijdschrift voor Filosofie, 25ste Jaarg*, 3: 605–623.

Levinas, Emmanuel (1969) *Totality and Infinity: An Essay on Exteriority*, trans. Alphonso Lingis, Pittsburgh, Pennsylvania: Duquesne University Press.

Levinas, Emmanuel (1988) 'The Paradox of Morality: An Interview with Emmanuel Levinas', trans. Andrew Benjamin and Tamra Wright in R. Bernasconi and D. Wood (eds), *The Provocation of Levinas: Rethinking the Other*, London and New York: Routledge, 168–180.

Levinas, Emmanuel (1979) *Le temps et l'autre*, 3rd edition, Paris: Presses Universitaires de France.

Levinas, Emmanuel (1990) *Difficult Freedom: Essays on Judaism*, trans. Sean Hand, Baltimore, MD: Johns Hopkins University Press.

Levinas, Emmanuel (1994 [1949]) *En découvrant l'existence avec Husserl et Heidegger*, 5th printing, Paris: J. Vrin.

Levinas, Emmanuel (1998a) *Otherwise than Being, or Beyond Essence*, trans. Alphonso Lingis, Pittsburgh, Pennsylvania: Duquesne University Press.

Levinas, Emmanuel (1998b) *Entre Nous: On Thinking-of-the-Other*, trans. Michael B. Smith and Barbara Harshav, London: The Athlone Press.

Levinas, Emmanuel (1998c [1930]) *The Theory of Intuition in Husserl's Phenomenology*, trans. André Orianne, Evanston, Illinois: Northwestern University Press.

Levinas, Emmanuel (1999) *Alterity and Transcendence*, trans. Michael B. Smith, London: The Athlone Press.

Levinas, Emmanuel (2003 [1935]) *On Escape/De l'évasion*, trans. Bettina Bergo, Stanford: Stanford University Press.

Levinas, Emmanuel (2006) *Humanism of the Other*, trans. Nidra Poller, Urbana and Chicago: University of Illiois Press.

Levinas, Emmanuel (2013) *Oeuvres 3: Eros, littérature et philosophie. Essais Romanesque et poétiques, notes philosophiques sur le theme d'éros*, Volume published under the responsibility of Jean-Luc Nancy and Danielle Cohen-Levinas, Paris: Bernard Grasset and Fasquelle/IMEC.

Lévi-Strauss, Claude (1973) *Totemism*, trans. Rodney Needham, Harmondsworth, Middlesex, England and Ringwood, Victoria, Australia: Penguin University Books.

Lévi-Strauss, Claude (1974), *The Savage Mind* (La pensée sauvage), trans. from the French, second impression, London: Weidenfeld and Nicolson.

Lévi-Strauss, Claude (1997) 'Selections from *Introduction to the Work of Marcel Mauss*', trans. Felicity Baker in Alan D. Schrift (ed.), *The Logic of the Gift: Towards and Ethic of Generosity*, New York and London: Routledge.

Marin, Louis (1988) *Portrait of the King*, trans. Michelle Houle, Minneapolis: University of Minnesota Press.

Marsden, Jill (2004) 'Bataille and the Poetic Fallacy of Animality' in Matthew Calarco and Peter Atterton (eds), *Animal Philosophy: Essential Readings in Continental Thought*, 40–44, London and New York: Continuum.

Marshall, David L. (2010) 'The Polis and Its Analogue on the Thought of Hannah Arendt', *Modern Intellectual History*, 7 (1): 123–149.

Marshall, Thomas Humphrey (1977) 'Citizenship and Social Class' in T.H. Marshall (ed.), *Class, Citizenship and Social Development*, 71–134, Chicago: Chicago University Press.

Marx, Karl (1977) *Capital Volume Ill*, trans. Ernest Untermann, New York: International Publishers.

Massumi, Brian (2014) *What Animals Teach Us About Politics*, Durham: Duke University Press.

Mauss, Marcel (2008) *On Prayer*, trans. Susan Leslie, New York, Oxford: Durkheim Press/Berghahn Books.

Mauss, Marcel (2009) 'Techniques of the Body', trans. Ben Brewster in Marcel Mauss (ed.), *Techniques, Technology and Civilisation*, 77–95, New York, Oxford: Durkheim Press/Berghahn Books.

Mayr, Ernst (1981) 'Introduction' in Charles Darwin (ed.), *On the Origin of Species*, A Facsimile of the First Edition, 6th printing, vii–xxvii, Cambridge, MA and London: Harvard University Press.

Merleau-Ponty, Maurice (1992) *Phenomenology of Perception*, trans. Colin Smith, London: Routledge, reprinted.

Merleau-Ponty, Maurice (2003) *Nature. Course Notes from the Collège de France*, trans. R. Vallier, Evanston, Illinois: Northwestern University Press.

Mondzain, Marie-José (1996) *Image, Icône, économie. Les sources byzantine de l'imaginaire contemporain*, Paris: Seuil.

Morphy, Howard (2008) 'Some Concluding Anthropological Reflections' in Marcel Mauss (ed.), *On Prayer*, trans. Susan Leslie, 139–154, New York, Oxford: Durkheim Press/Berghahn Books.

Morris, Sarah (2009) *Beijing 2008* [film]. Selected images available at: https://vimeo.com/14837950 (Accessed on 10 August 2016)

Motluk, Alison (2005) 'Execution by injection far from painless', *New Scientist*, 14 April. Available online at: http://www.newscientist.com/article/dn7269-execution-byinjection-far-from-painless.html (Accessed 3 August 2016)

Nancy, Jean-Luc (1990) *La communauté désoeuvrée*, Nouvelle édition, Paris: Christian Bourgois.

Nancy, Jean-Luc (1993) *The Experience of Freedom*, trans. Bridget McDonald, Stanford: Stanford University Press.

Nichols, Robert (2014) *The World of Freedom: Heidegger, Foucault and the World of Historical Ontology*, Stanford: Stanford University Press.

Nietzsche, Friedrich (1968) *The Will to Power*, trans. Walter Kaufmann and R.J. Hollingdale, New York: Vintage.

Nora, Dominique and Coutier, Bruno (2015) 'Alimentation du future: Des Croquettes de scarabée au menu', *L'Obs* (Paris), 2637 (21–27 May): 51–52.

Noys, Benjamin (2002) 'Time of Death', *Angelaki*, 7(2): 51–59.

Oliver, Kelly (2009) *Animal Lessons. How They Teach Us to Be Human*, New York: Columbia University Press.

Oliver, Kelly (2012) 'See Topsy "Ride the Lightening": The Scopic Machinery of Death', *The Southern Journal of Philosophy*, 50 (Spindel Supplement): 74–94.

Onians, Richard (2011[1951]) *The Origins of European Thought: About the Body, the Mind, the Soul, the world Time, and Fate*, paperback edition, Cambridge: Cambridge University Press.

Palmatier, Robert A. (1995) *Speaking of Animals: A Dictionary of Animal Metaphors*, Westport, CT: Greenwood Press.

Patton, Paul (1989) 'Taylor and Foucault on Power and Freedom', *Political Studies*, XXXVII: 260–276.

Patton, Paul (2007) 'Agamben and Foucault on Biopower and Biopolitics' in Matthew Calarco and Steven DeCaroli (eds), *Giorgio Agamben: Sovereignty and Life*, 203–218, Stanford: Stanford University Press.

Perkins, Hetti and Fink, Hannah (eds) (2001) *Pupunya Tula: Genesis and Genius*, Sydney: Art Gallery of New South Wales.

Perretti, Jacques (writer and presenter) (2015) *The super-Rich and Us* [TV programme] BBC2, January–February.

Peterson, Keith R. (2004) 'Translator's Introduction' in Friedrich Wilhelm Joseph Schelling, *First Outline of a System of the Philosophy of Nature*, trans. Keith R. Peterson, Albany: State University of New York Press.

Pitkin, Hannah Fenichel (1995) 'Conformism, House Keeping and the Attack of the Blob: The Origins of Hannah Arendt's Concept of the Social' in Bonnie Honig (ed.), *Feminist Interpretations of Hannah Arendt*, 51–82, University Park, PA: Penn State University Press.

Pitkin, Hannah Fenichel (1998) *The Attack of the Blob: Arendt's Concept of the Social*, Chicago: Chicago University Press.Plato (1980) The Collected Dialogues of Plato, Edith Hamilton and Huntington Cairns (eds), 10th printing,

Princeton, NJ: Princeton University Press, Bollingen Series LXXI.

Plumwood, Val (2002) *Environmental Crisis of Reason*, New York: Routledge.

Raber, Karen (2015) 'Shakespeare and Animal Studies', *Literature Compass*, 12(6): 286–298.

Rancière, Jacques (2004) 'Who Is the Subject of the Rights of Man?', *The South Atlantic Quarterly*, 103(2/3): 299–310.

Roberts, Ben (2005) 'Stiegler Reading Derrida: The Prosthesis of Deconstruction in Technics', *Postmodern Culture*, 16(1): [electronic journal].

Rolland, Jacques (2003), 'Getting out of Being by a New Path' in Levinas, Emmanuel (ed.) *On Escape/De l'évasion*, trans. Bettina Bergo, Stanford: Stanford University Press.

Rousseau, Jean-Jacques (1964) *Œuvres complètes III: Du contrat social*, écrits *politiques*, Paris: Gallimard, 'Bibliothèque de la Pléiade'.

Rousseau, Jean-Jacques (1982) 'A Discourse on the Origin of Inequality', trans. G.D.H. Cole in *The Social Contract the Discourses*, reprinted, London: J.M. Dent, Everyman's Library.

Rousseau, Jean-Jacques (1986) 'Essay On the Origin of Language' in *On the Origin of Language (Two Essays)*, trans. John H. Moran and Alexander Gode, Chicago: Chicago University Press.

Ruin, Hans (2008) 'The Destiny of Freedom: In Heidegger', *Continental Philosophy Review*, 41(2): 277–299.

Russell, Nerissa (2002). 'The Wild Side of Animal Domestication', *Society and Animals*, 10(3): 285–302.

Sahlins, Marshall (1974) *Stone Age Economics*, London: Tavistock.

Schaap, Andrew (2011) 'Enacting the Right to Have Rights: Jacques Rancière's Critique of Hannah Arendt', *European Journal of Political Theory*, 10(1): 22–45.

Schelling, Friedrich Wilhelm Joseph (2000) *The Ages of the World (Fragment), Third Version (c. 1815)*, trans. Jason M. Wirth, Albany: State University of New York Press.

Schelling, Friedrich Wilhelm Joseph (2004) *First Outline of a System of the Philosophy of Nature*, trans. Keith R. Peterson, Albany: State University of New York Press.

Schelling, Friedrich Wilhelm Joseph (2006) *Philosophical Investigations into the Essence of Human Freedom*, trans. Jeff Love and Johannes Schmidt, Albany: State University of New York.

Serres, Michel (1991) *Le Tiers-Instruit*, Paris: François Bourin.

Simmons, William Paul (1999) 'The Third: Levinas' Theoretical Move from An-Archical Ethics to the Realm of Justice and Politics', *Philosophy and Social Criticism*, 25(6): 83–104.

Simondon, Gilbert (1989) *L'Individuation psychique et collective à la lumière des notions de Forme, Information, Potential et Métastabilité*, Paris: Aubier.

Simondon, Gilbert (1995) *L'Individu et sa genèse physico-biologique*, Grenoble: Jérôme Million.

Simondon G (2011) *Two Lessons on Animal and Man*, trans. D.S. Burk, Minneapolis: Univocal Publishing.

Simondon, Gilbert (2012) *Du mode d'existence des objets techniques. Nouvelle édition revue et corrigée*, Paris: Aubier.

Simondon, Gilbert (2013) *L'Individuation à la lumière des notions de forme et d'information*, Grenoble: Jérome Million.

Smith, Bernard (1983) *European Vision and the South Pacific*, New Haven and London: Yale University Press.

Smith, Daniel (2003) 'Deleuze and Derrida, Immanence and Transcendence: Two Directions in Recent French Thought' in Paul Patton and John Protevi (eds), *Between Deleuze and Derrida*, 46–66, London and New York: Continuum.

Snapper, Ernest (1979) 'The Three Crises in Mathematics: Logicism, Intuitionism and Formalism', *Mathematics Magazine*, 52(4): 207–216.

Spindler, Fredrika (2010) 'A Philosophy of Immanence' in Jonna Bornemark and Hans Ruin (eds), *Phenomenology and Religion: New Frontiers*, Huddinge: Södertörns Högskola, University Södertörn Philosophical Studies.

Sreekumar, T.T. (2011) 'Mobile Phones and the Cultural Ecology of Fishing in Kerala, India', *The Information Society*, 27: 172–180.

Stibbe, Arran (2001) 'Language, Power and the Social Construction of Animals', *Society & Animals*, 9(2): 145–161.

Stiegler, Bernard (1996) *La technique et le temps, 2. La désorientation*, Paris: Galilée.

Stiegler, Bernard (1998) *Technics and Time, 1: The Fault of Epimetheseus*, trans. Richard Beardsworth and George Collins, Stanford: Stanford University Press.

Stiegler, Bernard (2001) *La technique et le temps, 3. Le temps du cinéma et la question du mal-être*, Paris: Galilée.

Stiegler, Bernard (2011) *The Decadence of Industrial Democracies*, trans. Daniel Ross and Suzanne Arnold, Cambridge, UK and Malden MA: Polity Press.

Talebinejad, M. Reza and Dastjerdi, H. Vahid (2005) 'A Cross-Cultural Study of Animal Metaphors: When Owls Are Not Wise', *Metaphor and Symbol*, 20(2): 133–150.

Tambiah, Stanley J. (1969) 'Animals Are Good to Think and Good to Prohibit', *Ethnology*, 8: 423–459.

Taminiaux, Jacques (1996) '*Bios politikos* and *bios theoretikos* in the Phenomenology of Hannah Arendt', *International Journal of Philosophical Studies*, 4(2): 215–232.

Tanzer, Mark (2016) 'Heidegger on Animality and Anthropocentrism', *Journal of the British Society for Phenomenology*, 47(1): 18–32.

Taylor, Charles (1984) 'Foucault on Freedom and Truth', *Political Theory*, 12(2): 152–183.

Tell, Dave (2012) *The Sacrament of Language: An Archaeology of the Oath* (Review), *Philosophy and Rhetoric*, 45(4): 452–459.

Trigg, Andrew B. (2004) 'Deriving the Engel Curve: Pierre Bourdieu and the Social Critique of Maslow's Hierarchy of Needs', *Review of Social Economy*, 62(3): 393–406.

Tsao, Roy T. (2002) 'Arendt Against Athens: Rereading *The Human Condition*', *Political Theory*, 30(1): 97–123.

Tyler, Tom (2005) 'Like Water in Water', *Journal for Cultural Research*, 9(3): 265–279.

Vernant, Jean-Pierre (1965) *Mythe et pensée chez les Grecs, I*, Paris: Maspero.

Villa, Dana (1996) *Arendt and Heidegger: The Fate of the Political*, Princeton, NJ: Princeton University Press.

Villa, Dana (2007) 'Arendt, Heidegger, and the Tradition', *Social Research*, 74(4): 983–1002.

Von Uexküll, Jakob (1921) *Umwelt und Innenwelt der Tiere*, Berlin: J. Springer.

Walsh, Philip (2015) *Arendt Contra Sociology: Theory, Society and Its Science*, Farnham, Surrey, UK and Burlington, VT, USA: Ashgate Press.

Weber, Max (1964) *The Theory of Social and Economic Organization*, trans. A.M. Henderson and Talcott Parsons, New York: Free Press; London: Collier-Macmillan.

Weber, Max (1970) *From Max Weber: Essays in Sociology*, trans. Hans H. Gerth and C. Wright Mills, London: Routledge and Kegan Paul.

Weber, Max (2001) *The Protestant Ethic and the Spirit of Capitalism*, London and New York: Routledge.

Wolin, Sheldon S. (1983) 'Hannah Arendt: Democracy and The Political' *Salmagundi*, 60: 3.

Wood, David (1999) '*Comment ne pas manger* – Deconstruction and Humanism' in H. Peter Steeves (ed.), 15–25, *Animal Others: On Ethics, Ontology and Animal Life*, Albany: State University of New York Press.

Wood, David (2004) 'Thinking with Cats' in Matthew Calarco and Peter Atterton (eds), *Animal Philosophy: Essential Readings in Continental Thought*, London and New York: Continuum.

Ziarek, Ewa (2008) 'Bare Life on Strike: Notes on the Biopolitics of Race and Gender', *South Atlantic Quarterly Winter*, 107(1): 89–105.

Index